Eagle Pond

Books by Donald Hall

POETRY

Exiles and Marriages
The Dark Houses
A Roof of Tiger Lilies
The Alligator Bride
The Yellow Room
The Town of Hill
Kicking the Leaves
The Happy Man
The One Day
Old and New Poems
The Museum of Clear Ideas
The Old Life
Without
The Painted Bed
White Apples and the Taste of Stone

PROSE

String Too Short to Be Saved
Henry Moore
Dock Ellis in the Country of Baseball
Fathers Playing Catch with Sons
The Ideal Bakery
Seasons at Eagle Pond
Here at Eagle Pond
Their Ancient Glittering Eyes
Life Work
Principal Products of Portugal
Willow Temple
The Best Day the Worst Day

Eagle Pond

Seasons at Eagle Pond

Here at Eagle Pond

Daylilies on the Hill

News from Eagle Pond

DONALD HALL

Illustrations by
Thomas W. Nason

A MARINER ORIGINAL
Houghton Mifflin Company
Boston New York
2007

Visit our Web site: www.houghtonmifflinbooks.com.

Library of Congress Cataloging-in-Publication Data

Hall, Donald, date.
Eagle Pond / Donald Hall.
p. cm.
ISBN-13: 978-0-618-83934-6
ISBN-10: 0-618-83934-8
1. Hall, Donald, date.—Homes and haunts—New Hampshire. 2. Poets, American—20th century—Biography. 3. New Hampshire—Social life and customs. 4. Country life—New Hampshire. I. Title.
PS3515.A3152Z46 2007
811'.54—dc22
[B] 2006034288

Book design by Anne Chalmers
Typeface: Filosofia

Printed in the United States of America
MP 10 9 8 7 6 5 4 3 2 1

The author and the publisher wish to thank the family of Thomas W. Nason for permission to reproduce the wood engraving illustrations from prints courtesy of the Boston Public Library.

For Carole and Steve Colburn

Contents

III. Daylilies

IV. News from Eagle Pond

Introduction

For thirty years, I have lived in the New Hampshire house, white clapboard and green shutters, where my grandmother was born in 1878, my mother in 1903. Great-grandparents had bought the farm in 1865. By adding rooms for their numerous children, they turned it into the familiar New England extended farmhouse. The original Cape had been built on the Grafton Turnpike, which became New Hampshire Highway Number 4 and devolved into U.S. Route 4. Shortly after I moved in, I had the old chimneys replaced—they were pretty well burned out—and found on a brick from the eldest chimney the date of its fabrication: 1803. I keep this brick, as my ancestors kept everything that ever entered this house. In the attic, or in an unfinished loft the family called the back chamber, there remain dozens of broken rockers and knocked-down beds, highchairs, oil lamps, chamber pots, pretty boxes, tools, catalogues, postcards, toys, sofas, butter churns, yellow newspapers, lasts, spinning wheels for wool and flax, books, rusty stoves, cranks for machines of inscrutable purpose, broken dolls and dolls' furniture, bundles of letters, and chests of dead people's clothing. Only in the rural South, and in rural New England, do American houses willfully contain the history of a family.

In 1975 my wife and I moved from Michigan to Eagle Pond Farm in Wilmot, New Hampshire. For me it was coming home, and it was coming home to the place of language. Years before, I had written a reminiscence, *String Too Short to Be Saved*, about the childhood summers when I hayed here with my grandfather. When I was twelve and thirteen, it was here that I began writing poetry. This farm provided subject matter for the first poems I published, when I was sixteen, and shows itself frequently in the four hundred and thirty-one pages of *White Apples and the Taste of Stone*, the selected poems I published in 2006, when I was seventy-seven. In 1986 I put together a book called *Seasons at Eagle Pond.* In 1990 I collected miscellaneous New Hampshire essays for *Here at Eagle Pond.* The relationship between essay and farm is symbiotic. Because I make my living by freelance writing, magazines that ask me to write about Eagle Pond Farm help pay its mortgage. In *Eagle Pond* I add a long poem—which belongs here rather than in a selected poems—and a few essays I wrote after *Here at Eagle Pond.* I have revised everything, to diminish repetition. I do repeat myself, when repetition is necessary to the structure of the essay. Still, this harvest of thirty years remains diverse. I reprint a piece of largely objective prose cheek by jowl with sarcasms about Vermont and enthusiasms over New England weather. But these different voices are each my own voice—and Picasso said that every human being is a colony. Often books try to abide by a neoclassic unity of character; such a notion is unreal: On a given day, a woman or a man speaks in one voice (diction, syntax, gesture, tone) to the folks in the mailroom, in another to the CEO, in another when giving instructions to an assistant, in another to the same assistant met on the street, in another to spouse, in another to children.

Thinking of what I do, as I gather these pieces together, I come upon an analogy that pleases me. My ancestors who lived here made their livings by freelancing as farmers, by harvesting small crops for diverse markets. They raised chickens to trade eggs for salt and coffee, sheep for wool and meat, cattle for milk and meat; they raised vegetables, they cut timber, they harvested cider, maple syrup, and honey. They never accumulated much money, but they paid their taxes by the various products of their repeated labors. Thus I gather for the reader mutton, zucchini, apples, eggs, milk by the hundredweight, sweetness in two flavors—derived from trees and from insects—and a barrel of vinegar.

. . .

These essays are also letters to friends, and they become letters to strangers. When I left teaching and moved here, to support myself by writing, my friends were anxious: How would we live? What would our lives be like, living here at Eagle Pond, in solitude among relicts and memories, in a countryside of birches and GMC pickups? Some of these essays answered their questions, almost like those photocopied annual reports that people include with their Christmas cards. And some of these essays, I believe, climbed from the pages of real letters to friends.

My letter writing, real and metaphorical, came naturally enough out of my family. The women of Eagle Pond Farm worked as hard as the men did—an equality not of ownership or political rights but of toil. One relaxation in the women's long day was writing letters. My grandmother Kate Wells sat in the kitchen window to write daily letters to the three daughters who grew up at the farm just east of Eagle Pond, daughters who journeyed to far-off Lewiston, Maine, to attend Bates College, and who later moved to southern places: my mother Lucy to Connecticut, my aunt Caroline to Boston suburbs where she taught school, my aunt Nan to Northfield, New Hampshire. Sometimes Kate's letters were postcards, a penny each, but she could pack a letter's worth onto the oblong with green Ben Franklin in the corner. Letters or postcards traveled south past Mount Kearsarge to daughters bearing news of *home*, for so she referred to Eagle Pond Farm, not for herself only but for her daughters, for her older sister Nannie, for her older brother Luther, and for her one grandchild. When she was past ninety she quizzed me elaborately to make sure that, in my absence from the farm—I was absent, then, three hundred and sixty-two days in the year—I referred habitually to this place as home.

Returning letters arrived daily, exclaiming on the Eagle Pond weather report, carrying climate's intimate news—"The perspiration just *dripped* from my nose." "It was *glare ice.*"—from the daughters of the diaspora back to the high priestess in her rocking chair. With her lips pursed in a scant smile, her brow furrowed, she concentrated on reading her daughters' words. As an old woman, Kate never read anything *except* letters. Young, she was a student: Her report cards from Franklin High School, always quick to hand, demonstrated her A's in Greek, Latin, and everything else; but after she had graduated, at the end of the nineteenth century—or maybe after courtship and babies—she stopped reading. She darned and daydreamed in the evening while my grandfather reread *David Harum* and giggled.

Her only literature was letters, but what a letterist she was. Nor did it start with her. In the back chamber, in old chests and boxes, along with diaries and slates and chalk and pens and dried inkwells, there are bundles of letters and postcards—Civil War letters, letters dispatched before stamps existed, letters of great formal intimacy often addressed to names I cannot place from names I cannot place. Nor did it end with her. I inherited the matter of Eagle Pond letters. I annoy my friends by answering their letters immediately. I puzzle publishers and magazine editors and impresarios of the poetry reading by writing instead of telephoning. I loathe the damned telephone; I prize the bundle of envelopes left each day in the outsized mailbox. Every day is Christmas, as I settle back into my blue chair and hear my friends out, knowing that late in the day I will talk back to them. Last time I counted, I was talking (I dictate) four thousand letters and postcards a year.

If I go away for a week, the mail punishes me when I return. Years ago, I left for seven weeks on a trip to China and Japan, and the mail that welcomed me home filled seven cardboard boxes. Travel can be a burden, and who wants to leave Eagle Pond anyway? My grandmother never did. Of course it takes all kinds, as we like to say. My grandmother's three girls all left, thus (*felix culpa*) providing her license to write them letters from Eagle Pond every day for fifty years. By pocket calculator (and mild exaggeration) that's 54,750 postal items.

THE FIRST ESSAY of *Here at Eagle Pond* is "Why We Live Here," and so is the second, and so is the third . . . These pieces begin with the bliss of return, and later they add anxiety to joy. The predictable armies of development and overpopulation heave into sight on the southern and western horizons. Thus I join the chorus: *I got here. Everybody else stay out!* Sometimes when I praise where I live, in this old family house, I'm afraid that I sound like a cartoon that Herblock drew while Barry Goldwater was running for the presidency. Herblock had the senator, a fortunate son, snapping at the beggar, "Go inherit a department store." Reader, believe me: I know I am lucky. Every day, I know that my intimate connection with the family past, in this place, depends upon a series of accidents and not upon my virtue. Also I know that we do not require ancestors in order to connect, joyously, with a place and a culture. I see all around me emigrants from other places who belong more preciously to this place than most old-timers do. But I see as well—by looking afield to Nashua or Burlington—that overpopulation with its suburban density can disconnect us all from the land and its history.

I

Seasons at Eagle Pond

Winter

In New Hampshire we know ourselves by winter—in snow, in cold, in darkness. For some of us the first true snow begins it; for others winter begins with the first bruising assault of zero weather. There is yet another sort, light-lovers, for whom winter begins with dark's onset in mid-August. If we wake as we ought to at 5:30, we begin waking in darkness, and dawn turns throaty with the ululations of photophiliacs, noctophobics, some of whom are fanatical enough to begin lamentation late in the month of June—when dawn arrives at 4:32 A.M. and the day before it arrived at 4:31:30. On June 22 my wife Jane exchanges postcards of commiseration with a fellow in Michigan who is another amorist of light. Fortunately this mountain has an upside as well as a downside. When in January daylight lasts half a minute longer every day, Jane's faint green leaves take on color; she leans south toward Kearsarge and the low, brief but lengthening pale winter sun. An observer can spy the faint buds that will burst into snowdrops and daffodils in April, tulips in May.

Some of us, on the other hand, are darkness-lovers. We do not dislike the early and late daylight of June, whippoorwill's graytime, but we cherish the gradually increasing dark of November, which we wrap around ourselves in the prosperous warmth of woodstove, oil, electric blanket, storm window, and insulation. We are partly tuber, partly bear. Inside our warmth we fold ourselves in the dark and its cold—around us, outside us, safely away from us; we tuck ourselves up in the long sleep and comfort of cold's opposite, warming ourselves by thought of the cold, lighting ourselves by darkness's idea. Or we are Persephone gone underground again, cozy in the amenities of Hell. Sheltered between stove and electric light, we hollow islands of safety within the cold and dark. As light grows less each day, our fur grows thicker. By December 22 we are cozy as a cat hunkered under a Glenwood.

Often October has shown one snow flurry, sometimes even September. For that matter, it once snowed in New Hampshire every month of the year. In 1816 it snowed and froze in June, in July, in August—the Poverty Year, season of continuous winter, when farmers planted over and over again, over and over again ripped out frozen shoots of corn and pumpkin. An 1815 volcanic eruption in Indonesia did it—though at the time our preachers thought the source more local and divine wrath explicit.

Winter starts in November, whatever the calendar says, with gray of granite, with russet and brown of used leaves. In November stillness our stonewalls wait, attentive, and gaunt revenant trunks of maple and oak settle down for winter's stasis, which annually mimics and presages death for each of us and for the planet. November's palette, Braque's analytic cubism, squared with fieldstones, interrupts itself briefly with the bright-flapped caps of deer hunters and their orange jackets. Always it is modified by the black-green fir, enduring, hinting at permanence. Serious snow begins one November afternoon. South of us Mount Kearsarge gradually disappears into white gauzy cloud, vanishing mountain, weather-sign for all of us to its north. For one hundred and eighty years the people of this house have looked south at dawn's light and again at sunset to tell the coming weather, reliable in 1803 when the first builder put in the south windows and reliable still. When Kearsarge disappears the storm comes closer. Birds gather at the feeder, squabbling, gobbling their weight. When they are full they look for shelter, and we do the same, or at least we bring wood from the shed to stack beside the old Glenwoods and the new Jøtul.

Every year the first snow sets me dreaming. By March it will only bring the grumps, but November snow is revenance, a dreamy restitution of childhood or even infancy. Tighten the door and settle a cloth snake against the breeze from the door's bottom; make sure the storms are firmly shut; add logs to the stove and widen the draft. Sit in a chair looking south into blue twilight that arrives earlier every day—as the sky flakes and densens, as the first clear flakes float past the porch's wood to light on dirt of the driveway and on brown frozen grass or dry stalks of the flower border. They seem tentative and awkward at first, then in a hastening host a whole brief army falls, white militia paratrooping out of the close sky over various textures, making them one. Snow is white and gray, part and whole, infinitely various yet infinitely repetitious, soft and hard, frozen and melting, a creaking underfoot and a soundlessness. But first of all it is the reversion of many into one. It is substance, almost the idea of substance, that turns grass, driveway, hayfield, old garden, log pile, Saab, watering trough, collapsed barn, and stonewall into the one white.

We finish early in November the task of preparing the house for snow—tacking poly over the low clapboards, raking leaves against the foundations as high as we can rake them. When the first real snow arrives, no dusting half inch but a solid foot, we complete the insulation, for it is snow that keeps us warm. After a neighbor's four-wheel-drive pickup, plow bolted in front, swoops clean our U-shaped driveway, and after we dig out the mailbox for Bert's rural delivery, it is time to heap the snow over leaves and against poly, around the house, on all sides of the house, against the granite foundation stones. Arctic winds halt before this white guard. When bright noon melts inches of snow away from the house, reflecting heat from the snowy clapboard, it leaves cracks of cold air for us to fill when new snow falls all winter long.

But November, although it begins winter, is only winter's approach, with little snow and with cold that announces itself only to increase. The calendar's winter begins at the solstice, Advent's event: the birth of the child who rises from winter to die and rise again in spring. November is autumn's burial, and the smoke of victims sacrificed is thanks for harvest and magic as we go into ourselves like maples for winter's bear-sleep. We make transition by way of feast and anticipatory snow, toward the long, white, hard hundred days, the true winter of our annual deaths. We wait for December to feel the *cold*, I mean COLD, for longer than a week, but now we are ready for snow.

THE FIRST big snow accumulates one night. Kearsarge may disappear at noon, and darkness start early. In teatime twilight, big flakes slowly, as if hesitant, reel past the empty trees like small white leaves, star-shaped and infrequent. By bedtime, driveway and lawn turn shaggy with the first cover. It is good to go to bed early in winter, and tonight as we sleep our dreams take punctuation from the thudding of snowplows as they roll and bluster up and down Route 4, shaking the house yet comforting our sleep: Someone takes care, the solitary captains in their great snowships breasting through vast whiteness, cleaving it sideways into gutter drifts. If we stir as they thump past, we watch revolving yellow lights flash through our windows and reflect on the ceiling. We roll over and fall back into protected sleep. In a house full of pets we sleep not alone, for the snowplows that reassure us frighten our dog like thunder or rifle fire; cats crawl between our warm bodies under warmer electric blankets.

When we become aware, by the plows' repeated patrols, that the first deep snow accumulates, when the first intense and almost unbreakable sleep finishes and we climb to the frangible second story of the night's house, I pull myself out of bed at two or three in the morning to inspect the true oncoming of winter's work. I walk through the dark house from one vantage to another—parlor window that looks west toward pond, kitchen from which I look toward Kearsarge, dining room that gives on the north and, if I twist, back to the slopes of Ragged Mountain rising east above us. The night's flaking air breaks black sky into white flecks, silent and pervasive, shuttering the day's vista. This snow fills the air and the eyes, the way on spring nights peepers fill the ears. Everywhere I look, limited by snow-limits, cold dewy whiteness takes everything into itself. Beside the covered woodshed, side by side, I see the shapes of two small cars rounded and smooth like enormous loaves of dead-white bread. Where the woodpile waits for final stacking in the shed, a mound rises with irregular sticks jagging out of it. Up on the hill the great cowbarn labors under a two-foot layer of snow, its unpainted vertical boards a dark upright shadow in all the whiteness, like the hemlocks above it on Ragged's hill. Although snowplows keep Route 4 passable, they do not yet scrape to the macadam: In the darkness the highway is as white as the hayfields on either side. Down the road the white cottage disappears against the white field, its green shutters a patch of vacancy in the whiteness. In the stillness of two A.M., in a silent unlit moment with no plows thudding, I regard a landscape reverted to other years by the same snow, and I might be my great-grandfather gazing from the same windows in 1885. Or it might be his mother's eyes I gaze from, born on a Wilmot hill in 1789. Or maybe I look, centuries earlier, from the eyes of a Penacook wintering over the pond.

But now the snowplow's thunder signals itself, and I watch the revolving yellow light reflect upward into white prodigious air, and hear the great bruising barge roar and rumble past the house as a steel prow swooshes high waves of whiteness up and over the gutter almost to the front of the house, and buries the mailbox.

ONE YEAR the first great snow came Christmas Eve after the family had struggled to bed. When we lit the tree in the morning, the day past the windows was thick and dark, and as we opened our presents the snow deepened in yard and hayfield outside, and on Christmas Day, all day, the great plows of state and town kept Route 4 clear. Snow stopped at three in the afternoon, and when Forrest rolled in to plow the driveway in the early blue twilight, Jane heaped slices of turkey between homemade bread to comfort him in his cab as he drove over the countryside digging people out.

The next morning was cold, thirty below, cold enough to notice. January in fact is the coldest month, although many would argue for February. Usually our cold is dry and does not penetrate so much as damp cold. December of 1975, our first full winter here, I tried starting the Plymouth one morning with normal confidence in the old six and without cold-weather precautions; I flooded it. When I looked at the thermometer I was astonished to find it seventeen degrees below zero, for my face and forehead had not warned me that it was *cold.* I had recently spent my winters in Michigan's damp cold; Ann Arbor's occasional zero felt harsher than New Hampshire's common twenty below.

Later that winter we did not complain of mildness. In January of 1976, morning after morning was thirty below; one morning on the porch the thermometer read thirty-eight degrees under—a temperature we did not equal until 1984. My grandmother had just died at ninety-seven, and she had spent most of her late winters going south to Connecticut. The house had grown unaccustomed to winter, the old heavy wooden storm windows broken, no central heat, and no insulation. Jane and I had never lived without central heat. Now we had a parlor Glenwood stove for heating, two kerosene burners in the kitchen, and on occasion an electric oven with the door open. This twelve-room house, in January of 1976, dwindled to a one-room house with a kitchen sometimes habitable. Working at the dining room table twenty feet from the living room's Glenwood, I felt chilly. At the time we were too excited or triumphant to complain: We were camping out; we were earning our stripes. The next summer we added aluminum combination storms and screens together with some insulation; we added two more woodstoves, one for each study, so that we could each work despite the winter. (My grandparents survived with only two woodstoves because they bustled around all day; in our work we sit on our duffs and require extra stoves.) When February came we learned we had passed our initiation, for it had been the coldest January since New Hampshire started keeping records more than a hundred years earlier. In all my grandmother's ninety-seven Januarys she had not known so cold a month.

My grandfather Wesley Wells worked all day without any heat except for the bodies of his cows. While he sat at morning and evening between two great steaming black-and-white Holstein hulks, pulling the pale thin tonnage of blue milk from their cud-chewing bodies, he kept warm. Other chores were cold. I can remember him, on my winter visits to the farm as a boy, scurrying into the house for a warmup between his outdoor tasks, rubbing his hands together, opening the drafts of one of the woodstoves and looming over it for a moment. Early and late, he moved among cold sheds and unheated barns. In the cowbarn he fed the cattle hay, grain, and ensilage, and provided his horse Riley with oats and hay and water. He let the Holsteins loose to wander stiff-legged to the old cement watering trough next to the milk room, from which he first removed a layer of ice. Their muzzles dipped one by one into the near-freezing water. And he fed the sheep in sheepbarn and sheepyard. From the sheep's trough he scooped water for the hens who lived next door to the sheep, and he carried feed for his hens from the grainshed beside the cowbarn.

He would start these chores early, most days of deep winter, rising at four-thirty, perhaps three hours before the sun, to do half the daily chores of feeding and watering, of milking and readying milk for the milk truck, because the special daily chores of winter were the year's hardest, the pains of minus twenty exacerbated by hard labor. To chop wood for next year's stove, the farmer stalked with his ax into his woodlot after chores and breakfast, and often marched far enough so that he carried with him his bread and butter, meat, pie, and thermos of coffee for dinner. Setting out with a great ax, usually working alone, the farmer chopped a tree down, trimmed branches, cut the trunk into four-foot sections, and stacked it. Later he would hitch oxen to the sledge and fetch the cordwood downhill to the barnyard for cutting to stove-length pieces and for splitting. Maybe ten cord of a winter for the house—more for the sugaring in March.

In January he harvested another winter crop, the crop that people forget when they think of the needs of an old farm—the harvest of ice, cut in great oblongs two or three feet thick from Eagle Pond, ox-sledded up to the icehouse in back of the cowbarn's watering trough, packed against warm weather six months hence. Each winter the farmer waited for a cold stretch, augering through the pond ice to check its thickness. Then he cut checkerboard squares with an ice saw. He kept himself heavily mittened not only against cold and wind rattling over the open desert lake, but also against the inevitable clasp of near-frozen water. A crew of them—neighbors cooperated to fetch ice—sawed and grappled, lifted and hauled, hard work and cold work. In the icehouse they stacked layers of ice, thickly insulated with sawdust, to last from the earliest warmth of April through hot spells of June and the long summer hay days of July and August through autumn with its Indian summer, until the pond froze again. In the hot months my grandfather brought one chunk a day downhill from the icehouse, great square balanced with ice tongs on his shoulder, to the toolshed behind the kitchen where my grandmother kept her icebox, drip drip. Most ice went to cool the milk, hot from the udders of Holsteins, so that it would not spoil overnight in summer. July and August, I was amazed every time we dug through the wet sawdust in the cool shade of the icehouse to find cold winter again—packed silvery slab of Eagle Pond preserved against summer, just as we hayed to preserve summer's grass for the winter cattle. On the hottest days when we returned sweaty from haying, my grandfather cracked off a little triangle of ice for me to suck on. Every January when he dug down in the icehouse to bury his crop of new ice, he found old ice underneath. After all, you never wanted to find yourself all out; some years, there might be hot days even in November when you would require a touch of ice. One long hot autumn he found at the bottom of the icehouse, farther than he ever remembered digging, a small coffin-shaped remnant from times past, ice that might have been five years old, he told me, maybe older.

And my grandfather told me how, in the state of Maine especially, in the old days, sailing ships loaded ice and sawdust in winter and sailed this cargo—transient mineral, annual and reproducible reverse-coal tonnage—down the East Coast to unload its cool for the South, which never otherwise saw a piece of ice: ice by the ton for coastal cities like Charleston, South Carolina. Sometimes they sailed all the way to the West Indies with their perishable glossy cargo: Maine ice for the juleps of Charleston, northern January cooling Jamaica's rum.

BY TRADITION, the hard snow and heavy cold of January take a vacation for the eldritch out-of-time phenomenon of January thaw. Sometimes the January thaw comes in February, sometimes it never arrives at all, and on the rarest occasions it starts early and lasts all winter. Mostly the January thaw lives up to its name. Some strange day, after a week when we dress in the black of twenty below, we notice that we do not back up to the fire as we change our clothing. Extraordinary. Or at midday we pick up the mail in our shirtsleeves, balmy at forty-two degrees. (It is commonplace to observe that a temperature which felt Arctic late in August feels tropical in mid-January.) Icicles drip, snow slides off the south roof in midday sun, and mud takes over the driveway. Snow melts deeply away from clapboard and poly. Or the January thaw comes with warm rain ("If this was snow we'd have twelve feet . . ."), and if warm rain pours for three January days, as I have known it to do, Ragged's melt floods our driveway, snow vanishes from all hayfields, and water drowns the black ice of Eagle Pond. Our small universe confuses itself with false spring. Bears wake perplexed and wander looking for deer corpses or compost heaps, thinking that it's time to get on with it. I remember fetching the newspaper one morning at five-thirty (I pick up the *Globe* outside a store that does not open for customers, slugabeds, until six o'clock) on the third day of a warm rain. Chugging through deep mud in my outboard Nissan, I pulled up at the wet porch to see a huge white cat rooting about in perennials beside the walk, a white pussycat with black spots . . . Oh, no. I remained in the front seat quietly reading the paper, careful not to make a startling sound or otherwise appear rude until the skunk wandered away.

Until we replaced rotten sills three years ago, a family of skunks lived in our rootcellar every winter. We never saw them but we found their scat; we found the holes by which they entered and exited. Of course we confirmed their presence by another sense. In the spring they sometimes quarreled, possibly over the correct time and place for love, and we could hear them arguing and discovered that skunks used on each other their special skunk equipment: Once a year in February or March we needed to throw all windows open. On one occasion, Ann Arbor friends visited in March, dear friends notable for an immaculate house in a culture of unspotted houses. When we brought them home with their skis from the airport, we opened the door to discover that our rootcellar family had suffered domestic disagreement. We opened all downstairs windows although it was fifteen below; as we prepared to take our friends up to their bedroom, where the air would be purer, we opened the hallway door to discover a dead rat on the carpet, courtesy of a guardian cat. Welcome to the country.

January thaw is dazzling but it lasts only a moment. If this were January in England we would expect crocuses and snowdrops soon; here we know enough to expect replacement battalions of snow's troopers following on coldness that freezes the melt, covering it with foot upon foot of furry whiteness and moon-coldness. We return to the satisfactions of winter, maybe even to the deliverance and delirium of a full moon. In New Hampshire the full moon is remarkable all year long because we suffer relatively little from garbage-air and less from background light. The great cloudless night of the full moon is werewolf time, glory of silver-pale hauntedness whenever it happens but most beautiful in winter. I set the internal alarm, maybe three or four nights in a row, and wander, self-made ghost, through pale rooms in the pewter light while the moon magnifies itself in bright hayfields and reflects upward, a sun from middle earth, onto shadowy low ceilings. High sailing above, higher than it has a right to, bigger, the February full moon, huge disc of cold, rides and slides among tatters of cloud. My breathing speeds, my pulse quickens; for half an hour I wander, pulled like a tide through the still house in the salty half-light, more asleep than awake, asleep not in house or nightshirt but in moon, moon, moon . . . What old animal awakens and stretches inside the marrow of the bones? What howls? What circles, sniffing for prey?

IT'S NO WINTER without an ice storm. When Robert Frost gazed at bowed-over birch trees and tried to think that boys had bent them playing, he knew better: "Ice-storms do that." They do that and a lot more, trimming disease and weakness out of the tree—the old tree's friend, as pneumonia used to be the old man's. Some of us provide life-support systems for our precious shrubs, boarding them over against the ice, for the ice storm takes the young or unlucky branch or birch as well as the rotten or feeble. One February morning we look out our windows over yards and fields littered with kindling, small twigs and great branches. We look out at a world turned into one diamond, ten thousand carats in the line of sight, twice as many facets. What a dazzle of spinning refracted light, spiderwebs of cold brilliance attacking our eyeballs! All winter we wear sunglasses to drive, more than we do in summer, and never so much as after an ice storm, with its painful glaze reflecting from maple and birch, granite boulder and stonewall, turning electric wires into bright silver filaments. The snow itself takes on a crust of ice, like the finish of a clay pot, that carries our weight and sends us swooping and sliding. It's worth your life to go for the mail. Until sand and salt redeem the highway, Route 4 is quiet. We cancel the appointment with the dentist, stay home, and marvel at the altered universe, knowing that midday sun will strip ice from tree and roof and restore our ordinary white winter world.

ANOTHER inescapable attribute of winter, increasing in years of affluence, is the ski people, cold counterpart to the summer folks who fill New Hampshire's Julys and Augusts. Now the roads north from Boston are as dense on a February Friday as they are on a July, and late Sunday afternoon, southbound Interstate 93 backs up miles from the tollbooth. On innumerable Toyotas pairs of skis ride north and south every winter weekend; at Christmas vacation and school holidays every hotel room fills all week with families of flatlanders. They wait in line at the tows, resplendent in the costumes of money, booted and coifed in bright petrochemical armor. They ride, they swoop, they fall, they drink whiskey, and the bonesetter takes no holiday on a New Hampshire February weekend, and the renter of crutches earns time and a half. Now that cross-country rivals downhill, the ski people grow older and more various. Tourism, which rivals the yard sale as the major North Country industry, brings Massachusetts and New York money to fatten purses in the cold country. In the fashionable areas—much of Vermont and Waterville Valley in New Hampshire's White Mountains—restaurants and boutiques, cute-shops and quiche-cafés buzz like winter's blackflies.

Few natives ski, though some have always done, and in our attic there are wide heavy wooden skis from the time of the Great War on which my mother and her sisters traipsed all winter, largely doing cross-country but perfectly willing to slide down a hill. Old-timers remember the horse-as-ski-tow, pulling adventurers uphill.

The motorcycle roar of snowmachines, from a distance indistinguishable from chainsaws, interrupts the downy quiet of midweek evenings, as kids roar along disused railroad tracks and over the surface of frozen lakes. Older folks, men mostly, park their bobhouses on frozen winter lakes, saw holes through the ice, light a fire, warm themselves with a pint of whiskey, and fish for the wormless perch of winter. Like deer hunting in November, this fishing is not mere sport; it fills the freezers of shacks, trailers, and extended farmhouses. On Eagle Pond we count six or a dozen bobhouses each winter, laboriously transported by pickup and slipped across the ice to a lucky spot.

After the labor of cordwood and ice in the old days, as the winter ended, followed the great chore of maplesugaring. It still arrives, though without so much labor. Usually it comes in one stretch of March, but on occasion the conditions for sap turn right for two weeks in February, go wrong for twenty days, then right themselves again—a split season for sugaring. Right conditions are warm days when snow melts followed by cold nights when it freezes.

Nowadays people suction sap from the sugarbush with miles of plastic tubing. In the old time, syrupers pounded the spigot into the tree—several of them in a good-sized three-hundred-year-old maple—and hung a bucket from each for the sap to drip into. My grandfather trudged from tree to tree every day, wearing a wooden yoke across his shoulders; long pails hung from the ends of it, narrow on top and wide on bottom, for collecting sap from each bucket. He emptied these yoke pails into a great receptacle sledged by an ox—oxen were especially useful in the winter, slow but unbothered by snow—and when he filled this great sledge kettle, his ox pulled it to a funnel and pipe whence the sap flowed downhill to a storage tank behind the saphouse. Gathering sap was a third of the work, or maybe a quarter. There was cordwood to cut, to burn under the trays boiling the sap down. Someone tended the fire day and night, watched and tested the sap on its delicate journey to syrup. In 1913 my grandfather corked five hundred gallons at a dollar a gallon, big money in 1913, with the help of his father-in-law Ben Keneston, cousin Freeman, and Anson the hired man. Remember that it takes about forty gallons of sap, boiled down, to make a gallon of syrup.

Not only the cash was sweet. To maple syrup and maple sugar my grandfather and grandmother added honey from the beehive beside the barn and the hollyhocks; they grew and produced their own sweetening. But big money from syrup bought land and paid taxes. Often their tax was little or nothing, for in the old days many farmers paid their taxes by doing road work—scraping and rolling the dirt roads, filling in with hardpan, and in winter rolling down the snow of the road to make it fit for the runners of sleighs, taking on a mile of Wilmot's Grafton Turnpike.

MARCH WAS ALWAYS the month for blizzards. Still is. It is the time when we all tell ourselves: *We've had enough of winter.* Old folks come back from Florida and Hilton Head; younger ones, fed up, head off for a week where the weather performs like May or June in New Hampshire. Every morning the *Globe* measures a word from Florida: *baseball* . . . In New Hampshire, tantalizing melt is overwhelmed by four feet of snow, drifts to twelve feet . . . We comfort each other, when we use the form of complaint for our boasting, that even if we lost the old outhouse yesterday or the '53 Buick that the chickens use for summer roosting, what comes quick in March goes quick in March, and three or four days from now it'll melt to reveal the lost Atlantis of the family barnyard. Then three or four days later we wake to another four feet.

In the 1940s, the old people still bragged about the great blizzard of '88. My Connecticut grandfather and my New Hampshire one, who shared little, shared the blizzard of '88: a great watershed for bragging or for telling lies about. And I still ask old people what they remember that *their* old people told them about '88, much as the '88ers themselves asked their old-timers about the Poverty Year of 1816. Paul Fenton told me a story he heard as a boy, not about '88 but just about "the big snows we used to have back in the old days." It seems that a bunch went out after a heavy snow, dragging the roads with the help of oxen so that people could use their sleighs and sledges, when one of the oxen slipped and got stuck, couldn't move at all, got a hoof caught in something . . . Well, they dug down, dug around, trying to free the ox's hoof, and what do you know . . . That ox had stuck its foot into a chimney!

Now, the blue snow of 1933 is *not* a lie. I am sure of it because of the way Ansel Powers tells me about it, because his wife Edna confirms it, because Les Ford from Potter Place, who has never been known to collaborate on a story, remembers it just as well and tells the same stories. It may be hard to believe, *but it was blue.* You stuck a shovel in it and it was *blue,* blue as that sky, blue as a bachelor's button. It fell in April, a late snow, and it fell fast. Les remembers that he'd been to a dance at Danbury, and when he went to bed at midnight, the sky was clear and full of stars; when he woke up in the morning, there it was. The snowplows were disassembled for summer; the road agent had to start up the old dozer and go patrol the road with it to clear a way for Model T's—and a few shiny Model A's. Sam Duby, the same blacksmith who made the first snowplows in Andover, woke up at two or three in the morning and had to do something, you know. Well, the outhouse was across the road in the barn and he went out to the end of the porch and it was snowing to beat the band and he just dropped a load right there . . . He's the only one who saw it snow; the rest of us went to bed under stars, woke up to the sun shining on three feet of blue snow.

In *The Voyage of the Beagle* Charles Darwin wrote about finding red snow, *Protococcus nivalis,* on the Peuquenes Ridge in Chile in 1835. "A little rubbed on paper gives it a faint rose tinge mingled with a little brick-red." When he examined it later, Darwin found "microscopical plants." As far as I know, no one took our blue snow into a laboratory.

Of course it snows in April every year, most often white, but you cannot call it winter anymore. Snow sticks around, in the north shade, most years until early in May, but it is ragged and dirty stuff, and we overlook it as we gaze in hopeful amazement at this year's crop of daffodils. Every year the earlier daffodils fill with snow, bright yellow spilling out white crystals, outraged optimism overcome by fact, emblem of corny desolation. And the worst storm I have driven through, after ten New Hampshire winters, occurred a few years back on the ninth day of May.

But annual aberration aside, March is the end of winter, and the transition to spring is April's melt. One year not long ago we had an open winter, with very little snow, *no* snow we all said; we exaggerated a little, for we had an inch here and an inch there. The winter was not only dry but mild, which was a good thing, for an open winter with cold weather destroys flowers and bushes and even trees, since snow is our great insulator. As it was, in our open winter we suffered one cold patch—twenty below for a week—and in the spring that followed, and in the summer, we discovered winterkill: A few rosebushes and old lilacs, plants and bulbs that had survived for decades, didn't make it that year. When spring came without a melt, when mild days softened with buttery air and the protected daffodils rose blowing yellow trumpets, we felt uneasy. All of us knew: Lacking the pains of winter, we did not deserve the rapture and the respite of spring.

Our annual melt is the wild, messy, glorious loosening of everything tight. It is gravity's ecstasy, as water seeks its own level on every level, and the noise of water running fills day and night. Down Ragged Mountain the streams rush, cutting through ice and snow, peeling away winter's cold layers: rush, trickle, rush. Busy water moves all day and all night, never tired, cutting away the corrupt detritus of winter; fingers of bare earth extend down hillsides; south sides of trees extend bare patches, farther every day; root-pattern rivulets, melting, gather downhill to form brief streams; dirt roads slog and driveways turn swamps.

Then it dries; last snow melts; trees bud green; soft air turns. Who can believe in winter now?

All of us. We know that winter has only retreated, waiting. When the bear comes out of its winter sleep, winter itself goes into hibernation, sleeping off the balmy months of peeper-sing until the red leaf wakes it again and the white season returns with the New Hampshire winter by which we know ourselves.

Spring

SPRING is the least of our seasons, and it has built no constituency in New Hampshire. Our countryside attracts leaf people in autumn who gape with good reason at the fauve hillsides; winter's skiers who drive north from Boston, skis atop Audis, and whole families over Christmas and schoolbreaks who break rich ankles; uncountable summer people who laze a permitted annual dally on the shore or in sailboats or simply in sun and play bridge at night by the light of state-liquor-store gin. But New Hampshire's spring people distinguish themselves by nonexistence. In April our restaurants and motels close for the month as weary industrialists of tourism take holiday in Carolina, Georgia, or Florida. For motelers and maitre d's, spring floats a brief intermission between the anxieties of ski time, when everything glides on the temperature, and the certain labors of long summer. Real spring people, often identical to our own summer people, gather at Hilton Head or sniff the sweet air of Savannah. Spring is long, tender, and luxurious in the Southeast, where the crocus shoves up its head in January and the flowering shrubs, like rhododendrons at the Masters in Augusta, waft rich odoriferous air through the warm nights.

Of the world's seasons spring has the best press. Where are the songs of spring? Everyplace. It is when the voice of the turtle is heard in the land. A later poet told how a young man's fancy lightly turned; another called April the cruelest month; another claimed always to mourn with ever-returning spring; still another, resident of Italy, protested, "Oh, to be in England now that April's there."

Now, I have never spent a whole spring in Carolina or Georgia, only flown in for a brief hallucinatory visit from chill muddy April or pestiferous May to hover a moment in the saccharine air of Milledgeville, Macon, or Charlotte. But in England I have spent four springs; I count them as a miser counts gold: two at Oxford, two in a village called Thaxted, not far from Cambridge. In England sometimes a January day can be purest spring: warm, muddy, lazy, sunny, with crocuses starting up. Correspondingly, in weird Albion, a gale always whoops out of the northeast early in August after a warmish week, gritty wind thrashes rain through the Doctor's Garden Fete, and somebody says, "It was rather a short summer but quite a nice one . . ."

But in England April, May, and early June are lemony days of velvet-green grass in the Fellows' Garden with bowls and croquet; evenings lengthening like the promise of an afterlife; balls at the colleges that end with a group photograph in the quadrangle at six in pale dawn; ten million daffodils by the Cam at the backs of the Cambridge colleges; and at Oxford the year's climax is Eights Week, early in June. The eights are crews competing on the Isis, but never mind. Pubs stay open, girls bloom into English roses, promise gilds itself in the golden sun of arrogant youth brazen with promise, the sun never sets, the sky never clouds, strawberries and champagne endlessly arrive carried by dutiful and conservative servants who know their place. We know: The beastly Huns, not to mention the Irish and the Working Classes, will never disturb our tranquil luxury.

In New Hampshire spring begins with rain and melt. For that matter, it continues to snow, at least from time to time, late in March through April. Spring snow rattles winter's death—or is it the triumphant final tour of winter? Well, *almost* final: perhaps *one* more go at Hedda, for charity of course. Or winter returns like a forty-four-year-old relief pitcher who has been practicing a knuckler in the backyard, throwing it to his mother. Now we become impatient: Let us give winter its gold watch; let us award it an honorary Oscar or a day of its own at Cooperstown; let us push it off to a condominium in the keys of Antarctica and stop all this damned nonsense about a comeback.

Water begins it, warm rain over the wasted gray drifts of March. Long days and nights of rain wear dingy ruts in our snowfields, or warm days of early sun release meltwater from crystals of hill and meadow, and the great crashing melt dozes creeks and streams, raising instant rivers where summer's gulch is dry. Water is never lazy, never quiet; it talks all day and gossips all night, chattering down hills through gullies to ditches at roadside. On the ponds ice rots and gray stains spread over level white. Provident ice fishermen have removed their bobhouses by early March, but every spring on New Hampshire's lakes some of these shacks tilt and sag and tumble through cold water to lake bottom. How many small huts, like outhouses *d'antan,* rot on pond bottoms? Ice leaves the lake one day when we do not notice; for weeks it has crept out from the shoreline, frayed from its muddy border, but when we gaze from the bridge to the pond's center, the ice looks steady and unbroken still. Then it is suddenly gone, for it sinks to the bottom while we are never looking.

Now pond and lake swell, rise, widen over meadow and bogland, lift picnic tables from the old year's summer and carry them a rod like pranksters, or misplace canoes, rafts, and docks improperly secured. Birch and popple that start at the water's edge now loom from water itself. Long ago our market town of Franklin routinely flooded in spring, the Pemigewasset widening and lifting into low-set workers' housing near the mills. Now a dam constructed by Army engineers in 1940 backs the water into a valley near the town of Hill.

During wet, melt, and high water, beavers chew at anything arboreal that appears attractive. At the south end of Eagle Pond they populate a boggy place and make it boggier with dams; nearby groves prickle with cone-shaped pointy stumps. Sometimes they leave behind a tree they've chewed down if it's too big to pull, or maybe they only wanted to strip bark off. There's a worked-over beaver plantation near the house at the north end of the hayfield between Route 4 and the railroad. These must be tasty trees, popple and gray birch, because the creatures bypass wood closer to their pond home in order to harvest this little grove. I've counted forty-seven chewed-off stumps. The railroad trench cuts deeply below this patch, and there's a rusty B & M fence to get through when the beaver transports his timber to the pond. Near the fence a well-worn trail looks like a cowpath or a lane trodden by habitual human feet—except that this path goes under a strand of wire ten inches off the ground. Here I've found a good-sized tree caught in the fence, hanging a third of its length into the air over the track; beavers are smart but they can't solve everything. Also I've found a tree hauled a long way from its stump but caught and wedged unmovable between other stumps. When I look at the trail that the beavers wear by their haulage I'm dazzled: After they roll the treetrunk down the sandbank, they must carry it across tracks, up another bank, then down a steep slope to Eagle Pond.

We never see beaver, except a distant nose sticking up from the water, leaving a V behind it as it swims across the pond carrying a stick. When we first moved here a cousin came to the kitchen door asking permission to trap beaver on our land. I signed the paper out of family feeling and cowardice, but I felt sorry for Bucky. It took six months before rage took guilt's place: I wanted to advance my cousin capital for more traps. Beaver chewed down four birches by our swimming place and let them rot; elsewhere they flooded gardens and hayfields by building dams. The fish-and-game people spend half their working hours blowing up beaver dams with dynamite. Lately the price for pelts has dropped like a chewed popple and my cousin has stopped trapping and beaver multiply.

As THE air warms, houseflies wake from their winter sleep and congregate at upstairs windows. For a week of this weather houseflies are the only pest, unless the driveway is a pest, for it becomes momentarily impassable, scourge of transmissions. Mud season's yellow viscosity churns under struggling wheels without exhausting itself to a solid bottom. We stay off the dirt roads that climb Ragged and circle the pond. Bert the RD lets air out of his tires for traction but gets stuck in mud season as he never sticks in blizzards or ice storms; it is the worst driving and the worst walking of the year. Sometimes the mud freezes at night, a grid of frozen seaways, torture for the shocks of cars; then by noon it melts back to colloid obscenity.

Sometimes this condition lasts for weeks but usually it is quick, and when it dries the air warms and the light turns yellowish, as if the mud's churn buttered the air. For a few days we enjoy the classic look of high spring. Crocuses stick their heads up opening fragile tentative mouths; daffodils climb beginning to unfold; the tulip rises with promise of outrage. Jane casts off winter gloom and works at the garden in a frenzy—swooping away gray leaves matted over the borders and against the house, raking twigs broken off by ice and gravel shoved everywhere by the snowplow. Jane frees soil for the grandeur of crack and blossom, enabling flowers. She works in such a frenzy for good reason: One day when the sun passes Ragged's edge and warms the air midmorning, suddenly *the blackflies are among us.*

For a day or two they don't bite. Then they start biting. Our Egyptian plague, blackflies annually destroy New Hampshire's spring. A bumper sticker turns up, NUKE THE BLACK FLIES, but drastic as the suggestion may be, it's pointless: After the last war only blackflies will prove nasty enough to survive, to evolve over a million years their own malicious culture. Oh, they bite. You hardly see them (no-see-ums is one of their names) but they have been with us forever. As Francis Parkman describes it, in the seventeenth century—and doubtless ever since they wandered this way from the Bering Strait—Indians lived in teepees dense with smoke to discourage blackflies and mosquitoes.

In New Hampshire although the air is balmy now we wear armor outdoors: long thick socks rolled up over heavy jeans, gloves, long sleeves rolled down, and for many a beekeeper's mask and hat. Otherwise flies get in our hair and smuggle themselves into the house. We don't always feel them hit but we know afterward: Great red welts rise on our skin. My mother-in-law was once bitten between her eyes so that her two eyes shut. Dogs go raw on their bald bellies.

We dab dope on face, neck, hair, hands, wrists, and ankles; it helps, if we keep on doing it, but it does not satisfy. Blackflies buzz around us forming an angry mobile helmet; they swarm and wheel within half an inch of our faces. Sometimes in spring I umpire softball games at the village school in Danbury, making crazy signals as my hands flip in constant involuntary motion warding blackflies. Similar wild signs emanate from pitcher, batter, and outfielders. It is spastic baseball, and if we were major leaguers we would be signaling—*Take! Hit! Steal! Bunt! Run! Don't run!*—on every pitch.

Mostly we stay inside. Jane makes desperate forays into her garden, transplanting this, fertilizing that, watering hastily; then she comes inside and takes a shower. Meantime tulips rise in their splendor, and daffodils that couldn't care less about blackflies dance their yellow dance on the granity hill behind the house. By the playhouse my cousin Freeman built for my grandmother Kate when she was five in 1880, with a noble slab of glacier-granite beside it, the ten thousand (really about two hundred) golden or gold-and-white daffodils raise bright agreeable faces. Uphill by the barn, and beside the woodshed under a sugarmaple near another boulder, and at the margin of the hayfield that runs south toward Kearsarge, Jane's daffodil armies march, onward floral soldiers. Oh, most wonderful of flowers, suncolored welcoming the sun, vigorous handsome energetic golden trumpets of spring heralding summer! I stare at them dreamily all day, happy to accept their wild generosity, safe behind panes of glass.

When blackflies start to diminish mosquitoes arrive, and spring is the least of our seasons. Here we don't suffer quite so much from mosquitoes; they are not so numerous as blackflies: As if to compensate for their numbers, of course, one mosquito can wreak havoc on a picnic or a night's sleep. But now I have gone on into summer. Fair enough: So do the blackflies.

. . .

THE FIRST vegetable to plant is peas; we scatter the pale round seed on top of March's rags of snow. My mother remembers planting them regularly on Saint Patrick's Day, for peas like it damp and cold. When it warms in April and May the little bushes rise among blackflies, and covered with dope we pick fresh peas for the table late in June.

In the old days April and May were heavy farming times, made heavier by mud and flies. It was time to cart manure into cornfield and vegetable garden and plow it under. The big cowbarn that my great-grandfather built in 1865 still stands, south of the house a little above it. Huge blocks of granite shore its east side against Ragged's mudslide, blocks so huge you would swear cranes must have hauled them, not oxen. West the barn drops away downhill. Its main floor is the second story, and as you look up from the house, the hill slopes enough so that there's a place to store a carriage under the grainshed that extends by the barnfloor. East of that door is the tie-up from which Holsteins strolled out to Ragged, which was their pasture, past the room for straining and cooling milk and the icehouse where we buried January's pond under sawdust for summer. Over the cows hay lofted two stories up.

And under the cows, west of the granite wall on bottom level, heaped the manure pile. Twice a day after milking we lifted long planks behind the cattle—rounded boards split from straight 1865 treetrunks, fastened to fixed floorboards by leather hinges made of worn-out harness—and slipped them over to open an eight-inch strip of lateral hole, the length of the tie-up. We scraped manure through this crack: Ranges of bovine excretion, down below, grew Alpine by April. For two weeks then—depending on snow, melt, and mud—my grandfather spent his days knee-deep in cowmanure. He kept a wagon for spreading it, which remained all year under the barn next to the manure pile, used every year for this one purpose only. The dump-cart remains there still, in good shape; if we wet the wheels to swell the wood tight inside iron rims, we could use it today. A small wooden seat rides on a spring next to a lever that lifted the truck bed up and slid manure off. The dump-cart under the barn flings its forearms down (arms that clutched the bony ribs of Riley and Roger, Ned's big bones, Nellie's black and Lady Ghost's pale gray) as if in despair on the humusy dirt of the floor where my grandfather let them fall in April of 1950. Beside it slope the diminishing alps of manure from later that year, before his heart attack in November and the cows' December departure forever and ever. We use it still; it makes great topsoil.

He carted many loads to fertilize his fields. In the last decades of his life he did it alone, except for a few years when Anson came back, the hired man who had worked for them when my mother was a girl. He departed, one day in the 1920s, for twenty-five years. Anson suffered from a learning disability; in the old days we used a scientific term that we pronounced *mow*-ron. My grandfather wore boots and overalls, which hung on a hook under the barn, used only for this purpose, and with his shovel filled the cart and then drove it into the fields he planted with millet and fieldcorn and to the big garden plot. He spread it with the aid of gravity, and sometimes Anson, and with one shovel. When some was left over from the cropfields, he spread it on hayfields.

Mostly it was cowmanure. The horse's stall got dug out once or twice a week, horsemanure shoveled through a trap door down beside the Holsteins'. From the sheepbarn once or twice a year my grandfather extracted the rich mixture of sheepmanure and straw;

my grandmother used some for her flowers. The crazy compost of the chickenhouse floor was too strong—chickenmanure, straw, and the decomposed detritus of all the garbage the hens had pecked at over the year: dry skeletal corn cobs, pale shreds of carrot tops and pea pods, even specks of old eggshells—and it would burn seed up.

There was even a little nightsoil, for my grandfather never quite accepted the indoor bathroom. In 1938 my grandparents added this innovation, struck off from the dining room: a narrow cold dingy miraculous toilet, wash stand, and bathtub perpetually in trouble, water freezing in the winter and spiders working their way up from bathtub drain all summer. The bathroom supplemented but did not replace the outhouse. This old facility did not require a trudge through rain or snow. Although suitably far from living quarters, it situated itself under the continuous roof of the extended farmhouse. To reach it we exited the kitchen through the door to the toolshed, then through another door into the woodshed; we turned a corner at the back of the woodshed, and the outhouse door took the farthest corner. My grandfather, however, kept a roll of toilet paper near the cowmanure under the barn, and during chores if he was taken short he squatted there. I think he preferred the barn. Surely the notion of indoor defecation seemed obscene; even the outhouse was a little close to home. When he was old and sick he used the plumbing, I think with some distress.

When manure was spread on the fields, it was time to pull the plow from the long shed between chickencoop and sheepbarn where he stored plow, hayrack, mowing machine, and horsedrawn rake under cover from winter weather. I suppose he plowed five acres for garden, fieldcorn, and millet. I never knew my grandmother to buy a vegetable. Row after row of peas, beans in many varieties, bush beans and pole starring Kentucky Wonders, beets, tomatoes, carrots, parsnips, potatoes, and Golden Bantam corn. Millet, or sometimes Hungarian, was sweet heavy-grained grass that he scythe-mowed every afternoon in July and August for his cattle; it helped to persuade the cattle down from the hill's sweet grass for afternoon milking: Apparently millet and Hungarian were cow-delicious. (I tried them myself and they were sweet.) Fieldcorn, chopped up and siloed in September, provided nutriment for cattle all winter long.

After plowing when the time was right—usually after the last full moon around Memorial Day—it was time to plant. Soon enough it was time to weed, long hours with a hoe—my grandmother too—making sure that the vegetables started strong. No help from a rototiller, but horse and harrow helped out between the spaced rows of corn.

LATE WINTER and early spring was the time for new animals. Chicks were easiest. Before my time the hens hatched their own. At some point around the Great War the chicks began to come by parcel post, and in spring the P.O. down at Henry's store filled up with noisy rectangular boxes, cheep-cheep-cheep. Everybody kept chickens. We brought ours back to the shed and opened the boxes, each packed to sequester a hundred live chicks. Brooding factories packed the eggs before hatching, and the tiny creatures cracked through their shells on their journey here, in the baggage cars of trains or in depots and post offices. The factories packed more than a hundred to be sure they delivered a hundred. Always a few eggs arrived unhatched and dead and one or two neonates lay stiff and dry among the riotous throng that rolled and teetered and chirped infant cries. We kept them warm and noisy in the shed until the nights were warmer; then they thrived in the yard behind the henhouse, a hundred new lives pecking into ancient dirt, eating grain from V-shaped feeders, drinking water I carried from the trough at roadside.

My grandfather bred his sheep so that lambs came in May after the mothers were out to pasture and the nights warm, but sometimes a lamb was born in the barn while it was still cold, which distressed him. New births every spring were economically essential; sheep brought money disproportionate to the time they took, and twin lambs were a cause for rejoicing.

In the winter the quantity of milk decreased rapidly as the great Holsteins swelled up with their babies, to dry out in the weeks before birth. Earlier when each cow came into heat, my grandfather left his bull alone with the chosen member of the black-and-white seraglio. Cedric Blasington, the farmer just down the road, lacked a bull himself; from time to time he led a distraught cow to our barn. My grandmother took her daughters up-attic to distract them while the service was performed, but they knew something was going on; they peeked to see cows jumping about in excitement. In spring when the cows birthed my grandfather midwifed, tying a rope around the emerging calf to pull as the bossy pushed. Sometimes he had to enter a cow as far as he could reach to assist in a breech or posterior birth. One of the great sights on a farm is the joy of the Holstein sisterhood when a calf is born. Not only does the mother lick the child; the whole herd tries to, and the community celebrates, enormous black-and-white bovines leaping as much as they are able and bellowing out of their collective triumph.

When the first vegetables edge up from cracked mud and earth, the farmer's enemies assemble: weeds, drought or flood, slugs and cutworms, an entomologist's army of insects—and the imperturbable tribe of the woodchuck. Other pests include deer that browse a vegetable garden to devastation; chipmunks and moles that eat the bulbs of flowers; bears that prefer the hives of the honeybee; foxes, weasels, fishers, and skunks that kill chickens; dogs and coyotes that kill sheep and lambs; and coons, shrewdest of vegetarian predators, that harvest our corn, taking the ripest ears on the morning before we boil water and walk into the cornpatch to pick supper.

Woodchucks are season-long, beginning in late spring as soon as peas emerge, and do battle with the superiority of numbers, reinforcements, and stupidity. I don't suppose that my grandfather had much trouble from chucks until sometime in the 1920s when he understood that he could no longer keep a dog. A dog that runs loose eliminates the woodchuck problem; woodchucks have a dog problem. Hunter and Tripp herded sheep and helped find the cattle when they stayed up-mountain eating on late summer afternoons; they also protected vegetables and chickens from predators. But cars proliferated on Route 4 and got faster and faster until they reached speeds like 35 mph. At the north end of the farm a car approaches the house over a little ridge, unable to stop in time if the driver sees a creature in the road. The Model T killed Wesley's dogs. So my grandfather burying Tripp in his woe knew that the internal-combustion engine forbade him the pleasure, companionship, and utility of dogs.

It would not have occurred to him to keep a pet inside and walk it on a leash. He loved his dogs; they earned their keep. Cats did too. The notion of a cat *indoors* made my grandmother wrinkle her nose—something she did frequently apropos rum, baseball on Sunday, ballroom dancing, and Frenchmen—although on rare occasions the senior barncat might be allowed entrance early in autumn when frost chased fieldmice inside in numbers greater than traps could handle. Once the barncat ate improvident mice to its full, it was out on its ear.

The barn was dense with cats. Silage and grain encouraged rodent-presence, and without a resident cat militia, mice and rats would have eaten the grainshed hollow. My grandfather when he milked (like all farmer grandfathers everywhere) swiveled a teat and squirted milk into the gaped jaws of kittens and cats who sat waiting for his performance, a little row of organic Staffordshire cats with pink mouths stretched wide. In the 1940s one old gray mother-tabby, shrewd about Route 4 and automobile behavior, teats hanging low from three-litter years, held perpetual sway, but her cleverness was an acquired characteristic, not transferable by Lamarckian genetics to her countless kittens. As a boy I buried one a week in the cats' graveyard between sheepbarn and vegetable garden.

Now we reverse old ways. Cats and dogs live indoors and our barns loom gray and silent without animals; I walk Gus along Route 4 on his chain; every day Jane and I drive or walk him to the triangular meadow by the pond or to a flattish stretch of New Canada Road or to cut-over acres of woodlot—someplace where cars are few and Gus can run loose. Ada guards the indoor house as Mio, Catto, Bella, and Amos did before them, performing effective duty against generations of mice, moles, voles, chipmunks—and one rat.

WHEN WE moved here a dozen years ago, we planted a garden that became a Woodchuck Resources Center. As a boy I would sit for an hour at dawn and another at dusk until I got a good shot at a woodchuck. My rifle was a short-barreled handmade old octagonal Mossberg .22 carbine, built for target shooting mostly. I practiced my eye by assassinating tin cans with my father and then when I was in my teens killed many woodchucks and buried them among the roadkilled kittens. But now I lack patience to sit for an hour waiting for the fat imbecilic figure of a woodchuck to stick its head out of its hole, sniff the air, and draw fire. Without patience, without a dog, our garden disappeared down woodchuck jaws year after year—peas eaten down as they ripened, beets gnawed into the earth, Kentucky Wonders nipped in the bud. Old holes were reinhabited each year, and each year fresh sand heaped in fields near the garden reported growth in the chuck population. Suburban woodchucks from Massachusetts built second homes in New Hampshire. Five or six times a day I wandered across Route 4 swinging my elegant rifle, looking for a woodchuck to shoot. Usually I saw nothing; occasionally I shot from a distance and missed; once I killed a creature sunning himself behind the ruins of the sheepbarn.

Mostly they just ate us out. We tried folk remedies: dried blood, Kitty Litter, and planting marigolds. I bought one of the gas bombs Agway sells, but I wasn't sure how the subway system worked and I was wary of trying it. I raised a good fence, which helped, but I couldn't use an electric fence because of the difficulties of stringing wire across Route 4. I stayed away from leg traps. On a visit to Agway, complaining about our woodchucks, I heard a story from a clerk: A year before, somebody had dropped around for one remedy and another, continually complaining and failing, getting madder and madder. He tried gas bombs and lost some chickens; he tried a leg trap and took a neighbor's shepherd to the vet with a broken leg. One day he arrived as red as the beets he had lost and bought sticks of dynamite and caps and went home and blew up his garden and hayfield. His garden was gone, his fields looked like Saipan—but he sure got that woodchuck.

Finally I bought a Havahart trap, which has its heart by capturing the animal intact when he trips a pedal going after food. I baited it with vegetables and fruit and caught two or three woodchucks every spring. These captures discouraged the tribe and allowed us three quarters of our garden. Of course the trap leaves the gardener with a problem: What do you do with the victim? Rumor suggests that some folks sneak live woodchucks by night into the gardens of local Democrats. I solved the problem my own way. When I caught Woody I took my Mossberg out of the closet and shot him through the head as he quavered in my Havahart trap.

A cousin of mine used to eat one woodchuck a year. Because he lived by himself without an oven, he prevailed upon my grandmother to bake it. No one else in this house would touch the meat. Every spring when I shot my first woodchuck in the Havahart, I meditated eating him. I knew, after all, what filled his stomach and gave him leg muscle; I had ordered his victuals by seed from Burpee. Every spring when the first chuck lay dead but unburied, I would look again at Irma

S. Rombauer's woodchuck recipe in *Joy of Cooking*. Every year when I reread the part about wearing rubber gloves to skin the beast on account of the mites, I fetched the shovel from the toolshed and dug a hole deep enough so that dogs would not annoy the corpse.

I DO NOT FARM; less and less do I farm; physical work grows more and more alien. It isn't a general laziness; often I work a hundred-hour week. I keep a farmer's hours and a farmer's work week but avoid physical labor and raise no crops and milk no milk. I sit at my desk and put words on paper. When we first moved here to stay, I dreamed about replacing my grandparents. Mostly my dreams offered reasons and justifications: dreams for repairing trouble. My favorite was the morning when we woke (as I dreamed it) to discover that my grandfather and grandmother—very old but still living with us on the farm, still tending their hens, sheep, and cattle—were missing, nowhere to be found; what's more, the animals were gone. With the imperturbability that outfits some dreams, I decided that the old people must have dropped dead someplace while they were working; their bodies must be concealed by tall grass. We were about to give up the search and go back to our own work when we saw them coming toward us, still a couple of hundred yards away, walking up the narrow dirt road from Andover (the road was clearly dirt, road paved before I was born), waving and shouting to catch our attention: They were leading back to the barn a whole straggling line of ostriches, zebras, elephants, tigers, crocodiles. In my dream I understood that, because they were too old to continue farming, they had traded their Holsteins and merinos and Rhode Island reds for zoo animals, for orangutans and lions, and I knew as I woke that I felt poetry to be as exotic, beautiful, scary, and useless as leopards and peacocks.

IN MAY AND JUNE the green comes back.

Winter's white is beautiful when it begins but degenerates by

March to gray snow that melts mud-brown. Spring begins as monochrome as November, but from the gray-brown, faint green arises in grass that the sun heats. Then with more sunlight green mounts, gathers, swells, and explodes, its onrushing upthrusting fibrous joy cavorting from the ground, yellow-green to butter the soul's bread with. Down from the verdant twigs of the trees, green descends toward green uprising, dog's-ear leaves first unwrapping their tender delicate early edible green, pale and lemony spring-leaf green, later to darken or weather into the green-shutter leaves of August.

Not until spring's end does the bounty of summer foreshadow itself in knuckled fingers of asparagus that hoist themselves through tall grass underneath the lilac. After a rain and a hot day, asparagus leaps so rapidly that it goes by if we do not harvest it daily. Every year we miss a dozen that go to seed and grow tall as corn, wispy small trees in the breeze. The first freshness of the year's crop, they are green heaven to the mouth. And now peas bush and thicken, now rhubarb grows green elephant ears over its strange ropy red-corded stalks. Best of all, the old single roses by the driveway's bottom turn green-leafed and bud a thousand tiny green buds that will welcome summer, just after solstice every year, with pink flowers and white. When they bloom they overpower the air with sweetness, then shatter almost immediately. My grandmother loved her old roses, and her small round gardens, marigolds under the kitchen window and poppies at the edge of the hayfield by the barn. They rise green now making ready their sweet violence.

Spring's greatest outburst happened earlier in the old days, and because it was the greatest I have saved it for last. In April between mud and blackflies, just before manuring and plowing, my grandfather turned the cattle out to pasture. (Although it no longer happens on this farm, it never stops happening.) All winter they stood upright in their stalls daylong, tied to wooden poles by steel chains. They lay down to sleep; they had plenty to eat; twice a day my grandfather unchained them to walk a few feet from tie-up to watering trough. They walked stiffly, down the one step and across frozen mud to the cement oblong trough to dip their pink noses into the just-unfrozen water. The surface froze every night and my grandfather lifted out big oblong pieces of ice. In January, in the shade and short daylight, winter's icy litter left a series of trough-lids, like a sheaf of transparent pages. When the cattle drank their fill they stared around them, maybe dimly aware that they last saw this place twelve hours earlier, then each gave way to the next thirsty bossy and stiffly returned to the stalls where my grandfather left grain to encourage and reward their expeditious return.

One day in April their lives changed utterly. My grandfather kept an eye on the pasture grass, ready to spring his cattle loose. Snow and ice remained on the north side of sugarmaples and boulders, and in much of the pasture lowish sun penetrated only briefly and grass remained gray-brown, but where a clearing opened up in a high pasture, or where in lower patches new sun felt its way through a forest gap, live green grass rose edible in April. With crocuses came grass and with grass cows' paradise.

One day he untied them as if for the trough but maneuvered around them to open the pasture gate past the trough, portal to a hundred and thirty acres of Ragged Mountain: granite, hemlock, sugarbush, oak, elm, birch, and abundant grass. At first when he pushed and whooped them toward the gate they moved sluggishly. When they discovered themselves let out to pasture again, free to wander, free to eat all day long, their capacity for joy—these slow-moving mountains that usually made a name for lethargy and passivity, stoic mothers untouched and unflappable—turned huge as their bodies: They jumped, they rubbed great sides against treetrunks, they leapt, they bellowed abruptly, they bounced. For a few moments the great Holsteins were eight kittens frolicking on the stomach of mothercat Ragged Mountain, play-fighting and romping. Then they let down their great heads into the sweet tender upgrowth of new grass and fed on the green milk of spring as we all do, even in New Hampshire where spring is the least of our seasons.

Summer

THE LONGEST DAY is the best day, when June twenty-second's pale light lasts into evening. In New Hampshire we are north enough to believe rumors from Scandinavia and Shakespeare about the madness of midsummer night's eve. Even contemporary England turns wild. I lived for a while in an East Anglian village where the morris men performed the Abbots Bromley Horn Dance on midsummer night's eve. They waited until the ghostly late twilight of ten-thirty to wend down from the immense church on the hill—fifteenth century, with holy carving in stone and wood—through the graveyard already straggly with weeds, past the chestnut tree, almost as huge and old as the church, down Stony Lane past beetling medieval cottages that stonemasons working on the church inhabited for five generations. First danced the vicar playing a fife, followed by fiddlers in green, a dancing man suited up as a deer wearing green, two others carrying stags' horns, and at the rear two dancers with bows and arrows. Clearly the old religion survived at the solstice and the green man would be pierced by an arrow like William Rufus mistaken for a hind. We spent one year there in a 1485 house opposite the guildhall and from our balcony watched the old troupe emerge from Stony Lane jigging to the eldritch tune. We sat with a poet friend visiting from England's north whose hair stood up as straight as grass. The next day as we walked between the church and the windmill a black cat streaked across our path and my friend leapt in the air; it was, he explained, the vicar.

The old religion stays underground in New Hampshire, or deep in the woods with Goodman Brown, but even here June twenty-second lofts gently out of this world. It begins early in the spirit-light of three-forty-five or so. When we are lucky the whippoorwill wakes us with his three syllables as brilliant as crystal, calling again, answering the call of a distant other, from the grass beside our bedroom window. The insistent triad continues for twenty minutes—*wake*-up-*now, wake*-up-*now*—and sets slugabeds cursing on every dirt road in New Hampshire. But if late sleepers erupt from their beds with mayhem on their minds, they are out of luck: The whippoorwill is elusive and we seldom catch glimpse of it. Brown, unpretty, it soars away to doze in its ground nest through sunlit hours.

Not only the whippoorwill wakes us on this long day and its briefer cousins of high summer. Every bough bends with feathered guests singing of summer in full-throated ease. Now the bluejay squawks and the fat crows caw—big as hens and black as evil where they gather on roadkills or on seeded fields—and the small birds trill, chirp, and exult or appear to exult; at least we exult as the pale light rises early casting a pink-yellow glow on the eastern slopes of Kearsarge. I walk outside blinking and stretching with the dog that blinks and stretches, performing The Dog from his yoga class, sniffing with total concentration. For him the nose and its pleasures and codes of knowledge are ten times more intense than my delighted vision. In dog language there are two hundred words for squirrel piss.

Now I inhale cool morning air and feel cold wet dew on my toes in summer sandals. The brief black tide of night withdrawn, the wet sand of morning emerges in vague light. An early squirrel tries the feeder that hangs from a branch on the great maple, squirrelproof squirrelsource, and gobbles his fill. Why not feed squirrels? I love these lithe tree-rats with bright eyes and nervous head-jerks that leap and run and fill mouths with grass for their nests and chase each other on the great trunks of old trees. Everywhere on lawn and hayfields we find round holes neatly cut into the ground, black Métro entrances for chipmunk, snake, mole, and vole. Gus the dog tries to give chase, which is why I leash him. Ada the cat spends all day on the breadbox watching birds; her life list fills a dozen pages. In the back garden where Jane tends flowers there is a stone retaining wall turned into cliff dwellings by chipmunks, skittery and quick, their furred cheeks bulging with tulip and crocus bulbs. Maybe the hummingbird is even more wonderful: In the hollyhocks, at the hosta, hummingbirds hover and flash. These overgrown bumblebees, biodegradable helicopters, athletes of stasis, fly or stand vibrating on air inches away from us all summer long.

Summer is one continual morning under greeny leaves looking across greeny hayfields. When it diminishes it diminishes slowly, like our own aging and indistinguishable from it. When we claim that things aren't what they used to be we are always correct, though we may mistake diminishment's provenance. On the other hand, some things *do* get worse, even in the world outside: The whippoorwill is gone or going. My cousins who live on a dirt road away from our busy Route 4 still wake to hear him sing, but less often now. Four years ago we heard one whippoorwill, and since then none; ten years ago he was loud and many. Because he is shy, he is apt to avoid the highway, but traffic has not scared him away. He dies, he and his race; his old sap-sucker generation narrows to disappear. How many years has DDT been prohibited? Yet DDT endures in the earth where we spread it once, and rises from the earth in blackfly livers that the whippoor-will eats. DDT thins whippoorwill eggshells so that they crack and the embryo dies that will not wake us in the morning to sing and to breed more whippoorwills. People sleep later in the morning.

Summer morning has its birdsong still and its clear pitchforks of energy. Then the day lengthens in silence and we work at our desks while the sun struggles past Ragged to rise in the sky. Because we are protected by Ragged and by outspreading elderly maples we don't take the sun's brunt until afternoon. The old house stays cool, even cold most mornings: a fire in the Glenwood. Usually once or twice in

July and August I scrape thin ice from the windshield at five o'clock. On the hottest days, when the New Hampshire midday reaches the nineties, our house stays cool except for upstairs late in the afternoon. Occasionally it's humid but night cools down and by dawn it's cold; even during a hot patch we sleep breathing cool air.

Afternoons we go down to Eagle Pond; elsewhere it would be Eagle Lake, for this is not a circle of water with a few ducks in it; it's forty acres, shaped like a humpback whale, shallow and muddy at its edge and deep in the center. Half a mile northwest is Eagle's Nest, a small camelhump hill where the bird lived that fed from the pond twice a day in my great-grandfather's time; Ben Keneston named our house Eagle Pond Farm when he moved here in 1865. He was thirty-nine years old, a sheepfarmer from Ragged with four children and more to come. My grandmother Kate, born at this place in 1878 when her father was fifty-two, never knew the eagle.

My great-grandfather owned the land around the pond. When my mother and her sisters went to Bates College and my grandparents needed cash for tuition, they sold land on the west side of the pond to provide space for a boys' camp; my mother remembers when they grew potatoes there. Over the years the camp expanded, buying land to the north that belonged to my uncle Luther's son-in-law Jesse Johnson, and from my grandmother a large patch to the south end of the pond where we once pastured sheep, where they built a companion girls' camp and tennis courts. We still own the east side from the bridge by the beaver bog past a triangular field, then past a narrow steep slope where the railroad trench cuts near the pond, a few hundred yards north to a corner that belonged to Kate's older brother, my uncle Luther, a Congregational minister who pastured his sheep beside the pond. Now it's the Eagle Pond Motel.

Pond afternoons begin at the end of June, maybe the first days of July, after the blackflies have largely departed. At the little beach we cut into the east side of the pond tall hemlocks and oaks screen out the sun until one or two in the afternoon. We walk down a steep slope over slippery needles and weathered oak leaves to our clearing on the mossy shore. A dozen birches lean out over dark water. The water is dark with minerals; exiting the pond as it goes south under the bridge, it turns into the Blackwater River. By the pond's edge under a birch a tiny ancient rosebush blooms pink and brief at June's turn into July. Ferns and oak saplings upthrust every summer. Moss sinks under our bare feet and sends up tiny red flowers. We sit in canvas sling chairs beside the picnic table or lie in the sun on Newberry's plastic chaises taking the breeze and the warmth. These afternoons I stare a lot, imbecilic with pleasure, at birches and ferns, at Eagle's Nest in the distance, and at campers. The camp is remarkably unobnoxious. When I was a boy it permitted me notions of superiority as I watched boys my own age marching to an indifferent drummer, or at least hiking under the direction of a counselor. They didn't feed chickens, load hay, or listen to old poems recited by a man milking Holsteins in a tie-up. They played games, went on hikes, practiced crafts, and sang songs; worst of all, they were stuck with each other's company.

The camp is a comfortable affair where children from prosperous suburbs (on Parents' Weekend the camp road jams with Mercedes-Benzes) visit our countryside. A congregation of four hundred children remains quiet, polite, and tidy: They don't litter; they don't vandalize or make trouble. If we hear reveille from an amplified tape in the morning and taps at night before we go to sleep, these sweet sounds raise a frail frame against our improvised day unstructured by clocks. The only unpleasant sound from the camp arrives during our pond afternoons when the girls waterski; the motorboat growls and makes waves that erode our shoreline. Still, the one motorboat on Eagle Pond interrupts us for only an hour, as we observe the gaiety and terror of ten-year-old girls holding on for life. I tried feeling grumpy about it, but the pleasure of watching pleasure—all these skinny daughters—won me grudgingly over.

Otherwise, our afternoons at the pond are silent. I gaze at the landscape and at clouds; I look at a book; occasionally I write a line, or a note toward a line, but I don't call it working. Jane reads and soaks in sun. We swim a little, but mush and mussel shells underfoot, not to mention green corpsefinger weeds straggling in our faces, make swimming less than perfect. With summer guests we laze talking and eat slow picnic suppers. Mid-August the campers leave. Jane turns melancholy as their departure plays taps for summer, but there are compensations, like perfection of quietness. Great oaks rise moving uphill from the birches by the shore. These trees protect us and hide us. I like swimming out fifty yards so that I can turn around, float or tread water, and stare back at the place I mostly stare out from—at the succession or hierarchy of trees, from delicate ghost birches leaning so decoratively, to the brave hemlock, tall and straight like a tree destined to become the mast of His Majesty's frigate that will blockade the Spanish ports, to the great irregular oaks and the intermixture of smaller ash and popple. At the hilltop by the railroad rises a birch a yard thick.

Late August, early September, the last afternoons punctuate themselves with sounds of falling acorns. I make my annual acorn collection; I stare at them and try to understand why I love them so much. Often they come two together, tiny metallic smooth green breasts with sharp nipple points, knitted caps on top to end breasthood. I hold them, rub them, shine them; I take my favorites home to put on my desk where they turn brown and I throw them away.

Lying still we watch squirrels gathering acorns. Sometimes if we keep quiet we spy a quick mink scooting under ferns and low bushes. We hear frogs chatter. If I walk back and forth along the water I cause a continual series of frog-splats by the startle my footsteps make; it is as if I were beating a drum. Now that the pond is depopulated we may see an enormous loon or jump at its terrifying cry. We have watched ducks all summer, little platoons of ducklings hiding in coves from motorboats and campers, now growing larger. Canada geese fly over in huge flotillas, heading south.

FISH, FLESH, and fowl commend all summer long whatever is begotten, born, or dies. All summer the creation thrives, wasps and roses. Tiny ants plague the kitchen. A bundle of wasps models a new nest under an attic eave. By the road at the end of June single old roses that budded late in spring burst forth with petals pink and white for the briefest season, ancient flowers my grandmother loved as a girl a century ago, doubtless sniffed by early settlers born in the eighteenth century. Shy small frail petals outcurl only to fall, to litter the green earth with their iridescence, making another beauty for an hour. While they bloom we hover above them, taking deep and startling breaths, for their odor is all the perfumes of Arabia, ambergris of all whales of all Pacifics, wave upon wave of velvety sensuous sweetness. We bend, sniff, shake our heads, walk away, and return for more. We cut a few—as abundant as they're brief—to take to church or float in a bowl on the black Glenwood. Quick and fragile as the flowers are, the bushes are durable. All winter snowplows heap dirty drifts on them thick with salt. Sometimes the plow gouges their earth; we think they must have been damaged this year, but come the end of June they raise to the summer air their proliferate odor.

Although the old farmers weren't known for their devotion to beauty, they loved their flowers. While I hayed with my grandfather, working as hard as he did he would pause stock-still from time to time—maybe as we worked the Crumbine place and looked across the valley toward Vermont's hills—and sigh and praise the glory. My grandmother interrupted the million tasks of her household—making soap, pies, bread, doughnuts, jam, and jelly; canning, sewing, darning, knitting, crocheting, egg gathering, washing, ironing—to tend her flowers. She kept a small round garden in front of the kitchen window over the set-tubs where she spent so much of her life. I remember marigolds there, zinnias, pansies early, hollyhocks. Across the yard, past the far driveway at the lip of the hayfield, she tended a circle of poppies that dazzled their Chinese reds against the long wavy gray-green grass. Some summers now a lone poppy rises in the field. In a tiny round bed by the road I remember my grandmother placing, among the green things, silvery burned-out radio tubes that she found beautiful. She loved a crockery birdbath that she ordered from Sears and set in front of the house and kept full of water where small birds routinely bathed. Also she stuck in the lawn painted wooden ducklings following a mother duck. In our back garden now we keep a wooden cutout of a girl in clogs watering a wooden cutout tulip. In front we favor whirligigs—a woodchopper, another milking a cow.

We say that the old farmers weren't known for their devotion to beauty, with their long workdays and their residual Calvinism, but perhaps their inattention allowed them to cultivate beautiful things without self-consciousness. The shape of an old Cape is handsome—and the wooden-carved pillars at the corners of Greek-temple farmhouses, and the elegant joints of barn beams, and the coherent stonework of walls. An old flower garden is not useful, but as you walk in the dense woods of New Hampshire in summer you know you are close to an old farmstead when you find the lilac and the old roses growing; the house is collapsed and even the cellarhole hardly distinguishable, but the farmwife's flowers endure.

Nor was it only in gardens and architecture that art showed itself. Theater groups in the villages put on annual performances. Yearlong, groups met once a fortnight to speak pieces, play the piano, and sing. We found in an old desk an 1890s record book containing the minutes of the South Danbury Oratorical and Debating Society, where my grandparents performed and courted. My grandmother played the piano; my grandfather spoke pieces, the same story-poems I heard in the tie-up fifty years later. After an hour in which citizens played, sang, and showed off for each other, they took coffee and then debated a topic like "Resolved: That the United States should cease from further territorial expansion." Maybe they were more political than aesthetic—they were certainly more passionate about national politics than most of their descendants—but it is remarkable how much art and beauty entered their daily lives, whatever they called it. Shaker design is elegant, simple, clear, durable, classic; this austere sect never consciously sought beauty.

The Shakers who fascinated Hawthorne were numerous not so long ago. My mother remembers fainting once in Enfield when she was a girl; two Shaker ladies alighted from a carriage to help her. Although the women had difficulty climbing into and out of the wagon, and lifting my mother, the two Shaker men up front could not assist them because they could not touch them.

In front of the porch Jane grows tulips, poppies, thermopsis, campanula (*C. carpatica, persicifolia, lactiflora*), phlox, daffodils, crocus, Siberian iris, dwarf German iris, peonies, foxglove, coral bells, old-fashioned single hollyhocks, bleeding heart, astilbe—as well as lavender, lovage, thyme, and oregano. At the house's front on Route 4 she grows daylilies, ajuga, Shasta daisies, yarrow, watermelon poppies, and some poppies without names that Mary Jane Ogmundson gave her. In back she tends a secret garden paved with brick she laid; it is hidden enough from the road so that she can sunbathe. Here the old wellhead raises a platform that she covers with pots of basil, geraniums, strawberries with alyssum around the edge, fragrant acidanthera, lobelia, nemesia, and browallia. There is a bench, a chair, and a pretty chaise; she has a cement swan-pot here, a cement lion, a terracotta putto, a sundial, and a tall iron potholder spilling over with bleeding hearts. In the interstices of the bricks, Jane plants glory-of-the-snow. Around the base of the wellhead she grows buttercups.

Against the retaining wall that holds Ragged back she plants heather, peonies, veronica (Crater Lake Blue), evening primrose, lamb's ears, artemesia (Silver Mound), dwarf asters, bee balm, *Lysimachia clethroides* (gooseneck loosestrife), Jacob's ladder, more phlox, more campanula, and more Siberian iris, red-twigged dogwood, and roses. On the hill above the wall, shading back to the ferns, oaks, and sugarmaples of Ragged Mountain, the spring's daffs defer to wave after wave of daylilies, the regular orange kind so common we forget how beautiful they are, yellow trumpets from White Flower Farm called Hyperion and planted in memory of John Keats—daylilies plain and fancy. All winter I sense Jane's silent presence in the dining room where she stands many-sweatered in the gloom, peering out into the back garden where bench and swan and sundial stick up through snow. She daydreams summer, daydreams seeds and plants she will order and tend; her mind blooms with bright petals in gray February.

Where she grows her lilies my aunts in the 1930s made a rock garden. I remember masses of pinks. Neither Caroline nor Nan married young. Both schoolteachers, occasionally they traveled in summer, and Caroline took an M.A. at Yale Summer School, but mostly they returned to Eagle Pond Farm, to their father and mother and nephew. The sisters cleared a beach near our swimming place, which they called Sabine, and when I was little, before I started haying with my grandfather in 1941, I spent my afternoons paddling and swimming with them, collecting mussel shells and turtles, scaring frogs.

THE GREATEST CROP in New Hampshire's July and August, for the last one hundred and forty years, is the summer people. I date them from the railroad but they came even earlier by stagecoach and horseback. Mid-nineteenth-century prosperity in the manufacturing North brought them before and after the Civil War. The poets and essayists of New England came to New Hampshire, and America's Alps sponsored a White Mountain School of painting. Nathaniel Hawthorne, who wrote many stories out of his New Hampshire trips—"The Great Stone Face" about the Old Man, "The Ambitious Guest," "The Great Carbuncle," "The Canterbury Pilgrims" about a Shaker settlement south of us—died in a hotel in Plymouth on his way to the mountains for a holiday with his old Bowdoin classmate the ex-president of the United States Frank Pierce. Ralph Waldo Emerson had nasty things to say about citizens of New Hampshire because he was annoyed with Daniel Webster, the Massachusetts senator who was born here. Melville and Thoreau came on foot and rowing a boat. William James had a summer place up north, and Henry visited him and wrote beautifully in *The American Scene* about New Hampshire's summer countryside. Henry Adams's great friend John Hay—Lincoln's private secretary and biographer, later secretary of state under McKinley and the first Roosevelt—spent every summer on Lake Sunapee, west of us.

They came by the thousands, women and children first, up by trains from Boston away from the heat. Their husbands followed on weekends and for two weeks in August. At Potter Place stages took them to New London, and to Elkins on Pleasant Lake. My mother remembers when Harry K. Thaw, famous murderer of Stanford White over the girl in the red velvet swing, parked his private railroad car at Potter Place, and with his keeper—Clarence Darrow copped an insanity plea for him; sprung from the insane asylum, he was required to keep a keeper—climbed Kearsarge and slept at the New London Inn. From West Andover's depot the stage took them to Springfield. Although there were lakes here and there, swimming was still an exotic pastime. People did not come north for water sports, nor for tennis or golf or anything except cool air. Huge old wooden inns rose on every hillside, some still standing, and the richest folks kept their own houses, or cottages as they called them. Halfway up Kearsarge, where the CCC made a parking lot and picnic area before the Second World War, stood Winslow House where the stage deposited Bostonians with trunks full of their clothes and even their china. Many visitors simply boarded at farms where they added plates to a table already large, occupied a spare room, and shared the outhouse.

Summer people were essential to the economy even before the collapse of farming. At the Pleasant Lake Inn—handsome with all its gables at the west end, with a splendid view of Kearsarge rising beyond the water—my great-aunt Nanny cooked all summer. Families spent summers at the same address for a hundred years. Children from Massachusetts and New Jersey grew up identifying July and August with Lake Sunapee, with Springfield or Danbury or Enfield.

These months make islands of guiltless hours away from school and the rules of winter; the summer place becomes a mental state, a name for sweet freedom, innocent irresponsibility, imagination's respite, time for loafing and inviting the soul. Poets of place hymn paradisal castles of summer: Poets as diverse as Charles Olson and T. S. Eliot write eloquently of their different Gloucesters. Now in our backwoods of New Hampshire, many permanent citizens are emigrants or descendants of emigrants from city and suburb, and a small but valuable contingent are children of the summer vacationers who came to love the landscape not only as interchangeable scenery—cards in a deck that flip through Switzerland, Mexico, Ireland, Peru, and Hilton Head—but as the heart's green and granite, and who, exposed to the rural culture, chose to join it.

On the other hand, many summer visitors care nothing for place or people—and people return the gesture. Every June we complain, at first of traffic and then of bad manners, discourteous behavior in the aisles of the supermarket, condescension, and arrogance. We have become The Natives, amusing rustics perhaps, more likely vendors suspected of exploitation. Year-rounders turn grumpy. Of course it is a perennial conflict wherever tourists congregate, as ineluctable as town-and-gown in the neighborhood of a college. When I feel scorn for July's hordes I try to remember that I started that way. Or almost. I grew up living the school year out in suburban Connecticut, Ardmore Street in Hamden—four miles from the center of New Haven, two miles from the Brock-Hall Dairy Company, which my grandfather co-founded and where my father worked. When I came north for summers I was not exactly a vacationer: I didn't go to a hotel or a rented cottage or a lakeside camp; I went to the house where my mother and my grandmother were born and grew up; I worked in the hayfields; briefly I joined the backcountry culture that was so alien to Spring Glen Grammar School and the values of the blocks. I inhabited for a while the universe of church suppers, Christian Endeavor, outhouses, cowmanure, chickens, Civil War stories, whitewash in the tie-up, cellarholes, fishing, poverty, straw-chewing, and Rawleigh's Salve.

It was not only a farm in the country I went to; it was an entire dying world. When I took the New York, New Haven & Hartford to Boston, from South Station to North, I crossed a line almost century-wide. The train I climbed onto in North Station was a time machine and the conductor a hundred years old; he wore a handkerchief between his collar and his neck for the sweat. The benches were hard in the old cars, and the Boston & Maine train, after leaving suburban Boston and southern New Hampshire, stopped every two miles. This was the Peanut, last passenger train of the afternoon, originally the next to last, because its name derived from *pénult.* While we chugged north, layers of Hamden peeled away from me as if I shed a skin: Concord, Penacook, Boscawen, Franklin, East Andover (called Halcyon), Andover, West Andover (called Gale)—and the old handkerchiefed conductor set the yellow step on cinders and I alighted to find my grandfather grinning as he whispered comforting words into the ear of a bony horse harnessed into the arms of an ancient carriage. Soon the train puffed away on its journey north—three miles to South Danbury (called Converse), just past the church—and with my suitcase lodged in back of the seat, behind Riley we started the mile journey home. My world was transformed: no car, no tractor, no school, no classmates. The whole summer I joined the historical past, entered it as if through a door, took part in it, played the part, lost myself in it and in love of it.

My old world I preferred to my new. From the moment of the depot until the moment ten weeks later when I reversed the slow melancholy journey, taking the morning Peanut for Boston, I joined the country of the grandparents—I have written this before; before I die I will write it again—and I loved it a thousand times more. Here was diversity: old and young, sick and healthy, rich and poor, all together. One definition of the suburbs is segregation: The greens live on one block and the blues on another. Here was eccentricity, affection, humor, freedom, and stories. Here of course were grandparents, not parents; this place had not been freedom for my mother. This place was not innocent irresponsibility or imagination's respite for the farmer who grappled yearlong in its sandy soil.

All summer I worked but I did not work hard. The chicks were my domain, and I brought them water and grain at morning and at night. Afternoons were haying. I stood atop the old rack with its split-pole rails while my grandfather pitched hay up and I tucked it in place and trod to weave it together. On the way to the hayfield and on the way back my grandfather talked, told stories, and recited poems. This was the best part, but even the work was good. I keep bright intact recollections of these afternoons: On a hot day I stand in the breeze on top of the hayrack looking down on valley and pond; I am thirteen and my grandfather will never die.

Because I did not belong to the country the whole year, the whole life, I was a summer person. A suburban child, I preferred the rural, archaic, old, and eccentric. I took my mother's New Hampshire over my father's Connecticut. I chose it and I choose it. When I was eleven or twelve I daydreamed living here year round, a lonely trapper on the hill like all the bachelor solitaries who lived cramped into tumbledown shacks. By the time I was sixteen I daydreamed of living here as a writer; in my twenties I learned that this was impractical; in my forties I did it. Now if I grumble about summer people, doubtless I protest in order to separate myself from what I was or partly was. It is easy to make stereotypes, harder to make distinctions. Many long-term summer people feel connected to landscape and to people by way of rural culture; their summers are not only climate, pond, and hill but islands of country ethic and culture, which they cherish against the life they lead at other times. They return to old cottages they renew each year, and they pay taxes and keep up their own land. Although in the stereotype summer people are rich, in truth many are not. I think of Clarence and Katherine Grimes, who came to Stinson Lake for fifty years. Clarence taught German and French and music at Hamden High School in Connecticut where I spent two years; Katherine was a painter and a cellist. On a high school teacher's salary they bought land in the 1930s and built a camp and brought their children every year and later their grandchildren, and when Kay died in 1985 Clarence buried her in a tiny graveyard over their camp where he stays summers still, lonely in his ninth decade.

On the other hand, a new breed buys condos and cuts off our view of the blue mountain. They purchase air and sun for their pleasure, as if the creation were not common inheritance, glory, and obligation. Greed is not only theirs but also the farmer's who sells his land and the developer's who subdivides it—but it is also theirs who grant the farmer and the developer their money; their greed is for exclusiveness. On the west side of Newfound Lake there's a patch of road where I used to drive, looking across choppy blue water at firs and hills on the other side, but now sawtooth brown-shingle condos, between road and water, remove Newfound Lake from public vision. They bought the view; for the first time in millennia, since the glacier set it there, the lake and the land are split apart.

JOHN MORSE hays our fields at June's end, cutting, turning hay that gets rained on, raking and baling it with a series of machines hooked up to his tractor: very like a horse. When he and his strong boys gather the bales onto a pickup truck, they work a long day shirtless in the bright sun and in the early evening stand resting in the long shadows. (In the fall after slaughter John returns our grass transformed into lamb roast and steak.) The stubble hayfield looks brown for a week or so; then it softens into green again, rises, and waves when the wind blows. Where the long grass ripples my grandfather grew tall field-corn; every summer when I was small I lost myself in it on purpose, in order to be frightened and enjoy the comfort of salvation.

For twenty-five years after my grandfather died hay remained abundant, growing from topsoil composed of a century and a half of Holstein manure. But underneath lies sand the glacier left. One year not long ago John stacked half as many bales as he had the year before, and we knew the goodness had leached out of the soil. Now John limes the fields in autumn; we talk of plowing, harrowing, replanting with new seed, and fertilizing. Whatever we do, we want to keep the fields. A hayfield grown up to bushes is melancholy. These summers I drive past dense groves of trees where I spent afternoons in the 1940s haying with my grandfather. Trees are beautiful and wood is useful but cleared land is a monument to the old settlers. Think of the labor that cleared it: cutting, stumping, burning the timber it didn't pay to haul; oxen sledding great stumps and granite boulders. How different the land looked a hundred years ago. On the slopes of Ragged, even of Kearsarge, stonewalls border deep forest. Stonewalls weren't built to keep pine trees in; somebody cleared it for pasture and kept it clear. Up on Highway 89 as you approach Hanover, great domed hills rise, clear with pasture and hayfield. The hills of our Ragged, and much of New Hampshire, domed clear and green under the yellow light of summer a century ago.

SUMMER is a series of special events. On the Fourth of July, little flags from Memorial Day still wave over the graves of the veterans, but Independence Day is less patriotic than it used to be. Maybe I remember it from an especially military time, 1942–45, but now it seems to be a child's day or a day to be childish on. Andover specializes in the glorious Fourth. There are crafts for sale, hot dogs and balloons, and at eleven we watch the long parade of floats, horses, bands, antique cars, and fire engines—the same ones that parade for Danbury at the Grange's Harvest Festival in September, that spend the year traipsing from parade to parade. Andover's own Lions Club parades a Concord coach hauled by a brace of horses, Leslie Ford as coachman, that galavants all over the state—at Danbury, at Warner's Fall Festival, at the Lions' soccer match between Vermont and New Hampshire. On the morning of the Fourth the Lions do a breakfast at Andover School—pancakes and sausage, real syrup—as they do on a Saturday in deer season. Lunch is everybody's chuck wagon. Supper is sometimes a church, sometimes the Volunteer Fire Department, back at the school about the time the midway opens: turtle races, a tethered balloon, try your strength, throw soggy baseballs at wooden milk bottles. When supper's cleared the bingo starts, also staged by the Lions, and when it is dark come the fireworks: sudden night-flowers, orange and red and green and gold and silver, erupting against the black of night.

Summer is also the South Danbury Church Fair, later in July. The committee that plans the fair meets a few weeks ahead. First we decide who's on the Supper Committee, because that's the biggest job, five or six women who will cook for a week, then dish it out, keep it flowing, and clean up afterward—three and a half frantic hours. The Supper Committee needs outside help. Every summer several of the hardest-working women are not churchgoers; they support the church that will bury them, working like crazy once a year, but they draw the line at sitting in a pew on a Sunday.

Our White Elephant Committee sells odds and ends; our Food Committee sells bread, brownies, and doughnuts. Another committee collects handicrafts and fancywork; we have a committee for grabs and another for tonic. Two or three husbands do setups the night before the fair, gathering picnic tables from all over town. On the fair Saturday, our tables open at four, followed by supper at five. People get in line by four-forty-five, and dishing up usually starts early; everything is early by New Hampshire time. (If friends are due at our house for a meeting at seven, we know to be ready for early arrivals at six-thirty.) During supper and after there will be homemade ice cream, always prepared and sold by Joe and Marilyn Bouley and Audrey Curren. Final event of the day is our annual auction. I'm on the Auction Committee, a male estate.

To cook for supper, I cross the line, contradicting a cultural gender-value, coming out of the closet with cooking. But I display no reticence: I walk up and down the supper line, urging, "Don't miss the turkey salad. Try the meatloaf." My cousin Ansel, who is a great baker, has always cooked quantities of magnificent rolls but they pass for Edna's. Mary Smith cooks prodigious amounts of everything. Doris Huntoon does also. Pies and casseroles and salads come from Bertha, Vicki, Jane Powers, Martha, Audrey, Dorothy, Ruth Houghton, Ruth True, Phyllis, Marion, Mary Lyn, Joan and Lois, Annie, Vera, Kendra, and Trudy. Along with pies and casseroles, Dot Heath makes funky beans, and equally funky, wholly different beans arrive from other kitchens.

Jane cooks a thousand loaves of French bread for the food table; she makes more rolls and three casseroles and salads of macaroni, fruit, and mixed vegetables. We have dozens of pies and cakes; Edna's red velvet cake annually shakes our heads with its startling deep crimson.

We dish supper outdoors in front of the church and eat at tables set around it. Every year we feed more than a hundred people for $3.50 apiece and less for children, cheap even for New Hampshire. Recently I heard of volunteer firemen charging $6 for a chicken barbecue supper. It must have been over by Center Sandwich. Last summer my wife read her poems there, a town of elegant, precise old Capes not far from Squam ("Golden Pond") and Winnipesaukee. In the audience every head was a distinguished gray, and the white ducks came from Brooks Brothers. Somebody said in the question period, "There's a lot of people in New Hampshire, but you never meet anyone who was born here." It astonished me to hear the line, spoken so often about California or Arizona, Colorado or Florida, applied to my state; and I shuddered to recognize the portent. In the Danbury crowd at our fair, most were born here; the bronze tablet at the Town Hall, where Danbury lists boys who fought in the Civil War, could almost be used for a list of voters. But in Wilmot or Andover, above all in New London, there are not so many natives; someday the South Danbury Church Fair will become an exercise in nostalgia.

Last summer it rained. We had to move the fair three miles north to the Grange Hall in Danbury Village. Sale tables occupied the auditorium upstairs; we ate supper downstairs at tables fixed in place next to the Grange's kitchen, handy except that it lacks water. I sat by the top of the stairs selling tickets for supper, which this year meant that I had to be a negative maitre d', holding the line upstairs when there were no more seats in the dining room.

When supper's over, and the exhausted kitchen crew finally eats what's left—beans, a corner of macaroni and cheese, some rolls, peach pie, carbs and more carbs—we hold our annual auction. Sometimes I auctioneer a little, but I am no good at it. This year, on the Grange's main floor, in front of the curtain with Kearsarge painted on it (normally we hold the auction in the little hillside amphitheater next to the church, where stables used to shelter horses and carriages from snow), my cousin Forrest filled in capably for Bill McKenzie, who had to be away. Strong and burly with a great mustache, Forrest is a comic: If there's a blouse to auction he will model it. We sell junk mostly—a lawnmower without the shaft, a wagon seat without the wagon, a dish strainer, boxes of Reader's Digest Condensed Books, radios and record players and toasters (handymen's specials) and a mixmaster with one beater missing. Three years ago we enjoyed a brief harvest of beds, bunk beds, tables, and chairs—big-ticket items—and we took in the dough. I act as changemaker, trudging up and down the little hill delivering goods; that was the year somebody with New York plates gave me a hundred dollar bill to change. (I had to crack the supper till.) Most years we make more laughter than money, as Bertha and Peter, who are brother and sister, bid against each other, as Pat challenges Ansel. Pat runs a perpetual yard sale and acquires stock every year from our auction. Toward the end, great boxes lump leftover items from the white elephant and the craft tables. One carton may gather a used whiskbroom, two pairs of ancient shoes, an issue of *Yankee*, sheet music from 1954, a three-way plug, two ashtrays, a package of pink sponges, a pale green crocheted pillow six inches by eight, a Snoopy washcloth, a cat's flea collar, part of an alarm clock, a broken cheeseboard, and three dozen plastic forks. This box goes for 25 cents, generally to Marge.

MID-AUGUST is Old Home Day, Danbury one Sunday and Wilmot the next. Each town alternates the location among its tiny centers: Wilmot Flat, Wilmot Center, or North Wilmot; Danbury Village or South Danbury. Wherever it happens it repeats certain rituals; wherever it happens it is a diminished thing. The governor proclaimed Old Home in 1899 because of New Hampshire's depopulation. For decades people had left the farms for the mills where the hours were shorter and the pay steady; then the farms became increasingly poorer because on better and flatter land to the west farmers could use more machinery and fewer hands.

My mother, born in 1903, remembers hordes arriving for Old Home when she was a girl. Wilmot's took place at the Methodist Camp Ground where cottages sprouted among tall pines like the mushrooms of a wet summer; the 1938 hurricane smashed pines onto the tiny cottages and ended the Camp Ground. (We still travel Camp Ground Road.) Even I can remember two hundred gathering there in the mid-thirties: My grandfather bought me vanilla cones, my uncle Luther the minister addressed the multitude, and on the bandstand the old men of Moulton's Band from Sanbornton, in blue caps and uniforms with red piping and epaulets, played marching songs and hymns that marched. In my mother's day, maybe until the Second War, local residents staged a play for the exiles' reunion, and a dance my mother couldn't go to. Rumor had it some of the fellows drank hard cider.

Stagecoaches and primitive buses waited at the depot for the diaspora's return. There were prizes for those who came from the greatest distance—Pennsylvania, Tennessee, Ohio, even Idaho; for the largest family groups, from great-grandparents to infants, thirty-seven at a whack; for the eldest attending, usually late nineties or a hundred, possessor as eldest citizen of the *Boston Post* cane, which persisted as badge of superior antiquity long after the *Post* died (my grandmother was proud of being eldest several years running); and for the youngest, always a babe in arms.

We still give the prizes but we are a remnant repeating a ritual after its purpose is mostly gone. Only forty of us gather. Although the eldest is still usually a nonagenarian, the youngest is sometimes four or five; the farthest journeying comes from Boston; the largest family may be six. The original emigrants are dead, and their children's children lived in seven cities before they were ten years old, none of them in New Hampshire. Still, Old Home Day remains another pleasant and innocent excuse for gathering. Always a few old friends and former residents schedule an annual visit to coincide with Old

Home. My mother who lives in Connecticut has not missed many. After the morning sermon we eat a picnic lunch and listen to the current Moulton's Band from Sanbornton playing Beatles songs adapted for brass—and John Philip Sousa also. After the band concert we move inside for a program. We sing songs like "Old New Hampshire" and "New Hampshire People," which goes to the tune of "Auld Lang Syne." We sing one called "Wilmot's Sons and Daughters," which Stella Collins wrote long ago:

> To the joyous din of welcome,
>   Wilmot joins with hearty voice
> As her fast-returning children
>   Make the old heart to rejoice.
> While Kearsarge still towers above us,
>   Strong and steadfast, calm and grand,
> To her absent sons and daughters
>   Wilmot holds a beckoning hand.

Usually there's a talk. Two years ago Walter Walker showed slides he'd taken at old Old Homes, a popular program. We sat in the Town Hall with shades drawn on a warm dry afternoon late in August looking at our dead in Ektachrome. Often on the weekend of Wilmot's Old Home the camps close down across the pond. Long lines of chartered Vermont Transit buses raise dust on Eagle Pond Road, and young campers crowd at the windows saying farewell for another year to Eagle Pond and Ragged Mountain.

We get to stay. We linger at pondside for a few more weeks of warm water in perfect stillness. Then one night, warned by the *Concord Monitor*, we cover tomatoes with poly, and in the cold morning I scrape ice from the windshield. Two or three icy mornings turn the pond chilly; along the shore we spy the first gay fires of fall.

Fall

WAKING in late September, we gaze south toward Kearsarge from the dawn window under the great maple that torches the hillside. Each morning is more outrageous than the one before, days outdoing their predecessors as sons outdo their fathers. We walk out over the chill dew to audit glorious wreckage from the night's cold passage—new branches suddenly turned, others gone deeper into ranges of fire, trees vying to surpass each other and their yester-selves. In the afternoon we take long walks with Gus, who is the color of oakleaves, who bounds ahead of us and leaps to chase a leaf falling. Maybe we take New Canada, the dirt road that climbs the northwest slope of Ragged Mountain, and promenade in a tunnel of red shade under oak and maple, under wide old birches with leaves a delicate yellow. On the downslope, as leaves fall away the valley opens, and for the first time since April we can look across toward hills of Vermont visible on the clearest day. As the dog bounces our hearts bounce also with a happy overload, our landscape turned into sensuous Italian crockery or grand opera staged by the cold hills.

Or we walk on the low dirt road that skirts Eagle Pond, and on the rattling bridge at the south end—over the Blackwater River's tributaries exiting the pond, by the beaver's bog where wet earth stabs upward with gnawed stumps of popple—we stand and stare with our jaws gaped at the tweedy circumference of the pond, low trees turned orange, Chinese red, pink, russet, together with silver-gray trunk and evergreen green, weaving the universe's most outlandish fabric, the whole more purple than not, although no part of it is purple.

Walking back to our house from any direction, we know again and always for the heart-stopping first time that our house sits floating in the center of autumn's flood: yellow-candle leaves against unpainted barn; wild fiery maple upshooting against the sprawling old white house with green shutters; the slope of Ragged rising behind with its crazy anthology of universal color, shade, and texture. We inhabit the landscape's brightest and briefest flesh.

Or we drive, dangerous as it is—who can watch the road?—to places we remember. Driving on I-89, up where the Connecticut River Valley opens, we ride high discovering enormous vistas of fall's bounty, the distant low hills giving off their variegated light. But middle distance is best. Close up we see the one leaf and the one tree, gorgeous but myopic; long distance makes a momentary uniformity; best middle distance offers tricks of focus, and as we drive by certain mild hills—mild the rest of the year—we take them in as leaf, as tree, and as expressionist wild canvas. The eye learns a rapid oscillation that makes all-parts and one-whole into yet another whole: creation's apotheosis and heaven on earth. Past Danbury east on 104 there's a moment of space, north of Ragged where the ski folks go in winter, where the land widens into a sudden plain, flat as water and the size of Eagle Pond. Here we park in October to stare. Over the brief plain the hills start again, bright in the middle distance.

Or driving back from Franklin, where we shop at the A & P or go to Keegan's Hardware, or from Tilton where Bob Beaulieu sells the best cheese and corns his own beef, we take the back road from East Andover to Andover Village. This narrow road rides straight up and down, past abandoned farms and great farmhouses, some with their elms surviving, one Victorian and huge where Governor Batchelder lived, some with stony pastures cleared two hundred years ago and not yet grown over. At the edge of this road stands a magnificent Federal house with a fanlight over the door, square and upright white clapboard, with a little family graveyard, with a view of noble Kearsarge and with Ragged's southern slope in the grandeur of middle distance.

Then leaves fall. They turn, they alter, and they fall. The trees that turn first drop leaves first, swampmaples shedding into their damp boggy earth, upsticking their twigs as the slower trees on the hills behind them start their journey. Then birch, popple, ash, and the great maple inaugurate their denuding, at first in the chill vinegary air one and two leaves spiraling; then by the dozen the colorful leaves diving and dancing down, divers and dancers staggering through air to rest on silvery grass; then by the hundreds the leaves reeling down, making the air solid with swirling leaf-confetti, sketching the wind's whirling shapes on a cool morning. Oh, to stand in the woods or by the house, with the chill wind in our hair, surrounded and gently touched by the continual descent of the multitudinous reds and yellows of the abundant and generous trees. Only the oaks hold on, cherishing still their crimped brown leaves through winter and even into spring.

Rain is the enemy of brilliance. Some autumns when the reds and yellows blaze their fiercest, three days of cold rain drain color out. Rain knocks the bright leaves down and removes their stain, so that if you kick at a leaf on the brown earth of the driveway, you find underneath it, like the imprint left by a child's cellophane transfer, the leaf's bright image intact and quick on the dirt. These years the pomp is brief, abrupt, and poignant. But autumn is always poignant.

Fall, I would rather call it, as in dying fall or the fall of man. I think it was September when Adam and Eve left the Garden, struggling as they walked on rough footing, the first time anyone did, uphill into the compromised world. Outside Eden the live pulsing green, thick flesh of leaf and stem, showed red wounds for the first time, withered beige and gray stalk, the bruised russet and yellow of dying vegetation. Against the uniform green of continual summer advanced the complexities of autumn, fall's multivalent messages of decay in color and shape, death's mothering sigh. A leaf falls, the year falls, men and women fall. And, *felix culpa,* fall is the most beautiful season—at least in New Hampshire.

Some of us spend our lives preferring fall to all the seasons, accepting winter's blank as the completion or fulfillment that our season presages, taking spring only as prologue, and summer as the gently inclined platform leading all too slowly to the annual dazzle. We are in love—not half in love, and not with easeful death—with the vigor of decay, as if we were philanderers bored by any gorgeous nineteen-year-old, all smooth skin and taut roundedness; merely tolerant of the *femmes de trente ans* whose bodies, softer and more serious, bloom with the secret growth of the sensual life; pursuing not young girl nor bloomed beauty but the gray-haired, stark-cheekboned beautiful woman of fifty.

For amorists of October, the red branch is the sign we seek. If we find it in May or June it only mocks us, for it is not earned and appropriate aging but disease, acid, blight, salt, herbicide, or a plague of beetles—mocking the splendor of autumn as progeria, wretched aging-disease of children, mocks residents of the nursing home. But in August we may reasonably look for a touch of the true and natural red that flames at a maple branch's tip; even in August, with vagaries of elevation, temperature, storm, and moon, a minifrost foreshadows splendor. Though noon be hot, though well dry up and hay turn brown, though we parch tossing bales and rush to the lake for cool, yet the air is cold every morning. We rise to light a fire in the Glenwood, taking the chill off and the damp of cold dew, and to glance outside through early mist: *Is there more red on the hill?*

Every August somebody's garden goes. By Eagle Pond we are protected from early frost by the water's heat. But north of us toward Danbury, and west at Wilmot Flat, we watch for August's autumn. When somebody loses her garden, we hear when we drop into the post office or the store: "Buck's folks got frosted out this morning." Driving past the Buck place, we see tall corn browning and withered, tomato plants blackening heavy with green-yellow globes. It is melancholy and no joke. From the peas planted early, scattered on snow in April; through the rototilled wet soil of May; through planting while blackflies assault the planter; through radishes, peas, frail carrot tops emerging, and beets; through struggles with woodchucks and deer onward to the battle with coons over corn; through weeding in July's heat and watering in the drought of early August—gardens are hard duty. A frost in late August or early September is enough to drive a family to drink, or to Arizona.

Safe with our garden, we look for the red branch. As September starts, we rise to white patches on grass that keeps its dark green. We glance at the tomato plants by the porch: They appear untouched; near the house and its reflected heat, sometimes they last into October.

Today it will warm up, and even turn hot for an hour early in the afternoon, but with a clear sky, tonight will be cold again. The million stars, so bright and harsh they prick at eyeballs, will see another frost. Somewhere somebody's tomatoes will blacken and sag. This morning, taking lunch at Blackwater Bill's, I hear one old man, entering, ask another old man at the counter, "How did your garden fare?"

From the red branch on the green tree, fall enlarges to become the red tree on the green slope, where one maple of a hundred chooses to charge first into the breach. Then in September, in the damp places where swampmaples flourish, gross splendor begins: Swampmaple leads the way, groves of the small bushes or trees, in spring and summer scarcely worth our attention as they plume their frail green in marshy land beside meadows, unremarkable in a landscape of great oaks, of elms rare now even in New Hampshire, and of true maples in the dark sugarbush. In September these weed trees take their brief hour on the stage. Swampmaples are the pioneers of autumn, Daniel Boones or even Columbuses of the new world to come. They blaze with their Chinese reds, brilliant enamels sudden on a cool morning. While their noble cousins-by-name, rockmaple of the hill, together with skinny poplar and pale birch, keep intact their dark almost black summer green, green-shutter dark, swampmaples explode like Fourth of July nightworks, small red-fire fountains on low land. Driving to the P.O., I watch for the boggy patch a mile this side of Danbury where swampmaples congregate; here, on a sharp morning, a crimson eloquence rises like Godzilla from the bog.

The oldest metaphor makes autumn a painter, Jack Frost with his manic palette. In the verdant context of August, when the first branch bursts red on the green tree, this quick eruption draws the eye as the hosta sucks the hummingbird in, and the hollyhock the honeybee. It is seductive enough, but it is subtle compared to the wild cacophony of late September and early October which blares and magnifies itself, synaesthetician mixing glaciers and violins, car horns and kangaroos, cowflops and electronic spacemusic. Deep autumn is a *beautiful* Godzilla, wildest of wild beasts. Abrupt shreds and edges of New Hampshire turn fauve, while most of the northern hemisphere remains vague, impressionist, and *pretty*. Here we become Van Gogh for the yellow of sunflowers, Gauguin for the skin of oakleaves rich and sensuous, Hans Hofmann for the loaded, overloaded, dripping explosions or onslaughts of RED.

In summer when cattle eat rich grass heavy with seed, their udders fill so tight that they drip milk while they wait their turn for milking; the colorist's autumn palette drips milk never white but red, sunflower yellow, green as pine or hemlock. Here in northern New England nothing is restrained—in a culture where restraint is rumored to be the tint of the soul. No, it's wild opera, all finale from overture on, and every leaf ranges through octaves from soprano to bass, Yma Sumac indeed, Yma Ash, Yma Birchtree, and above all Yma Maple—composer and company collaborating on arias brilliant with contrast, gross gorgeous vulgar screeches of color, unlimited banquets of edible sense. If it were a cuisine, New Hampshire fall would combine curry powder, maplesyrup, garlic, tutti-frutti, basil, scallions, chocolate black as the human heart, chile relleno, fresh pineapple, and Coleman's mustard—chopped and hashed together, mayhap, in the Cuisinart of the middle distance.

We are all art critics of the annual exhibition, and we are always mildly disappointed. "Why, sure," we say, "it's just *fine* . . . but it's not bright like it was *last* year." In the actual year, leaves never burn with a fire so wild as the conflagrations of the arch-year in the mind's gallery.

Of New Hampshire I speak, not of the Midwest, which is colorful but subdued, nor of the duochrome West Coast: California is green-if-it-rains, Arizona is brown-since-it-doesn't. Michigan's fall is like Europe's: burnished old gold; yellow harvest mellow with violins; autumn of the falling fruit and the long journey toward oblivion; muted and melancholy; that time of year when yellow leaves or none or few do hang; where looking on the happy autumn fields, we fall to thinking of the days that are no more. Autumn is English Johnny's, season of mists and mellow fruitfulness, gorgeous and monochrome. Or if autumn be French, let the long sobs of its violins pierce our hearts with languor and, indeed, monotony. Europe never reaches the cacophony of New Hampshire's October with its purple cymbals and vermilion kettle drums, with driving red trumpets and Edgard Varèse carcrash-codas of metallic jumble and roar. European autumn is a dust of centuries over the painter's light, brown cracked varnish aging, taking winter's oncoming darkness into itself.

In New Hampshire, October's detonation is flesh, opera, and expressionist cooking, but one must admit that it lacks structure. Like everything we love, this effect changes and turns into its opposite. By mid-November the cuisine alters to New England Boiled Dinner, wherein four hours of boiling blends corned beef and cabbage and onion and potato and turnip into the one salty tang. If Jack Frost starts expressionist, he ends constructivist. Braque the brief fauve takes a six-week journey to Braque the analytic cubist. Crazy gorgeous canvas turns wire sculpture, and Willem de Kooning becomes Naum Gabo.

By autumn's end all colors leave—or *almost* leave. To November's connoisseur the grades of beiges and grays, adjusting their textures, assemble colors as dear in their faintness as any orange whoops of September. Form, shape, and line take over, as egregious tweed hillsides shed orange, red, purple, and saffron. Darkening shreds of old leaves hang on the oaks, russet descending to earth-color, red-squirrel fur; then the gray-squirrel treetrunk advances with its frost-silver, vertical scored with vertical lines, against which rise vertical birches swooped and tilting (*Ice-storms do that*) with horizontal Mondrian-lines to contradict the white pillar of the trunk. And everywhere the rich dark evergreen. We assemble together, on the November canvas: green triangles, persisting serious heaving greens of hemlock, fir, and pine; vertical grays and vertical whites; slim horizontals of twig and birch-score; crumpled russet-gray of oakleaf and puffball. Now dead weeds straggle, gray stonewalls outline irregular rectangles, and emerging granite boulders push like whales with their great shoulders through the gray-brown sea of fallen leaves. Finally we reach the shape of the durable enduring world, fundament, skull underneath the flesh of shouts and colors. We arrive at line and form, without feeling except feeling for line and form, strong in what they omit and what they oppose: Son and daughter attack nothing so much as the loins they start from. Fall that begins as a Latin Quarter of passionate disorderly violent color—not so much French as Spanish, not so much Spanish as Italian, and not Italian of pope and doge, of Caravaggio and Michelangelo, but Italian of Cellini's breasted saltcellar and equally breasted self-esteem, or Italian of twentieth-century graveyard and wedding party—this fall dissolves flesh or flesh falls away to reveal that in proper Heraclitean fashion the bones under the flesh are flesh's opposite.

Order and taste turn Japanese, the garden that is the analytic palette a thousand years early: beige sand and gravel, raked for direction without motion, sand-sea or frozen desert against the arranged precise madness of miniature mountains, artificial Fujis of restrained romantic grays and gray-blues; meanwhile, on every side the framing gray-green moss, Kyoto's evergreen, and rocks that make more borders. New Hampshire's November is Zen cubist de Stijl.

EARLIER, Labor Day is a holiday truly celebrated hereabouts, for it is the day when THEY go home, the summer people who arrive blooming late in the month of June. Everywhere gross Oldsmobile stationwagons back up to cottages, loading leftover Stolichnaya, unread stacks of summer unreading, Port-Salut, golfclubs, tennisrackets, dental floss, and bottles of tanning lotion. At hundreds of lakesides Volvos lift wing-hatches; at mountain cottages fleets of BMWs load themselves with summer's surplus commodity fetishism. Then down the long I-ways—91, 89, 95—expensive cars crammed with tanned flesh creep toward the suburbs of Boston and New York, even unto New Jersey. THEY stretch and unload late at night in the blocks of neighborhoods among prosperous twelve-room houses and three-car garages . . .

While up north, in the countryside, air thins, lightens, chills, and cheers up. No more traffic jams down to the post office! No more bumping and shoving in the aisles at Cricenti's! Browning hayfields, mountain, dirt road, and stonewall return to us. The land is ours again, so far as it is anybody's. The annual long rental—essential to our economy for a hundred and fifty years—annually breaks its lease. Overnight, traffic on Route 4 diminishes by thirty percent. A few elderly summer people remain, not forced back to Lincoln by school-opening or the end of vacation, but THEY move more cautiously now, nervous and polite or more nearly polite. THEY know THEY are outnumbered now. But with the growth of retirement condominium barn-palaces, we begin to witness in New Hampshire the newest phenomenon: year-round summer people.

In Danbury the change is not so great as in some towns, because there are not so many summer people. Yet the village celebrates the end of summer, exodus and restoration, with the yearly Danbury Grange Harvest Festival and Parade, one Saturday soon after Labor Day. The harvest part is a show in the Legion Hall, melons and squash and tomatoes big and ripe, canning, pies—all displayed and judged. In the Grange Hall and Volunteer Fire Department there are crafts and sewing, watercolors, hot dogs and hamburgers, antiques, fudge, and penuche. In the afternoon horses compete at pulling weights and there is a baseball game; at five o'clock the Grange puts on its ham and bean supper.

The parade is the best part. We gather at the crossroads where 104 from Bristol and Plymouth hits Route 4 head on, between Danbury Center's two stores where Hippie Hill—people gather there, summer nights, to smoke funny cigarettes—occupies the raised spot beside the railroad—no train for five years. The parade is decorated bicycles; the fife and drum corps from Bristol in Colonial costume; girls riding horseback; men driving antique cars; politicians standing upright in convertibles; floats from the Grange, the Fire Department, the South Danbury Christian Church, the Jiminy Cricket Kindergarten, and the Little League; Willard Huntoon leading his Holstein oxen; and seven or nine fire engines from Danbury and all the little towns hooting their sirens, the volunteers throwing fistfuls of candy out windows to children gathered at roadside.

After the summer people have gone we enter a quiet time. Then at the end of September, throughout October and even into November, the leaf people come. They do not resemble the summer people. The leafers don't own, rent, or hold tenancy here: They buy a ticket, as if for the Whirl-O-Ride at the county fair. Most of them elderly, they peer from bus windows with good will and mouths that make O's. Young leafers from the flatlands drive their own cars and help support restaurant people, bed-and-breakfasters, inn-folks; for the tourist business, leafers cut the wedge of a season between summer and ski. They drive to the White Mountains in early September; later they mosey along little roads; they stop at the side of Route 4 beside our barn to photograph yellow popple against the gritty textures of unpainted vertical boards.

We like leaf people doubtless because we are also leaf people. In Andover down the road, the Lions Club annually rents a schoolbus and busdriver to take a load of Andover's senior citizens up north. Because we are lucky enough to live here, our ecstasy is annual, quotidian, and hysterical together, not once-in-a-lifetime as it is for the riders of the great land yachts with Texas license plates that wander for a week through Green Mountains and White, parking where it says Scenic View, where everybody whips out a Ph.D. camera (Push Here, Dummy) and shoots the leaf's red dazzle for taking back to Houston and San Antone. Sometimes these buses must have trouble with their WCs, because Gail down at the Blackwater Restaurant puts signs on her restrooms during leaf season, Out of Order; it is uncanny what a busload of eighty senior citizens can do for your septic system.

FALL IS the time of the McIntosh.

Apples remain a big New Hampshire crop, after the other farming has pulled up and gone west. In our cellar the row of barrels remains where the squeezed apples took their long journey toward vinegar, important to the diet in decades when a single orange was a Christmas treat. It was always on the table—good with beets, canned or fresh, and with cabbage and with red-flannel hash, a North Country soulfood that starts from the detritus of boiled dinner: Brown some salt pork in a skillet; grind up the leftover vegetables (cabbage, turnip, onion, potato, carrot); then grind up beets, which brings red flannel to the hash; and hash it together and serve it with a cruet of apple vinegar tapped from the cellar's barrel.

Our barrels have been dry, I suppose, for sixty years. The apple trees have gone that filled the barrels with cider and the bins with apples for the pies of winter. We put in new trees now, midgets for easy picking: old varieties like Sheep's Nose which we chose for their names, some McIntosh for serious eating, Northern Spy and Strawberry . . . Down the road toward West Andover, the remains of the Blasington orchard still attract deer in the autumn. Deer love apples—and hunters love abandoned orchards. Lately there are fewer deer, fewer hunters: An orchard a hundred years old loses flavor. For that matter, deer emigrate to the suburbs. Animals, like people, come and go, and deer follow the inhabitants who left, taking their cleared land with them. Two hundred years ago, when the farmers cut trees down for pasture and for grass, bear departed the cleared land for woods. Then the deer waxed. Now that farmers have left these narrow valleys, the deer wane and the woods return, bringing the bear back.

The farming that flourishes or endures in New Hampshire is special-crop and part-time farming: People grow herbs and strawberries—or maybe apples. Great hillside orchards snow petals in spring and dangle ripening fruit all summer. At Bone's Orchard they grow thirty-seven varieties but ninety-eight percent of the apples they sell are Macs. Late summer we drive past Bone's, watching the trees grow heavy with the dense globes of redness. We look for the day they start picking, and later for the day they start pressing cider. Early Macs aren't much better than Delicious or Granny Smith; the lover of the true McIntosh lives for a short season. Brevity sweetens the flesh, and nothing is so intense to the mouth as a ripe McIntosh that detonates with the sweet-sweet yet acidy harsh texture of the accurate apple, autumn's bounty. Or almost nothing. The textured flesh is a mouth's joy but the mouth or the mind's mouth craves the sweet torture of essence without texture, nervous pleasure-pain multiplied by abstraction: I mean *cider.*

THE FIRST TASTE of October's cider always recovers for me a single afternoon in the autumn of 1944, a long walk with a new friend and a day I cherish. There are days in a long life that are carved without pain in the heart's chambers, or with pain as sweet as cider's. In September of 1944, I left home for the first time and lived among the barbarians of adolescence all day and night at a prep school in southern New Hampshire where I studied Latin in hopeless panic and wept tears of solitude and loathed the blond thicklipped sons of lawyers and brokers who glared at me with insolence, with frigidity, and without acknowledgment. Once I asked directions from someone who looked depressed—the only facial expression I wished to address—and when he proclaimed his ignorance we began our friendship to the death.

My new friend and I took a hike on a Sunday afternoon, walking for four hours maybe in a circle of dirt roads around the town, past grown-over farms and farms mothballed for war, on roads no one traveled because of gas rationing. It was dry and dusty but there was chill in the air, apple weather, and we walked smartly as we talked about everything important—the war, what we would do in the war, what we would do after the war and after college, our parents, our Goals in Life . . . Gradually and tentatively under the bright blue air we spoke with trust of what we most cared for. We walked under the bonny elms that had never heard of Dutch elm disease, under oaks still green, weathering toward gray, and under maples splendid with carmine. Worn out, heading back to school, we took a narrow road so quiet that it seemed as if we discovered it—teenage Magellans sailing the New Hampshire fall, or maybe rediscovering it like a Mayan settlement grown over, for conquistadors to chance upon under jungle vines: architecture, temple, and aqueduct; for as we turned a curve we saw a great white farmhouse leading back from a wide lawn, and on the edge of the lawn at the dirt road's edge a table in the shade of an elm, empty glasses on it and a full tawny pitcher with a sign lettered on cardboard: CIDER 5¢ A GLASS.

It looked like the best idea the world ever came up with, cider in October on a dusty road, a miracle surely, and surely we were the first customers for thirty years or maybe a thousand . . . Then a screendoor banged on the porch above and a big old woman in a long housedress with a flowered apron over it worked her way over the grass, hobbling and smiling; she took our nickels and poured us cider; then she took a dime and poured us more cider; and then she took no more money but poured our glasses full until she emptied the pitcher.

We walked home as darkness started and red trees flared into the building dark. We walked with a light step in our friendship, tender and lively with the exquisite pain and excitement of cider wild in our mouths like apple fire. And if, thirty-five years later, my friend's wife found him prone on the staircase of their house, and if the lives lived have not entirely resembled the lives planned for on a Sunday afternoon in 1944, at least the lives had that day in them, that house, that long friendship, and that cider.

IN THE OLD LIFE of the farms, fall was a lazy season. *Relatively.* Late in fall the farmer cut down to eighty hours a week, maybe even to seventy-two.

First there was harvest. Come September my grandparents dug potatoes for the cellar and buried late carrots in sand; come October they picked apples for cellar and ciderpress. The busiest time was bringing the fieldcorn in. My grandfather gathered it himself. The great grassy stalks, green as bamboo and thick, fell like soldiers in the teeth of the horsedrawn mowing machine; he always nailed the tallest, maybe twelve feet, on the barn door. Then the ensilage crew arrived early one morning. They brought with them the gasoline-powered corn-chopper, a noisy rattling snarling belt-driven machine that gobbled whole stalks—white hard ears, green stalk, leaf and silk together. The machine blew the chopped mass into the silo, where my cousin Freeman tamped it down—Holstein granola for the milk of winter and pale spring.

When the fieldcorn was chopped and stowed, the machine disassembled and packed for its journey to the next farm, the hard part of the fall was done with. There was fruit still to pick and cider to press. If no frost killed the plants, there were tomatoes to can. After the first deep frost Kate and Wesley pulled up the remaining tomato plants to hang upside down in the shed where the green tomatoes blushed and turned edible. Now it was time to feed up the pig with corn for slaughter when it turned cold, to sell young roosters and wethers, to kill off old hens—one for dinner every Sunday—and settle pullets in the henhouse.

But none of these tasks was continuous, like haying all summer or woodcutting in winter. As soon as the grass stopped growing, cattle moved into the barn for winter, standing all day in the tie-up eating golden hay, ensilage, and grain. Before heavy snow it was time for fencing, to walk the perimeters of the two pastures for cattle and sheep. Always there had been patching in the summer when the sheep got out or maybe a cow or a heifer, or you could fence in July and August when the hay was too wet to bring in. But systematic fencing, mending wall as the poet says, occupied a few days between harvest and deer season; only suicidal farmers fenced during deer season. You hung a coil of wire over your shoulder, staples and hammer in overall pockets. Then you looked for places where a rock had tumbled loose or a tree, blown over in a thunderstorm, crashed across barbed wire. You set the stone back in place or chopped up the tree to clear the breach and strung more wire. And you looked around you in the October woods at the extended private exhibition, low pale autumn sunlight striking through the diminishing leafy air to catch on reds and yellows of the great woods. After hauling rocks it was good to catch your breath; it was good to look, and look, and look.

And everyone looked and still *looks.* Even people who have lived their whole lives here never become bored with this looking—the old farmers I remember; my cousins now. When I was young I thought maybe the old didn't see, didn't relish the beauty they lived in. Then I learned: For more than a hundred years, anybody willing to leave this countryside has been rewarded for leaving it by more money, leisure, and creature comforts. A few may have stayed from fecklessness or lack of gumption; more have stayed from family feeling or homesickness; but most stay from love. I live among a population, extraordinary in our culture, that lives where it lives because it loves its place. We are self-selected place-lovers. There's no reason to live here except for love.

At Halloween the mounded pumpkins of the roadside, carved, grin with candles from all the doorsteps, and the stuffed guys of the dooryards and all the ghosts of summer gather at October's end. According to the calendar, winter begins just before Christmas Eve, at the solstice of the twenty-second, but the soul's calendar, like the body's, knows that autumn dwindles by entropy into winter as Halloween turns the corner to November. In November we rake leaves for insulation against the sides of the house, as the grandfathers and great-grandfathers did forever in their northern houses, heaping the summer's warmth against the foundation stones and low clapboards.

Winter's onset is the theme of autumn after the glory's gone. Ice forms in the watering trough; we scrape ice from the windshield early in the morning. In the pale grays and browns of late October and November we tuck the house up, tamping her skirts down and bundling her tight against the winds of thirty below. We split and stack cordwood in the woodshed, splinter-time, packing the autumn wood as we used to pack hay in the summer's rick. Now the house's fall puts on weight and solidity, like the bear fattening himself for a long winter's sleep, and the house is protected by the collapsed summer's dead leaves, forearmed with firewood that is the stored heat of many summers turned into fiber by sun and rain through the agency of leaves. Trees warm the wooden house.

Thanksgiving's turkey is the fall's last fall: "Over the river and through the wood / To grandfather's house we go . . ." The horse knows the way, and so does the Nissan pickup. Though the turkey be frozen and the stuffing be Pepperidge Farm, the Pilgrims' late celebration of corn and apple and cranberry, of mince and turnip and cider, turns the last key in the door of autumn. At noon the potato mashes and the gravy thickens. In early dark we lie about, with football breaking its bones all over the living room, and we make Thanksgiving for one more cycle of the year gone through, ended with the great ghostdance of autumn, bright and pale wedded from September's leaf to November's early dark.

And although we may regret the darkening day, the beauty of late autumn is real and serious. With the leaves down, granite emerges from the hills, and everywhere we see again the hills' true shape and the stonewalls that the ancestors built—to enclose their animals and to clear their fields of rocks—making gray rectangles on the gray hillsides.

Late October or early November—after weeks of frost and the fields brown and the harvest long taken and the garden ripped up and dumped and the trees mostly bare and the house tucked up for winter—comes the moment of miraculous restoration, summer's curtain call or triumphal final tour: The wind relents, the sun rises, golden warmth risen from frozen acres, and Indian summer visits like a millionaire; the expensive stranger walks over Kearsarge and Ragged and spends gold sunshine on the unreceptive fields. Down jackets hang again from a brief hook; the summer's T-shirt reappears. Flies wake in the windows of the second story; a wasp rubs her lazy legs together. If the frost has not finished them, late asters and chrysanthemums hover in summery air along with other late survivors: maybe the spindly autumnal goldenrod. Soon, sure enough, frost will blacken fall's flowers and snow tamp them down with its orgy of sensuous deprivation, but now for five days or seven they float a warm raft of midsummer on the lake of fall's desolation.

II
Here at Eagle Pond

Why We Live Here

LATE SPRING and early summer, the whippoorwill wakes us at four-thirty. Gray light starts over the hills; thrushes sing from every branch; clouds snag like lamb's wool on blue Mount Kearsarge. Down by Eagle Pond, just west of us, pickerel leap for blackflies and when they splat on the still water wake frogs and turtles. It is a good hour for waking; we keep the green universe alone. But late September is the most beautiful time, and early October; sugarmaples flare a Chinese red; they combine with yellow birch leaves, russet oak, and evergreen to weave a wild tweed on hills in the middle distance. I grant that winter causes pain—in cold January sometimes I lie abed until six—but even winter is gorgeous; when the moon is high, I wake at midnight and wander through the farmhouse in gray, spooky light that illuminates every corner, the ceilings luminous with reflections from snowy hayfields.

We live where we live for landscape and seasons, for the place of it, but also for the time of it, daily and historical time. Although I keep a farmer's hours I farm no crops. Ancestors who took their turns inhabiting this house arose to milk cattle, to feed hens and sheep. I work on paper at my desk, in the room where I slept as a child—and I live here because it was my grandparents' place, which sets me into the decades. The original Cape was 1803. My sheepfarmer great-grandfather sold wool for uniforms, and in 1865 bought this valley farm next to the railroad, moving down from his steep Ragged Mountain acreage. Where once he pastured his merinos, now cables drag flatlanders uphill, wearing petroleum byproducts with a dollar value that would have sounded like riches in 1865.

We live here also for the solitude. Friends drive up from New York, admire the landscape, swim in the pond, wear us out, and as they are leaving ask, clearing their throats, "But, uh, what do you *do?*" Sometimes we wish we had a little *more* solitude. Maybe because we both write poetry, we are untroubled by the notoriety that hides J. D. Salinger behind fences up in Cornish . . . But occasionally somebody seeks us out. A few years back I heard a knock on the front door, through which nothing has entered or exited, except for corpses, since 1865. Two readers from California had tracked me down. The bold one took me out to the car to meet the shy one, who congratulated me (before I detached myself to return to my desk) "on your privacy and seclusion."

We did not come here for the social life, yet we found enough. We had not been here long before Jane found the word for Thornley's store, the general store just out of sight around a bend: Thornley's is a continual party. Go there any time of day and somebody is telling a story. At Thornley's you learn that it got so cold last week that Ansel saw two hound dogs putting jumper cables on a jackrabbit. At Thornley's you learn who's getting divorced, and maybe why; you talk politics, weather, old times, and what's for dinner down to the Grange in town.

"Town" is ambiguous. It is difficult, in the country, to give a straight answer when somebody asks where you live. Haying with my grandfather when I was a boy, I considered that we lived in West Andover because that was our post office. Now West Andover is gone except for houses, and our post office is Danbury. The telephone exchange, however, is Andover; we call the Danbury P.O. long-distance. On the other hand, Wilmot is the town of our town meeting, and the town we pay our taxes to. Wilmot is composed of Wilmot Center, Wilmot Flat, and North Wilmot—little centers mostly gone where West Andover went. We live in a flap of the town that tucks over Route 4 between Danbury and Andover, a flap that a hundred years ago called itself East Wilmot but never acquired the depot, inn, livery stable, fishmonger, butcher, and two grocery stores that made West Andover a quondam metropolis.

Besides continual parties like the store, there are special ones. South Danbury Christian Church, where I find myself deacon, has a coffee hour every Sunday. (Attendance has vaulted from an average of ten to an average of twenty.) Most towns specialize in one annual holiday. The most elaborate local celebration is Andover's Fourth of July. Last year it began with a pancake breakfast at seven, put on by the Lions Club. The flea market, art show, and midway got started a little later—hundreds of crafters with leather and ceramics, tables of junk, turtle races, hot dogs—before the parade at noon. Past the bandstand marched the Shriners' band, kids rolled decorated bicycles, floats celebrated American Pastimes, fire engines first-geared, a dozen old cars shone like new dimes, pickups crowded with Babe Ruth League teams slowed by—and riders on horseback, and a farmer leading oxen, and seven clowns throwing candy to children. Afternoon featured a town baseball game, pony-pulling, and a guitar player.

Until last year, the midway continued into darkness; for years I worked the booth where you throw soggy baseballs at wooden bottles, twenty-five cents for three balls, and if you knock down the bottles I give you a ten-cent prize. (This concession was property of the Andover Lions Club, of which I used to be a dilatory member.) At dark there were fireworks, but the year before last, some lout let off a canister of tear gas during fireworks, which ended the fireworks. Last year Andover's Fourth concluded with a barbecue chicken dinner, five to seven P.M., put on by the Volunteer Fire Department.

OF THE THREE towns we live in, Danbury is my favorite because it is the wildest, with most diversity of character, many eccentrics, and a few louts. The diversity of the country is its greatest quality, and nowhere outside the East Village of Manhattan are people so various as in Danbury, New Hampshire—lazy and industrious, rich and poor, aged and precocious, virtuous and wicked. Because much of the younger set is shaggy, with long hair and untended beards, the word "hippie" finds an afterlife here. In Danbury Center, across from Dick's Store, there is an elevated strip of land between Route 4 and the railroad where trains no longer run. Someone has spread wood chips, and there's a trash can and some trash chairs and milkcases to sit on. Here a portion of Danbury youth, up to the age of forty, spends mild summer evenings drinking Dick's six-packs and smoking hand-rolled cigarettes. This informal, privately operated recreation area is known as Hippie Hill.

Danbury Center includes the Grange, two churches, and two stores. Every September after Labor Day, Danbury's annual bash is the Danbury Grange Harvest Festival and Parade. Without many farmers left, maybe it celebrates harvesting the summer people, who are tucked back in the suburbs by this time. The American Legion Hall swells with prize vegetables, the Grange Hall with brownies and antiques for sale and with the work of local watercolorists. There are hamburgers and hot dogs for lunch, and in the evening a big dinner at the Grange. The parade features fire engines hooting—the same that rolled on Andover's Fourth, without hooting in staid Andover—a fife and drum corps from Bristol, Willard Huntoon's brace of Holstein oxen, and floats representing organizations; sometimes I ride in the back of a yellow Nissan pickup, the deacon waving from the South Danbury Christian Church's Sunday school float. There is also a float labeled Hippie Hill, which features young folk lolling on cut grass drinking six-packs at ten-thirty on a Saturday morning in September.

Between our house and Danbury Village, South Danbury is another disappearing town, whose remaining identity resides mostly in the white clapboard church that my great-grandparents helped to start after the Civil War. When we moved here nine years ago we decided that *they*—probably the dead—would expect us to go to church . . . Wearily we dragged ourselves there the first Sunday; the second Sunday we went less wearily; within a few weeks we got there early. Let me not go into theology. Let me mention that our minister—Jack Jensen from

Kansas City and Yale Divinity, who teaches at Colby-Sawyer College nearby—the first Sunday quoted Rainer Maria Rilke. Although the allusion pleased us, it was not excerpts from German poets that turned us into deacons. It started with community, and extended itself to communion. One side of the church, which Jane calls the gene pool, shares a couple of great-grandparents, but the true community is an extraordinary interconnectedness. We cover much social territory—age, occupation, politics, tone deafness—and we are also connected to the community of the dead, who lie in the graveyard up the road, and to the unborn. Funerals, weddings, and baptisms mark sensible boundaries.

Finally, we live where we live mostly because of a weird mixture: permitted solitude and strong society. Many Danbury families find their surnames on the bronze plaque outside the Town Hall that lists veterans of the Civil War, but others moved here last week; it makes little difference in Danbury. People move here because they want to live here—they don't come here for the wages, nor do companies transfer managers to Danbury—and people born here do not move away, to seek their fortunes, *only* because they want to live here. We associate in the shared love of place and in an ethic. When X's house burns down—say, someone widely disliked, a leading local Snopes—twelve pickups deliver household goods the next morning. It is what you do. You *are* your brother's keeper; you do it without needing to think about it, because it is an ethic that goes with the place.

Of our three towns, Danbury is the most country and the least Vermont. Heaven knows, Vermont is a beautiful state with pockets of real country remaining, but it is the chic northern New England rural retreat, and not New Hampshire. To Vermont go summering professors of philosophy and Dada poets from New Jersey. The result is Woodstock, where orthopedic surgeons wear checkered shirts from L. L. Bean and play at being country folk. Alas, patches of New Hampshire already approach Vermonthood. We have heard the sound of condosaurus slapping its beaverboard tail in distant meadows. Maybe one day Danbury will be digested by Yankee suburbia, and on Route 4 will arise boutiques, disguised as saphouses, that feature Venetian glass. By that time, I will have joined my ancestors down the road, and together we will haunt skiers and golfers with chain-rattling ectoplasm.

Keeping Things

The Back Chamber

On the second floor of our house there is a long, unfinished room that my family has always called the back chamber. It is the place the broken chair ascends to when it is too weak for sitting on; the broken lamp finds its shelf there, the toolbox its roost after the carpenter's death. You do not throw things away: You cannot tell when they might come in handy. My great-grandfather was born in 1826 and died in 1914; some of his clothes remain in the back chamber, waiting to come in handy.

His name was Benjamin Keneston, and he had two sons and three daughters, the youngest my grandmother Kate, who died at ninety-seven in 1975. Most of Ben's children were long-lived; when they survived their spouses they would come home, bringing a houseful of furniture with them. They never called this place anything but home, or used the word for any other place, though they might have lived and worked elsewhere for fifty years. Both Luther and Nannie returned to live in cottages near the farm, and Kate kept bedrooms at the house in their names—Luther's room, Nannie's room—for when they were sick. Their extra furniture went to the back chamber, or above the back chamber in a loft, or in the dark hole that extends under eaves in the old part of the house without windows or electric lights.

When we potter in the back chamber today, we find a dozen knocked-down double beds, one painted with gold designs and the slogan *Sleep Balmy Sleep* on dark veneer. We find something like thirty chairs: captain's chairs, rockers with a rocker missing, Morris chairs, green-painted kitchen chairs, pressed-wood upright dining room chairs, uncomfortable stuffed parlor chairs; most of them lack a strut or a leg but live within distance of repair. We find a sewing machine that my grandmother sewed on for sixty years and a 1903 perambulator she wheeled my mother in. Two sisters came after my mother, and the back chamber is well furnished with dolls' furniture: tiny chests of drawers, small rockers and small captain's chairs, prams, cradles, and a miniature iron cookstove, like the big Glenwood range in the kitchen below, with an oven door that swings open, a firebox, stove lids, and a tiny iron skillet that fits a stovetop opening. We find fat old wooden skis and sleds with bentwood runners. One ancient stove, with castiron floral reliefs, we cleaned up and use in Jane's study, which used to be Nannie's room. We find toolboxes, postcard collections, oil lamps, electric lamps, pretty cardboard boxes, books by Joe Lincoln and Zane Grey, cribs, carpetbags, loveseats, and a last for making shoes. We find three spinning wheels, two of them broken and a third intact, dispatched upstairs when Ward's replaced homespun; as the family remembers, Benjamin's wife Lucy Buck Keneston was a wonderful spinner. We find a dozen quilts too frail for cleaning, showing bright squares of the cut-up dresses of seamstresses born to the early Republic. We find six or seven chests full of dead people's clothing, Ben Keneston's among them. In a dark row stand four baby highchairs; one made from stout brown wood is more than seventy years old, first used by my mother's younger sister Nan, next by me, later by my children; two wicker highchairs are older, and a frail wooden one older still. I don't know which of them my grandmother sat in.

In the back chamber we keep the used and broken past. Of course it is also a dispensary. When my daughter moved from her University of New Hampshire dormitory to an apartment in Dover, she outfitted her flat from unbroken furniture out of the back chamber. With glue and dowels, the apartments of children and grandchildren could be filled for fifty years. In, and out again: the past hovering in the dusty present like motes, a future implicit in shadowy ranks of used things, usable again. We do not call these objects antiques; they were never removed from use as testimony to affluence. Twice a year, as I show somebody through the house, somebody decides that I am in need of counseling: "You've got a fortune here." I keep my temper. None of it would fetch a great price, but even if it would, I would as soon sell my ancestors' bones for soup as I would sell their top hats, chairs, tool chests, and pretty boxes. Someday when we are dead let them go to auction, if they are not repaired and dispersed.

Continually we discover new saved things, and my wonder is not for the things themselves but for the saving of them. Could Kate really have thought, when she put away a 1917 agricultural bulletin, that it might come in handy someday? The back chamber bespeaks attachment to the outlived world. On a long, narrow cardboard box an old hand has written, "Wool was from B. C. Keneston's sheep carded and ready for spinning at Otterville"—where there was a carding mill—"in 1848." When we open it, we find protected by mothballs a few pounds of one-hundred-and-forty-year-old sheep's wool, preserved for preservation's sake, so that we may touch our fingers to the wool our ancestor's fingers sheared. (Was 1848 his first crop from his first sheep? He was twenty-two that year.) This back chamber is like the parlor walls covered with family portraits, like the graveyard with its Vermont slate and New Hampshire granite; it keeps the dead.

The Saphouse

When we moved into the old house after my grandmother's death, it needed work. (She was seventy-four when my grandfather died. He had kept the house up, and after his death she could not afford to hire help. My mother paid to keep the house painted and the roof dry.) Now as we painted and shingled, dug out the cesspool, planted daffodils, put in a leachfield, fertilized hayfields, jacked up the woodshed for a new sill, replaced clapboards, and mulched old roses, our neighbors let us know that they were pleased. In this countryside, everyone over fifty had watched white wooden houses lose paint and tilt inward as their roofs sagged, and finally whole square-built houses collapse into their own cellarholes. Everyone here takes interest in preserving things, in landscape and buildingscape, even if everyone knows that in a hundred years fire will consume all these houses.

One outbuilding was too far gone for us to bring it back. Built around 1900 just north of the house, the saphouse had been the site of prodigious syrup making. Because it takes about forty gallons of sap to make a gallon of syrup—the pale sap is watery; it is hard to taste the sweetness—he hauled twenty thousand gallons of maple sap for the two or three weeks of sugaring. First he tapped the huge old trees of the sugarbush on Ragged Mountain, setting one or more buckets at each tree to collect the dripping liquid; then he visited each tree each day, emptying the buckets into twenty-gallon pails he carried on a yoke across his shoulders; then he walked through the snowy woods to the ox sledge, where he poured the sap into milk cans; when the cans were full he eased his oxen to a funnel uphill from the saphouse and piped his crop down to the saphouse's holding tank.

When I was little and visited the farm in March, if I hit upon sugaring time, I walked the sugarbush with him. The crop is best when days are warm and nights freezing. To keep the sap boiling, somebody has to tend the fire twenty-four hours a day; Freeman Morrison, my grandmother's cousin, who was a night owl, stayed up all night and much of the day to feed the fire. He pushed whole trees, foot by foot, over the snow through the saphouse's open doors into the firebox. Freeman and my grandfather had built the saphouse under the supervision of my grandfather's father-in-law, informally called Uncle Ben. (Formally he was Benjamin Cilley Keneston, to distinguish him from his father, who was plain Benjamin. When I was a child I liked knowing that I was part Cilley.) BCK died in 1914, sixty-six years after he sheared the sheep's wool in the back chamber. Although I never knew him, I have been aware of his presence since I was a child, and living in his house I feel him every day, not only in the photograph on the living room wall or the top hat under the stairs. If we find a tar-brand for sheep, it is *K.* He was diminutive and powerful, and it must have been hard for my grandfather Wesley Wells to marry his daughter, move into his house, and take direction from him. Yet I never caught a shade of resentment in the stories my grandfather told me.

We hated to pull the saphouse down. My grandfather used it last to make a few gallons in March 1950. That autumn he had a heart attack, sold the cows, and never used the saphouse again. He died in March 1953. When we moved into his house in 1975 we found an unopened quart from his last crop of syrup on a shelf in the rootcellar. Maybe if I had been truest to family practices I would have carried it up to the back chamber unopened but labeled for future generations to wonder at. However, we opened it, we ate it on pancakes, and when we had almost finished it, we poured the last drops into a store-bought gallon—figuring that for a few decades at least, if we continued emptying old gallons into new ones, we could imagine molecular survival for my grandfather's final quart.

The saphouse leaned over, a third out of the vertical. The shed-like door gapped loose. I no longer entered it, because sometime the roof would collapse and I would not let it collapse on me. Rot feathered the timbers up from the ground, the tarpaper roof was swaybacked, and the lead pipe sagged as it rose up-mountain from the rotten galvanized holding tank. Twenty years before, my grandmother Kate had sold the evaporator—big tin tray over the firebox—to somebody building a new saphouse; somebody else had bought the buckets. Every now and then a pickup braked in front of the house and a stranger offered to tear the house down for us, in return for the old wood that he could salvage. There's a market for old wood: beams for what is called restoration, planks to be cut up for picture frames. I refused these offers, wanting to keep the old wood, and probably because I inherited or acquired the desire to keep things. Also I remembered the sheepbarn. Two men tore it down for my grandmother when it started to lean over; they promised, as all the pickup people promised, to clean it up real good. But when these fellows had removed the solid wood they left a mess of rotten board and shingle that weeds grew to cover, a treacherous vegetal-archaeological heap you could break a leg in, where woodchucks bred for generations until we hired a dozer and a truck to haul the mess to the dump.

We tied a cable around the saphouse walls, hitched the cable to a four-wheel-drive pickup, and pulled it down. The frail boards stretched apart like a clasped bunch of straw when you unclench your fist. Sun touched bright unweathered boards that had seen no light since Wesley and Freeman lifted them from the sawmill's pile and hammered them in place. Store nails pulled from the corner four-by-fours. At the door we found long, irregular hammered iron pins, which Freeman had pounded out at his forge in the shop that stood not twenty yards away—the shop also gone now, all traces gone except the grindstone's base that leaned beside it.

We tossed rotten boards in the pickup's bed, stacked the good wood and hauled it for storage to the cowbarn with its kept-up roof. At day's end we drove the junk to the town dump. In a wheelbarrow we collected old bottles, one intact sap bucket, a float, an enamel funnel, and an elegantly shaped handmade shovel. Two huge tapered iron hinges bore a hammer's prints. We tucked the ironwork in a corner of the woodshed (where firewood covers it half the year) among ax heads, scythe blades, and the frail graceful trident of a pitchfork. Freeman forged some of this iron with his engineering-generalist's skill—who turned baseball bats on a lathe, tanned leather and made shoes, built ladders and hayricks and playhouses and wooden spoons and stonewalls, repaired cutlery and milk pails, moved rocks and pulled stumps—but some of the work is finer than Freeman's; I fancy the hand of John Wells, Wesley's father, who fought at

Vicksburg and returned to be blacksmith and farrier on a hill west of Danbury.

Soon grass and saplings would cover the debris we left behind, bricks and small pieces of wood, chowder of rusted metal, spread now in a drift of old leaves that blew into the saphouse autumns past, gray-brown and fragile. High in the center stood the one monument that remained like the saphouse's tombstone, the long brick hive of fire, firebox into which Freeman had pushed whole trees. Seventy-five-year-old mortar spilled at the edge of bricks pink as a baby's mouth. I remember hearing that BCK liked to butter bricks; he must have done this work. Maybe in a hundred years a hiker walking down Ragged Mountain will find this brickwork among new maples.

When we were done, birches cast late-day shadows across the little field between the house and the place where the saphouse used to be. Then we noticed an odd-shaped white stone where there had been a corner four-by-four. It was flat and looked carved. We lifted it up and saw that beneath it there was another piece just like it, and when we turned the top one over, we understood two things at once: The two pieces fitted where they had broken in the middle, and it was a tombstone. Cleaning it off, I read the name and dates of my great-great-grandfather, BCK's father, BENJAMIN KENISTON 1789–1863. Because I knew his grave in the old Andover graveyard, because I remembered the sturdy, legible stone above it, I understood that this was his *first* gravestone, that it had broken, that his son BCK had replaced it—and brought it home and put it to use.

The Bone Ring

The first month we moved here, going through an old desk, we found a yellowed piece of stationery headed by an indistinct photograph of Mount Kearsarge and the words *B. C. Keneston Eagle Pond Farm.* (It was BCK who changed the spelling of the family name, to distance himself from some Keniston cousins.) The pond is west of the farm, forty acres of water—a lake anywhere else. No one alive remembered that name for the place. Although it had not stuck, I decided to make use of it, not for piety of reference but to ease the minds of urban and suburban correspondents who find it hard to believe that a town's name can be address enough. So BCK solved a problem: All that first year, the dead helped out.

Mostly they demanded attention. I could not decide whether Freeman or BCK demanded more. (My grandparents, whom I knew so well and loved so much, demanded little; I thought of them without being reminded.) BCK, whom I had never known, had picked this place out; it was he who deserved credit for staking the claim to Kearsarge and to Eagle Pond. It was he who bought the pew at the South Danbury church he helped to found, where his daughter Kate played the organ Sundays from the age of fourteen to ninety-two. (Is seventy-eight years at the same organ a neo-Calvinist record?) It was fitting, then, that my one glimpse of his ghost, looking suspiciously like my favorite photograph of him, occurred in church one Sunday. He vanished as soon as I saw him. If every Sunday I caught sight of my grandmother's black sequined hat, bobbing next to the green glass lampshade above the organ, that vision seemed natural enough.

Freeman insisted on his presence in a manner perfectly material. He had stenciled his name all over the house. Cousin Freeman moved in as a boy when his family was burned out; he preferred Uncle Ben and Aunt Lucy to his parents and loved Kate like a little sister. His father took him away and put him to work when he was sixteen, but for the rest of his life he kept returning to this place that he loved. I remember him old and sick, wrapped in a blanket, tucked into the rocker by the kitchen range, attended by Kate grown old. He stenciled his name on the underside of stairs leading to the back chamber, which we could see as we walked down to the rootcellar. He stenciled his name on the bottom of a drawer in the pantry, on the underside of the windowsill in his room, and on shingles we found wedged under a box in the toolshed. When we turned something over or lifted something up, we half expected to see Freeman's name, as if his face with its playful eyes leapt up like a jack-in-the-box. He stenciled his name, as it were, on everybody who knew him.

My ghost stories are mostly unconscious memory. When we had lived here only a few weeks a stranger knocked on the front door; his trailer had broken down and he needed a large monkey wrench. I started to say that I had no big wrench, but before I could speak something took hold of me. Asking the man to wait, I gave myself over to whatever possessed me and let it direct me out of the kitchen, into the toolshed toward the woodshed door; my right hand rose unbidden toward a flat shelf over that door where the big wrench resided, and had resided forever, covered now with thirty years of dust and spiderwebs. Something similar happened when I bought a sickle at Thornley's store to chop down weeds in the barnyard. I cut Lexington plant until my back stopped me, then walked with my silvery crescent into the toolshed where I would find something to hang it on; I did not know why I headed for a particular place, but when I raised my hand toward the naily ceiling, I saw three frail rusted sickles hanging there already.

Not everything that happened was memory. Once my wife heard her name called repeatedly in the barn when no one was there to say it. Once after someone helping us cleaned a shed loft, and threw away old shoes and clothing we would not have thrown away, Jane felt in the loft some violence, anger, or even evil, as if something terrible had happened there; maybe it was only resentment over things lost. And there was something else soon after we moved in, although we did not hear about it for two years. It happened to a visitor—skeptical, secular, unsuperstitious, hesitant to speak of it, unable to understand what she saw. It was just a *seeing*. As she stood in our living room she saw someone in the doorway of the kitchen, someone who was not there: a short man, bearded, wearing overalls and a hat. Both BCK and Freeman were short, bearded, wore overalls and a hat.

These experiences virtually stopped after that first year, but there was an exception. When we had lived here six years, we finally afforded a new bathroom. The old one was Sears 1937: cold, shabby, showerless. We tore it off the side of the house and put a new bathroom (with shower and laundry) into our old bedroom, extending a new bedroom onto the north lawn. For warmth in winter we extended the rootcellar under the new room, which obliged us to raise the north side of the house on jacks and bulldoze underneath it. We dug out rotten sills and replaced them; ripping a wall from the old bedroom, we exposed 1803 carpentry; the wallpaper of the family Troy was nine layers deep; in one wall we found cardboard insulation from a box of breakfast cereal, Washington's Crisps, and a picture of the general with bright red lips.

It was the first major alteration of the house's shape since BCK expanded it in 1865, when it became the extended farmhouse familiar in New Hampshire—outbuildings not separated but linked one to one, moving in slow file backward to the hill. To haul firewood in winter we pass through a kitchen door into the toolshed, which is another repository almost like the back chamber: saws, levels, crowbars, old nails, screws, bolts, shovels, rakes, hoes, sickles, awls, drills and their bits, hammers, hammerheads, traps, stovepipe, lanterns, wrenches, screwdrivers; and the practice organ Kate learned to play on, moved from the parlor to the toolshed in 1927 when my mother and father displayed wedding presents in the parlor—and at the southeast corner of the toolshed we go through another door into the woodshed. This door is made from planks nailed to crossplanks, and it latches by a smooth oblong of wood—touched ten million times like Saint Peter's toe to a soft and shiny texture—which turns on a bolt and sticks at a thumb of wood below. Because we must carry wood many times a day, much of the year, we have unfixed the latch to open this door thousands of times, walked into the woodshed, loaded up with logs, and walked back out again, latching the door behind us. But while we were tearing things up, something new happened, not once or twice but seven times: While we were fetching logs, this woodshed door swung closed behind us, and the wooden latch turned by itself and locked us inside the woodshed.

It never happened once in the years before; in the years since we stopped sawing and hammering, it has not happened again. This locking up was not malicious, because it is easy enough to get out of the woodshed by a door that leads outside. Not malicious, just an annoying prank.

THE STEADIEST presence remains in the possessions, rooms, and artifacts of the dead. Living in their house, we take over their practices and habits, which makes us feel close to them and to the years that they knew. I always wanted to live in this house with the old people, and now I do, even though they are dead. I don't live in their past; they inhabit my present, where I live as I never lived before. I used to survive, like many people, half in a daydream of future reward that is a confession of present malaise: the vacation trip, the miraculous encounter. When I moved here, at first I feared the fulfillment of desire, as if I would be punished for possessing what I wanted so much; there was a brief time when I drove ten miles under the speed limit and buckled up to move the car in the driveway; but contentment was relentless and would not let me go until I studied the rapture of the present tense. It turns out that the fulfillment of desire is to stop desiring, to live in the full moon and the snow, in the direction the wind comes from, in the animal scent of the alive second.

The dead were welcoming. I worried about usurping their place until two dreams helped me. In one I discovered that my grandfather—who was working the farm, now, in my dream—had disappeared and I thought him dead, only to see him striding up the dirt road from Andover (a road paved before I was born), leading a file of zoo animals: ostrich, bear, elephant, lion, tiger. He had traded the cows and sheep for these exotic creatures, proving (as I take the dream) that I was permitted to raise poems on this farm instead of stock. The other dream was more to the point of disappearances; a large voice pronounced, "The blow of the ax resides in the acorn."

If there is no connected past, we lack the implication of persistence after our own death. The preserved or continuous past implies the possibility that oneself may continue, in place or object or even in spirit, a ring of time that revolves, revisits, and contains. As a child I heard about a bone ring. When John Wells fought at Vicksburg he stood next to a young man named George Henry Butler, who came from a farm on New Canada Road; people from the same neighborhoods fought together in that war. As they were shelled, Wells took cover behind a great tree, which allowed him to stand upright; Butler squatted in a hole beside him. When the cannonade continued Wells offered to switch places with Butler, to let him stretch for a bit, and when they had changed places, a cannonball crashed through the tree and took off the young man's head. My great-grandfather emptied Butler's pockets, and when he mustered out and walked home to Danbury turned over the dead soldier's possessions to his family.

John Wells's son Wesley married George Henry Butler's cousin Kate Keneston, and one object from those pockets came down to her. A few years ago it disappeared. No one could find it in the house, and we thought it was gone forever. We lamented the lost connection with a young man killed in the Civil War. Then we discovered it in a box of buttons in the back chamber: a finger ring carved out of bone, eight-sided, scratched with little decorations, small and yellowed—a bone ring I take as emblem of this place.

Perennials

I LIVE IN the house I always wanted to live in. When I was a boy, spending summers here with my grandmother and grandfather, I wrote poems and read books in the morning; in the afternoon I hayed with my grandfather, listening to his long, slow stories of old times. I loved him, and he gave me the past of his boyhood as if it were a fortune or a mild chronic disease. Over the years of separation, in a suburban world, I felt continuously connected with this land and with the dead who make it precious. Now I return full circle, except that I write all day and I do not hay at all. If I miss my grandfather and his stories, I do not miss him so much as I used to; he died long ago but he is no longer *missing*. As I reach the age he carried when I was born, I sleep in the bed he died in and I find him everywhere I look. In a cousin's cheekbone, in a turn of phrase, in a remembered quilt I find him.

Paul Fenton reminds me of my grandfather, with good reason. Paul's mother was Wesley's sister Grace, who died just three years ago. Paul is seventy now, a pacemaker in his chest, and he complains that although he can still chop wood all day, now he must pause sometimes to catch his breath, and the doctor can't tell him why. When I was a boy on the farm, my grandfather was in his sixties and seventies, while Paul was early in middle age. Paul and Bertha used to call on Wesley and Kate; my grandfather saved good stories for Paul, who liked hearing his uncle's talk. Now sometimes Bertha and Paul will call on us, driving over from the long farm where their son Dennis keeps fifty Holsteins, and Paul has a story to tell me.

When Paul was a boy, an old man told him this one, and the old man told Paul that he had heard it from an old man when *he* was a boy.

"So this one goes back some . . .

"Once there was a man living around here who filled his ox cart every year in the fall. He filled it with everything he and his family made over the whole year: things his wife and daughters sewed or knitted or crocheted, things like yarn and cloth, goose feathers for stuffing beds, linen and flax seed. Probably the man and his boys made shingles he put in the ox cart; young boys made birch brooms. And he put in the ox cart everything from his fields that would keep and that he didn't need: extra apples, potatoes, Indian corn, turnips, pumpkins, and squash; vinegar, honey in combs, dried meat, and maybe tanned deerhide.

"Well, he filled it right up with everything all of them had made or done or grown, leaving behind just enough for them to eat and wear all winter. Then he walked beside his ox, ten days maybe, all the way to Portsmouth, where there was a big market. (One year he went all the way down to Boston, to the market by the harbor.) When he got to market he sold whatever he had. There'd be sailors in Portsmouth then, and people came from all around to do their shopping. After he sold his potatoes he sold the bag he brought the potatoes in. If he had vinegar in a barrel, you know he'd've made the barrel too; so then he sold the barrel. When he sold everything out of his cart, and the cart was empty, he sold the cart. After he sold the cart he sold his ox, harness and all."

Paul pauses a moment, grinning, and looks at me to see how I like his story's twist. I like it. Paul goes on.

"Then he walked home. Maybe he bought things for his family with the money. Salt, an orange for each of them—they never saw oranges in those days—maybe needles or knives, things he couldn't make at his own forge. But he had his year's money, money for the year.

"Then when he came home he started everything over again, the young ox in the barn, the harness, the cart . . ."

Paul smiles, excitement in his face; he knows what he has given. Soon he must stand and leave, back to the chores by which he helps Dennis, his necktie and white shirt back in the closet until Sunday. He will wear overalls again, become farmer again—winter and summer, garden and cattlebarn.

He leaves me to early November nightfall and my dream of the ox-cart man. I see him walking home from Portsmouth Market, up Highway 4 from Concord through Penacook, Boscawen, Salisbury, Andover. On a narrow dirt road he walks steadily, coins heavy in his pockets, past forest and farm, pasture and cornfield, big houses and settlers' cabins. Now he walks through West Andover, almost home, and I see him down the road in the cool afternoon sun, slanting low from Vermont, lengthening shadows of cornstalks blackened with frost. Now he is home—it is this farm, as I dream it—and his family gathers around him as he gives each of them a gift from his great pockets, needles and combs for the women, a Barlow knife for each boy, and stashes the cash in the treasury crock, which he keeps under a stone in the rootcellar. Now they sit in the dark parlor in December, the family on chairs in a semicircle around the castiron stove, under high candles, working. The ox-cart man sews a harness. His wife and girl children sew, knit, spin, weave. His boys work with leather, carve, whittle. They work, and the years move on in paths and circles of work. From the dark underground of dead winter the year moves to woodchopping, ice cutting, deer hunting, tanning, coopering, sugaring, manuring, plowing, planting, weeding, haying, harvesting, slaughtering, and filling the cart again for the journey to Portsmouth.

I see that the ox-cart man is a perennial plant, divesting himself each year of everything grown, and growing it all again. When I dream his face I see Paul's face, who harvests a story for me, and I see my grandfather's face, who divested himself of everything he could gather, in his stewardship carrying all the past through winter darkness into present light. I understand: This duty is my duty also.

If people like Wesley and Kate, like Paul and Bertha, not only live out their lives but pass on the stories of their lives—their own and the stories dead people told them—by these stories our seasons on earth may return and repeat themselves in others.

Let the curve of my story meet the curve of your own.

The Fire That Never Went Out

WELL, it *did* go out, in summer's heat when only noontime dinner need be cooked and supper was cold, or in spring or autumn when the night would be mild and the range's heat unnecessary. In the 1930s and the wartime 1940s, we let the fire die down when we went to bed at nine o'clock, and we thundered it up again, five the next morning, with a cup of kerosene flung over kindling. Only in winter, perhaps, did the fire never go out. December into early March, my grandfather in overalls carried armfuls of maple and ash from the woodshed to fill the woodbox fitted between range and papered wall. Then my grandmother, the kitchen's broad and powerful matriarch, tended the range's firebox, alternating kinds and cuts of wood according to need. When she required high heat in the oven, for bread and pies, ash blazed; midafternoon, various hardwoods steamed the kettle slowly, at the ready for coffee. At night, tight maple or elm heated slow and reliable.

In the morning—after oatmeal, pork scraps, and fried eggs, sometimes with potatoes hot or cold, always with bread and yesterday's leftover pie—the stove heated to assemble noontime's dinner: potatoes again, vegetables out of the blue Ball jars that lined shelves in the rootcellar, maybe boiled beef or fowl, roast mutton, pork. Baking once a week collected breads and pies to store in the milk room. Supper was dinner diminished, cold in summer, in winter supplemented with hot beans from the oven or pies warmed up.

At summer's end, in August and hot September, the prodigious canning took all day, week after week. It had begun early in the summer with peas; now it was Kentucky Wonders, corn sliced from the cob, pickled beets, tomatoes—a thousand jars every summer. Women's faces and bare arms stayed red for weeks, and in the rootcellar shelves bent under the tonnage of ripe summer alongside bins for the storage of roots and apples in autumn.

IT IS A GLENWOOD RANGE, black and regularly blackened again. Dating from the first years of the last century, it is ornamental like Victorian houses and furniture, its squat, elegant lines floral with castiron relief. The draft system—multiple sliding panels, doors and levers for internal alteration—allows both subtle control and decorative business. The oven door opens by hand, or if hands be occupied offers a foot pedal. Six lids lift from the stove's top, two over the small firebox, four gradually receding from the hottest places. But the whole large surface is for cooking and warming, with further warming shelves extending above the surface at the range's rear. Farthest from the firebox is the well or reservoir that kept water warm day and night—for filling the kettle, for lowering the aluminum dipper into when you needed hot water to wash and rinse the dishes—almost as easy as the hot-water faucet that takes its place. If quantities of hot water were needed, when the great washing machine with its fitted mangle was rolled in from the shed, kettles over the stove's whole surface heated gallons.

What an American creation, what a system, what a technology, this wonder mechanical, visible, and tangible, this mystery huge, heavy, and ornamental!

MY MOTHER remembers when the stove arrived in a great Railway Express wooden box carted by a team of horses. She remembers also finding under the Christmas tree the tiny replica Glenwood that I mentioned now rests in the back chamber.

When my grandfather died, my grandmother was seventy-four, and kept the stove going until she was almost ninety, splitting wood herself for many years, and using the good help of cousins. Then another technology fitted two kerosene burners into the old firebox and threaded slender pipes through walls to an oil drum outdoors near the old well. After several years of this luxury, one day the firebox split and exposed flame. My mother was visiting my grandmother then and wrote me a letter about it. She'd found a good secondhand white enamel kerosene-electric stove. The men who brought it were good enough to haul the old Glenwood off to the barn until somebody could be found to drag it to the Wilmot dump. I was not to feel too bad; there was no way it could be repaired.

But my daughter, who was eight years old, told stories about that range to friends back home, and when they were incredulous, she required me to photograph it. No one in the suburbs had ever seen anything so grand. So I telephoned, so I wrote a letter: *Please keep the stove in the barn. Please don't dump it.* Thus when I returned to live here myself, I found the Glenwood a sagging hulk that looked frail and tiny detached from its function and its kitchen dominion, turned red like November leaves, piled in the corner the barn made where it joined the grainshed. Down the road in Potter Place I discovered a man who worked with metal, Leslie Ford, a blacksmith who also pumped out cesspools and repaired small engines, a wiry craftsman snappy and waggish in his mid-sixties, who looked over the rust heap and thought probably he could do something about it.

Les kept the stove six months, complained bitterly about the task's difficulty, added firebrick to the firebox, improvised a grill from somebody's old coal stove, delivered and installed it in the kitchen—from which it had absented itself only five years in the last eighty—and charged too little. Now the Glenwood takes its place again, with its old dignity, squat and horizontal, festooned with pedals and knobs, with its weightiness both literal and figurative. Its reservoir leaks but a hot-water faucet supplies our needs. Its firebox is narrow but we keep the stove going twenty-four hours a day only in coldest weather, when its fire allows habitation of half downstairs and prevents the kitchen water pipes from freezing. When it is thirty below I wake every two hours to feed it. Otherwise in winter we fire it in the morning (with twisted newspaper, not with kerosene) and let it cool down after dinner, which assembles itself again on the Glenwood's black surface.

Where my grandmother fitted small skillets into the round holes over the naked fire, we set the wok's inverted dome; stew bubbles all day; soup rolls its knuckles of boil and froth—on the fire that seldom goes out.

To Walk a Dog

Dogs give us an excuse for walking. They love us, we love them, and we walk them because it makes them happy.

Gus is a golden retriever–sheepdog cross, affectionate and agreeable, handsome and guilty, who presides over the walkable acreage of our hearts. Like most dogs Gus is an enthusiast, not least for perambulation. In our house as in many, when Jane and I plan out the day, we are reduced to spelling words out: w-a-l-k. For *us* it may be walking; for Gus it is running and halting, often combined in a cartoonish maneuver as Gus skids, stopping in midsprint, scattering gravel. His acute olfactory sensor has bleeped him information of irresistible fascination—some woodland creature, seldom encountered, has decorated a bush with its odoriferous Kilroy: coyote, skunk, bear, moose, otter, badger, raccoon, beaver, fisher, fox . . . Who knows?

Gus cannot run loose because our house sits beside a busy two-lane blacktop that killed my grandfather's dogs as early as the 1920s. Good walking, however, waits all about us. Our house sits like an egg in a nest of twenty dirt roads, from which old logging trails slant up-mountain. Often we walk Gus on New Canada Road, which lopes its cursive along the side of Ragged Mountain, up and down but mostly up in both directions. As we trudge New Canada, Gus flashes into the woods after a flickering chipmunk, disappears into hemlock or birch or ash, and then reappears fifty yards ahead, calmly sitting in the ditch to wait for us while we absurdly whistle for him into the dark shade where he vanished.

Watching him run is purest joy. I walk doggedly ahead while Gus loses himself in rapt contemplation of something about a stone that I lack equipment to contemplate. After five minutes of intense rhinal analysis, acute ecstasy of nose, while I have pumped ahead uphill puffing, Gus covers the distance in one eighth the time. I crave watching him. At the top of the hill, where I can see his whole trajectory, I whistle. Having catalogued five hundred items around the examined stone, he looks up and remembers me. He coils himself like a spring, flattens on the air, and breaks the all-world up-Ragged hundred-meter record—every afternoon, all over again.

While I trudge, or while I pause for him, my eyes perform like Gus's nose. On New Canada Road I can walk the same path, day after day, and every day uncover new glory of the creation. Over the divided seasons I study stonewalls, which used to keep sheep out of corn, as they extend into dense woods. I contemplate thick-waisted matronly birches, dark hemlocks, and every spring the fragile, indomitable ferns. Streams hurtle after spring rains and become dry stony gulches of August. Leaves fall, snow decorates, moss blossoms, and I walk each day through an anthology of natural growth, change, and stasis, pausing to stare at the same mossy granite that Gus pauses to inhale. Six legs walking provide pleasures for two grateful eyes and one lengthy learned nose.

Good Use for Bad Weather

My grandparents nailed two thermometers side by side on the porch of their New Hampshire farmhouse. One registered ten degrees cold, the other ten degrees hot, so that there was always something to brag about. Every morning when my grandmother sat in the rocker under Christopher the canary, writing three postcards to three daughters, she could say, "Thirty below this morning. Seems like it might get cold." Or, "Ninety already and the sun's not over the mountain."

In New England we take pride in our weather because it provides us with pain and suffering, necessities for the spirit, like food and clothing for the body. We never brag about good weather. Let Tucson display self-esteem over eighty-three days without rain. Let Sarasota newspapers go free for the asking when the sun doesn't shine. We smirk in the murk, superior. It's true that we have good weather; we just don't pay it any mind. When summer people flock north to the lakes and the mountains, they do not gather to enjoy our foggy rain. If they're from Boston, they don't come *for* bright sun and cool dry air; they migrate north *against* the soup-kettle mugginess of home. It seems more decent.

In good weather—apple days of October, brilliant noons and cool evenings of August—we remain comfortable despite our pleasure by talking about pleasure's brevity, forecasting what we're in for as soon as the good spell is done with. Winter is best for bragging. For a week or two in March, mud is almost as good. (Mud is weather as much as snow is; leaves are landscape.) "Tried to get the Buick up New Canada this morning. Have to wait for a dry spell to pull it out, I suppose. Of course, we'll have to dig to find it, first."

Black ice is first rate, but most of us who cherish difficulty will settle for a good ten feet of snow. We get up about five-fifteen, make the coffee, check the thermometer: ten degrees above. The warmth must account for the snow. Highway department plows blunder down Route 4 in the dark outside. We get dressed, dragging on flannel-lined chinos, flannel shirt, sweater, down jacket, and boots. Then we broom one car, headlights and taillights, gun it in reverse over the hump of snow Forrest's plow left, swing it up Forrest's alley, and swoop it down to the road, scattering ridges of snow.

Only two miles to the store. It's not adventurous driving, but it pays to be attentive, to start slowing for a turn a hundred yards early. The store opens at six. Because this is New Hampshire, somebody's bound to be there by five-forty-five. We park with the motor running and the heater on—it'll get warm while we pick up the *Globe*—to go inside. Bob's there with his cup of coffee, and Bill who owns garage and store, and Judy the manager who makes coffee and change. We grin at each other as I stamp my boots and slip my paper out of the pile. We say things like "Nice weather!" "Bit of snow out there!" "Hear we're getting two feet more!" but what we're really saying is *It takes more than a couple of feet of snow to slow us down!*

WEATHER is conversation's eternal subject, lingua franca shared by every New Englander with sensory equipment. When Rolls-Royce meets junker, over to the dump, they can talk about the damned rain. Weather talk helps us over difficult subjects. On one Monday morning some years ago, Ned said to Will, "Too bad about Pearl Harbor. I hear there's ten feet over on Five-A." Will said to Ned, "I suppose we'll lick 'em. They say a bread truck got through."

In a boring patch when the weather's mild, we talk about disasters and catastrophes of the past. As a child I heard endless stories about the blizzard of '88. My Connecticut grandfather belonged to a club that met once a year on the anniversary to swap reminiscences—by which, of course, we understand that they met to tell lies. As I stagger into codgerhood, I discover that my own blizzard of '88 is the great wind of 1938. I was in Connecticut for that one, which first visited our house in my father's disgust over his new barometer. He won it in a putting contest, and he was proud of it, pretty in its rich brown wood and bright brass. Then when he hung it on the wall it busted; at least it sank way, way down until the foolish thing predicted hurricane.

Most of the time, weather is relative. Every year when an August morning is forty degrees, we shiver and chill: It's *cold* out there! But when a February morning rises to forty, we walk around with our coats unbuttoned, enjoying the heat wave. Next day an ice storm, and we take relief in the return of suffering. It's true—if you don't have to drive in it—that there are few things in creation as beautiful as an ice storm. Much bad weather is beautiful: dark days when it never quite rains and never quite doesn't, English weather cozy around the fire; wild rains of summer after high heat, compensation and relief; drizzle in autumn that drains color from the trees, quiet and private; the first snow, which steps my heartbeat up; the first *big* snow, which steps it higher; winter thaw, with its hesitant promise; gothic thunderstorms with bolts of melodrama—we quicken, we thrill, we comfort the dog.

Every now and then we have an open winter, as we call it when we have no snow; it's psychic disaster, because we haven't suffered enough. The earth can't emerge because it never submerged. We don't deserve the milder air and the daffodils rising because we haven't lost our annual battles with the snow—fender benders, bad backs from shoveling the mailbox, rasp of frozen air in the lungs, falls on ice, chunks of snow down our boots. The only bad weather in New England is when we don't have any.

October's Omens

EVERYWHERE in the north, October is gorgeous and ominous. Red omens of the maple tree, firing wild flares into the soft early twilight, prophesy white frozen winter, zero of January and February's drifts, blocked turnpikes and the wretched gutter-snow of the city. In New Hampshire the warnings begin early. Even August flies winter's sign in its red branch; frost visits in hesitant September. But in October, auspices of winter show themselves as steadily as the onset of a head cold, a tightening behind the eyes and a tentative sniffle. Up early to drive for the paper, we scrape omens from the windshield of the car. On the same frosty morning late hollyhocks sag blown brown rotten trumpets from spindly stalks. But noon warms up, October's message relents, and chrysanthemums and asters will endure—for a few weeks.

At this time of year, the vegetable gardener undergoes the fear of frost. If one day we read in the paper that the first deep cold is on its way, our tomato vines always hang a hundred great green globes. We pull old sheets from the back of the linen closet, and blankets with holes in them, to drape our plants against frost's killing scythe. Usually we ignore widespread pumpkins and squash, because the gourd will survive though the vine-shrivel; if the zucchini expire we will feel only gratitude.

All night under the clear cold sky, starlight reflects from the ghostly white-sheeted tomato plants. Come anxious morning, we inspect the rows for green or brown; in lucky years our refrigerator-cold green tomatoes have survived. And if we endure a three-day flurry of early frost-fright, September or October, then maybe the sky will cloud up, ether will densen and warm . . . and Indian summer, lazing down Route 4, will redden the great globes of our tomatoes well into autumn—fresh red slices for sandwiches at lunch, beefsteaks and Better Girls for stewing up with onions at supper or for freezing toward the summery spaghettis of January.

If the vines die with hundreds of green tomatoes on them, the next morning we will rip up the tomato plants and hang them upside down in the cellar to ripen, or maybe we will pile green tomatoes in the shed wrapped in newspaper, or . . . There are as many solutions to the Problem of the Green Tomato as there are cures for hiccups. But it is a rule of October: No tomato picked green, however much it reddens in the afterlife of shed or rootcellar, will ever taste like a ripe tomato.

Frost-fears get us moving. It is time to check out the radiator coolant in the Saab, which overheated all summer, and test it for forty below; it is time to change plugs and points in the Nissan pickup, which retains old-style rear-wheel drive, so that we must examine the treads on snow tires. For many of us in New Hampshire, it is time to get the plow ready for bolting on to the V-8 four-wheel-drive truck; it is provident to grease up the snowblower, not to mention the snowmachine. It is time for everyone of a northern persuasion to switch wardrobes, to air the mothball smell out of a drawerful of sweaters, to stash the light khakis of summer and recover L. L. Bean's flannel-lined jeans from the shelf at the back of the closet. Blazer and light flannel climb attic stairs as tweed and whipcord descend. Summer's sandals pack themselves away. We clear spiderwebs out of felt-lined boots and set them under the closet's down jacket.

In New Hampshire we measure the year by the category of flatlander that the season elicits. When the leafers of autumn depart in mid-October, we know what we are in for. Deer hunters come in two formats: The local sort lives in a trailer down the road on Route 4, freezer packed with deer meat against a layoff at the shoe factory; the other sort drives up from Massachusetts, paunchy Rambo geared with red vest and cap, geared with .30-30 and Four Roses. When he hunts he is drunk by seven A.M., and every autumn he shoots two or three laid-off shoemakers trying to stock their freezers.

For this reason, among others, the two formats do not get along. Flatlander feels that countryman lacks the sporting sense; New Hampshire doubts Rambo's ability to distinguish a deer's track from a chipmunk's, or even a railroad's. My favorite sign of autumn was handwritten, irregular, indignant block capitals two feet high on a bedsheet stapled to a fence in Vermont. I saw it last November, just after deer season: THIS IS A DONKEY!

IN OCTOBER everybody in the northern half of the country prepares to heat houses. We check our furnaces, gas or oil or propane; if we heat by wood, we stack split logs—eight cord for the winter, maybe—and if we are sensible we clean the chimney. Then we hunker down. Everywhere winter approaches by its own weird routes. In northern Michigan and in Canada provident people test the electrical systems that, plugged in all night, keep their cars warm enough to start. In Florida they check out the smudge pots. I don't know *what* they do in Arizona. In California people look at the grass, hoping it may turn green this year, and if it does, and the rains keep coming, people watch in terror for the mountainous Godzilla of a mudslide ingesting Jacuzzi, carport, deck, and conversation pit. In West Texas, old desert reclaimed for cotton by irrigation and diminishing aquifer, people watch with irritation and annoyance as the single tree next to the house in the country drops brown leaves, littering the precious patch of lawn. Every year outside Lubbock a homeowner, outraged by the sheer mess of falling leaves, rents a chainsaw from Taylor's and saws down the old live oak that was planted and nursed, fifty years ago, by someone homesick for northeastern elms.

Here in New Hampshire, we would need to hire the province of Quebec to clear-cut the entire state if we wanted to prevent leaves from messing up our yards. Unwilling to undertake such a project, and putting a good face on things, we use our leaves. In November, maybe during deer season when we cannot walk in the woods, it is time to tuck up the house. Nowadays some of us are insulated, and the old house is tight, but tightness is not a property traditional among country houses, where icy winds at floorboard level riffle the braided rugs. To cut down on the breeze that blows through the clapboard, we rake maple leaves (oak, ash, anything) against the foundation stones of the house high onto clapboard. To keep the piles in place we cut hemlock branches, green on red, and lay them across the leaves. When the first snow comes we shovel it over the leaves and against the house, best insulation of all, and all winter when a thaw melts snow back from the wood, we shovel new snow into the cold gap. (Naturally all this damp rots clapboard; we need to replace boards every fifty years or so.) Often we tack poly around the base of the house before we pull leaves against it. We buy it down to the lumberyard in great rolls and wrap up the house with it, rural Christos, tacking it three feet high. Some folks prefer black tarpaper, some Reynolds Wrap. Houses on Route 4 sport extra socks and leggings like arctic explorers.

By October's end or early November we have checked out the heating, winterized the car, tucked up the house, switched clothing, and pulled up the garden. Now we are permitted to wait. One night we will wake conscious of a soft advent, quietness dropping from the air; we will gaze into darkness to watch the great white onset of winter. We will rise in the morning, virtue's reward, in a warm house to don warm clothing and to start a car that will start. The most foresighted among us will even have stationed snow shovels and pails of salt by the kitchen door. *Sigh* . . . It helps to remember that winter is ominous of spring.

A Good Foot of Snow

CHRISTMAS DAY, snow started before dawn. In the blackness of five A.M. we heard the snowplows rumble north and rumble south, shaking the oak sills of our farmhouse, comforting us in our beds. All winter, plows made cold thunder: up . . . down . . . up . . . down. Sometimes the vibration wakes us, and we roll over, under heaped blankets, snugly aware of where we are. Sometimes I rise, add wood to the fires banked in our castiron stoves, flip on the porch light to see our driveway's accumulation, and wait for the plow to turn and return. In the distance, like a freight train thirty years ago, the grunt and shudder begins; then the bright headlights illuminate snow; then, in a tidal wave of thrust whiteness, great Hokusai coils of dazzle fly gutterward, almost hiding the dark body of the truck; and in the upward light, snow falls as thick as cloth.

Christmas Day at five A.M., the plow's shudder waked six-year-olds up and down Route 4, to stretch and remember suddenly what *day* it was, to turn on a bedroom light and look for a full stocking. And the sea captains of the snow, great plowers over the road, never reached home until nighttime—cold turkey and stuffing among crabby children, toys already broken—for the snow kept up all day until night returned at five in the afternoon. All day the party lines trilled up and down the countryside, distant relatives deciding to postpone long trips, close brothers and sisters reassuring each other that the roads were fine, driveways dug out. All day the bright sky flaked white against the dark pine climbing Ragged Mountain behind us. All Christmas Day the snow mounted on barn roof, birdfeeder, and useless mailbox. All day we gazed at the white world. By nightfall the radio told us: We had accumulated eighteen inches of snow.

Snow turns us back two hundred years. When the plow disappears down the road, the road sinks out of sight between the whiteness of ditches and fields. Bright stillness thick with flakes hovers on tree and barn, hill, pond, and meadow. I stand in the white doorway, in front of the still house, squinting to take the country back before highways, trains, and snowplows.

Then a pickup crushes ahead over the plowed Route 4, carrying someone home for Christmas.

All Christmas Day we looked for Forrest to come and plow us out. My big cousin, contractor and carpenter and winter plowman, plows the parking lot at the ski slope on Ragged as well as numerous private driveways. At noon his pickup burst up one side of our U-shaped driveway and pushed the snow back once-over-lightly behind our cars; if we needed to go someplace, we could shovel a minute, back out, and swoop to the road. All day we waited for him to return, for the fifteen minutes of backing and charging that clears all portions of our driveway, pushes snow back onto leachfield and daffodil patch, up to woodshed and carriage shed. Sometimes when we've had thirty or forty inches without a melt, Forrest will hire a front loader to heap drift on drift, farther out into roses and asparagus, clearing space for the next accumulation. Although Forrest complains about cold and no sleep and long hours, I never see him so happy as when he is perched high over his blade—backing, gathering speed, changing the blade's tilt, and *whomp* into the plain of whiteness, shoving it around like a large child in the best sandbox.

It was pitch black early Christmas night, and we were ready for bed, when the sound of Forrest's plow came through to us, and high in the black yard gleamed the yellow eye of his truck's forehead. Back and *whomp.* Back and *whomp.* We watched him skillfully shift and back and thud and thud, with the grace of an ocean liner, of a 747, of a seven-foot tight end—anything huge and doing well what it loves to do. Forrest slammed into our eighteen inches, Forrest tucked it, Forrest treated it like a flurry.

Half done, he parked and paused, as he often does. Water boiled on the woodstove, and Forrest accepted the offer of a cup of coffee. And when he came in, his beard whitened, his eyes red, smiling and shaking his head, we heard him say, "Yes, that's a good foot." He paused for emphasis, repeated, "A *good* foot of snow."

Heman Chase's Corners

ONE DAY in August of 1983 I went surveying with Heman Chase, who has been measuring land in Vermont and New Hampshire since 1928. In order to start first thing in the morning, I stayed overnight in the house that Heman and Edith built in 1936, in the town of East Alstead, New Hampshire, where Heman has spent most of his many-sided life. Being a surveyor is only Heman's vocation; by avocation he writes books, runs a watermill, invents useful devices, philosophizes, and uncovers local history.

Surveying was the morning's task. After breakfast we descended to the under-house garage, where Heman keeps the truck he uses for surveying. His Bronco is twelve years old, with eighty-seven thousand miles on it. And this Bronco has a lot on it besides miles. Heman has equipped it as ingeniously as the British secret service outfits a sports car for James Bond. A clock, an altimeter, and a pencil sharpener are screwed to the dashboard. At the front of the hood he has fixed an antique bell from Manchester, Vermont, bartered from a dealer for whom Heman felled an elm. On the front bumper Heman has attached a telescoping device for pushing cars without doing damage to pusher or pushee. As he shows me how it works, Heman remembers a story. In 1928 his Model T got stuck in a snowstorm at Craig's Four Corners; he slogged uphill to Ike Craig's farmhouse, and Ike Craig hitched up his oxen to a logging chain to pull him out. When Heman tried to pay him, Ike waved him off. "Pass it on," said Ike Craig, and Heman has been passing it on ever since.

Surveying equipment fills the Bronco's truck bed. It will be a warm day, and Heman wears a tank top over his wiry chest and shoulders, heavy trousers against the brush, and old sneakers for his work in the woods. Today Heman says that he will use compasses, to save the client time and money. Machines that measure more precisely are expensive and time-consuming. "We are always being pushed to be more technological," Heman begins; he has arrived at a favorite subject. "A compass survey is accurate within one in three hundred and fifty or so, adequate where we're going. People who spend their time in an easy chair in an office now say we ought to get it one in five thousand." Heman snorts and seems to change the subject by referring to old-fashioned telephone operations. "Back when Mrs. Buzzle was Central, once I tried to get Mr. Marsh the minister. Mrs. Buzzle said, 'You'd better wait five minutes, he just walked past the window.'"

Heman looks over to see if I get the point; he had not changed the subject. "Maybe all this homogeneity," he says, "leaves us free to read poetry and do inward things." He is being ironical. It is not that Heman dislikes machines. In fact, he has invented many useful devices. As we get ready to back out of the garage, I observe a Chase invention: Heman pushes lightly against the garage door and it lifts up easily, its weight balanced by an egg-shaped stone fixed to the end of a twelve-foot wooden spoke. When the door is open, its granite counterweight poises in air like a dinosaur's egg over a cave mouth.

As we drive to Alstead Center, Heman discusses the appropriate technology of surveying, in his crisp, deliberate voice. He parks on a wood road by the parcel of land we will survey for possible subdividing and selling. Heman opens drawers and panels in the Bronco's back end—as compartmentalized as a Swiss army knife—and removes some tools of the trade: a compass on a tripod, a hundred-foot spool of metal surveyor's tape, a red-and-white-striped pole for sighting through the compass, a machete, and bug spray.

Now Hallie Whitcomb arrives, Heman's co-worker, a slim woman in her late twenties, strong, shy, friendly, giving off senses of both farm girl and intellectual. On his stationery Heman lists Hallie as his assistant. When he first told me about her, he spoke of Hallie as if she were a miracle. Six years back she dropped over, a total stranger *out of the blue,* to visit Heman and Edith. She had grown up on a farm in Springfield, Vermont, where she still lives, and had studied geologic mapping at Earlham College in Indiana; she thought she would like to try surveying for a while. After the visit Edith told Heman, "Give her a chance." Heman gave her a chance. "I call her a partner now," he says. "She just about as often tells *me* what to do as I tell *her* what to do." About one social matter Heman feels especially grateful. "I'm glad that I lived into an age—or *to* an age—such that it's not considered improper for her to work with me."

Heman has already explained the morning's task: We will follow the old backline through eight hundred feet of forest, and set a new corner for the putative subdivision. Heman leads the way. We set off for the place we will start from. We head into the woods; the woods take us over: up precipitous banks slippery with pine needles, down steep sides to streams layered with flat round stones as black as slate. We clutch at saplings; we dig our fists into cliff faces of needles. Our leader in his tank top wields his machete rapidly, cuts off sharp dead hemlock boughs with a quick powerful wrist stroke—intrepid, single-minded, and overheated.

A great hemlock marks the corner from which we begin to measure. Heman nails on the tree's trunk a metal plate that bears his name, the initials of the owner, and the date. From this tree we set out, Heman leading with his barber pole in one hand and his brush-cutting machete in the other, slashing blazes on trees on either side of his path, progressing at north fifty-four degrees west. Hallie takes up the rear with compass and tripod. When Heman has traveled eighty or ninety feet ahead, still visible, he stops for Hallie to check the line. She sights Heman's barber pole in the open sights of the compass and tells him to move a foot to the right, or six inches to the left. With his own hand-held compass Heman counterchecks the reading; if his compass differs, he moves to split the difference. The tape counts the distance traveled, and Hallie keeps track.

Sometimes I forge ahead with Heman, sometimes stay behind with Hallie. As I scramble up and down, following our bearing down gullies and up hills, I lose my reading glasses from my shirt pocket. This loss annoys me, because I was foolish to bring my reading glasses into the woods. Heman stops what he is doing and crawls around on his hands and knees searching for my glasses. "What color are they?" says Heman, and I tell him that the rims are gold. "Well," he says drily, "if I find any silver ones I won't pick them up." I think of how, in fifty years, someone surveying these woods again—or digging in a suburban garden, or starved and scrabbling for a root to eat—will discover a pair of old-fashioned glasses deep in leaf mold.

Finally I persuade Heman to return to the attack, and I talk with Hallie as he marches forward, carrying his skinny pole before him like a relay racer with a six-foot baton. At the family farm in Springfield Hallie keeps a big garden, she tells me, and surveying is a good job for her. She works no more than half-time, three or four days a week, nine months a year; she wants only as much money as she needs. She loves surveying, loves Heman, approves of using the compass. "He keeps the client in mind," says Hallie. "Land values are rising, though . . . We may have to be more precise." Maybe it's not only people in office easy chairs who want Heman to measure one in five thousand.

As we talk, we keep moving. Ninety feet and eighty-seven and ninety-four. We are two hundred and seventy-one feet toward our eight-hundred-foot goal, where we will make a corner and head for the road. Heman draws a line through trackless wood that was pasture once. This land was never cultivated. There are too many stones for that, granite and quartz, and there is no feel underfoot of ridges that a plow made. Its pasture days are a long way back, maybe fifty years, maybe a hundred. Old trees with trunks two feet thick have given up the ghost and lie across our path. Sharp branches scrape our skin. Though Heman hacks a gap, it is a Heman-sized gap, for a body smaller and suppler than mine.

Everywhere the prolix morbidity of the natural world has toppled old trees to the ground and started new ones up. No atom of space is unoccupied, by infant or by corpse, by needle or moss or tiny purple flower. Young trees stretch out in a row, pushed over by one gust; old trees root deep to endure. One hardy birch grips its root into earth around a round hunk of quartz the way a six-fingered pitcher might grasp a baseball. Everywhere among roots and in mosses there are holes for snake, mink, rabbit, skunk, and bigger holes for woodchuck. We find the droppings of deer and fox, yet nowhere do we see an animal; insects and the birds who eat them fly around us, but nothing larger shows itself.

Through it all—hacking, indomitable—Heman Chase draws a mapmaker's line, making a human mark on the vital, moribund, unstoppable energy and decay of the natural world. He draws a line through the wilderness, order imposed on chaos, the way a railroad draws a line through valley and forest, over stream and past meadow. I remember something Heman told me earlier, about a day when he and Hallie were setting a line. Deep in the woods, in bypassed rural New Hampshire, the old man and young woman found a stone culvert supporting abandoned railroad track and marveled at the beauty of its construction: "Cut granite stones about three feet by a foot and a half, laid up without mortar in an arch to support a deep fill, a hundred feet through." Marveling, they ate lunch together in the woods, Heman a sandwich, Hallie "some vegetable concoction." In summary, Heman tells me, "We go around and find out what history was."

WHEN HEMAN draws a mapmaker's approximate line through the moral wilderness, he does it by anecdote and by reference to his secular saints. The night before the survey, under trees near his house over Warren's Pond, he spoke about some of his professors at the University of Wisconsin. (He likes to say that his father thought Harvard the only place, his stepfather thought MIT the only place, and his mother packed him off to Wisconsin.) Professor Louis Kahlenberg was a moral example, an outstanding scientist who was forced to teach freshman chemistry—to the benefit of the freshmen—because he refused to work on chemical warfare during the First World War. Of course, a teacher can provide a counterexample. Another engineering professor, to whom Heman mentioned that he would take a philosophy course, observed, "All right, but it won't get you ahead."

For Heman the greatest ethical model is Henry George, the American economist and author of *Progress and Poverty*, who proposed a single tax on land. In Heman's first book, *American Ideals*, he connected George's idea with the society envisioned by this nation's founders. With land the ultimate determiner of wealth and power, George saw the concentration of land ownership as the greatest source of inequality and inequity in the world. If a land tax were our only means of revenue, then no one could aggregate masses of land and everyone could share in it—a democracy of small landowners. "George was the man who, more than any other, understood how the earth would have to be shared."

But Henry George's ideas do not find general acceptance among economists. One time Heman picked up a hitchhiking college student who majored in economics at Middlebury College in Vermont. Naturally enough, Heman asked his guest what he had learned in his classes about Henry George. The senior graduating in economics had never heard the name. Back home, after simmering down, Heman wrote a letter to the chairman of the economics department at Middlebury, offering his services as an unpaid lecturer on Henry George. After a long delay he was invited to address a class, and he enjoyed his visit to Middlebury, which ended in a long discussion with students who adjourned to the house of a history professor. Early on, however, Heman lost the class's economics teacher. He emphasized that under George's scheme there would be no income tax at all, and the professor, looking incredulous, asked, "Not even for Ted Williams?" Now,

Heman's interests were wide-ranging but not universal: He didn't know who Ted Williams was. From the tone of the question, Williams was obviously an important figure. In the recesses of his mind Heman suddenly recollected that Ted Williams belonged to the sporting world. Figuring that his ignorance would undermine his advocacy, he merely affirmed, "Not even for Ted Williams." The professor of economics allowed that he could not countenance any tax scheme that refused to tax an income of *a hundred thousand dollars.*

Supper done, we walked back to the house carrying trays. Heman always walks tilted slightly forward, as if he were trudging uphill. Or he leans like the tower at Pisa, as tough as Pisan stone, with abrupt angular energy. He speaks little of age. Sometimes he remembers that he is old—as if with surprise. Back in the house he told a story about a lawsuit in 1940 when he had been hired to map a crossroads where a young man and an old had collided automobiles. The young man sued and lost, but that was not the point of the story. When the young man testified he was asked his age, and he replied brightly, as if he were proclaiming virtue, "Twenty-seven!" When the old man took the stand he was asked the same question. As Heman mimicked his answer, the old man pronounced his years with a mixture of tones: bemusement, bewilderment, recognition that it did not matter, amazement that he should have lived so long. He said in a lingering voice, "Seventy-seven." As Heman told the story, he too was seventy-seven.

Before bed we visited Chase's Mill. One of Heman's books, *Short History of Mill Hollow,* tells the story of the various water-power mills that used Mill Brook or Warren Brook, flowing out of Warren's Pond. It is a remarkable essay, combining archaeological detective work with a spirited defense of water power. Now we visited the actual place, where hundreds of children and adults have learned the old ways of water power. Chase's Mill is a large building topped by a great loft with a fireplace, site of community gatherings. Outside, set into the ground, is an enormous gristmill stone from an earlier mill. On the ground floor above the mill's works is the shop, with water-powered lumber planer, large table saw, and jointer, together with electric-powered drill presses, band saw, table saw, wood lathe, machinist's lathe, and emery wheels. Here Heman and Edith have held shop classes for local children, teaching them to work in wood and metal.

As we entered the shop in August, I noticed a large woodstove back against a wall, out of the way. Heman showed how the castiron body pivots on skids into the room's center for the winter cold, its stovepipe artfully jointed to pivot in agreement. The shop is equipped to manufacture whatever ingenuity requires. Here Heman has implemented inventions: tripods for surveying, his own screw for splitting cordwood; he has made Windsor footstools and dumpcart bodies, trestle tables, cradles, and coffins for his mother and stepfather.

Heman stepped excitedly over the busy floor, pointing out, explaining; I realized that Heman is one of nature's professors, a doer who enjoys professing what he does. Although I am ignorant of mechanics and machines, enthusiasm pulled me in. I found myself watching intently as Heman cut a zigzag piece of brass, polished, trimmed . . . Then we descended to the floor beneath and moved inward toward the source of the old mill's power. The walls were rough stone, and I heard water dripping. Plunging in front of us, a nineteen-inch iron perstock channeled water to a turbine two stories down. At the moment the mill was quiet: alert, suspended, waiting. Lower down, at midlevel, we walked in a maze of pulleys, belts, and shafting, now silent as the works of a huge abandoned clock.

Then Heman pulled a lever: CRASH, and a hurtle of water deafened us as inside these deep, narrow chambers a liquid column smashed into the turbine, urging it into spinning life. All over the mill wheels whirled, cogs spun, gears groaned interlocking, long belts turned their quarter turns. An immense intricacy of mechanic power, loosed by Heman's hand on a lever, resurged the power of the clockmaker-engineer; we lived inside a clock of power, shaking, whirling with the force of twenty tumultuous horses straining to pull, smoothly and steadily, a system, a church, a cave, the thunderous center of the earth. And as Heman saw its effect, he grinned like a boy.

We descended toward the tumult of water. Heman recounted, shouting, a sequence of sluices: an old wooden one, an iron one that he rescued from an abandoned mill, this new one only seven years old. Then he pointed to another pipe, a second, smaller sluice, as if the big one had dropped a foal, which connected to a tiny version of the big turbine. Over the small sluice was a hand lever that Heman asked me to pull. When I did, water spun into the small turbine, from which a wire moved upward to a little machine on a level above. The little machine was a car's generator, and over it Heman had hung an electric light. As the small turbine spun it generated electricity; slowly, flickering at first, a lightbulb illuminated the deep hollow of Chase's Mill.

Heman offered congratulations: "You just lit a light by hydroelectric power!"

Now in the woods, surveying, we have come eight hundred feet, and it is time to make a corner. First we gather rocks, mostly lumps of granite from football size to the size of a basketball. To pry out medium stones, Heman wedges his machete under them. For larger rocks he takes a stick of hemlock, sharpens the end, uses another stone as a fulcrum, and lifts the rock out to roll it toward the pile. In twenty minutes we have collected a small quarry. Then Heman inserts a stout hemlock stake in the middle of the rock pile, big stones at the bottom showing their moss, smaller stones wedged closer in. Taking another metal patch from his pocket, he pokes his initials onto it and the date of this day and this year when we set out this line and made this corner.

Then we all stand back to look at it—a cairn of stones embodying purpose, a stick with a metal tag announcing a deed—and I feel for a moment as if I had taken part in a ritual, partly because this device resembles a grave. Out of the silence Heman's voice declares this sign a sacrament, and Hallie adds:

"Nobody makes a corner like Heman Chase."

Reasons for Hating Vermont

VERMONTERS lead quiet, introspective lives among the unspoiled splendors of their countryside, interrupted only by brunches, cocktail parties, and *Masterpiece Theatre.* Vermont invented the Young Rural Professional in 1972; in the same year, the yuppie invented Vermont. But it is not true that Vermonters live a serene existence without worries of any kind. The editor of a distinguished country journal once wrote a column about a typical Vermont dilemma. Which was better for starting the fire in your woodstove, he pondered, the *New York Times* or the *Wall Street Journal*?

New Hampshire is inhabited by real people who drive pickup trucks with gun racks and NRA bumper stickers; Vermont is a theme park full of Bostonians, New Yorkers, and Nebraskans dressed up in Vermont suits. When writers, intellectuals, violinists, and CEOs live north of Boston, they live in Vermont. If the oboe from the Indianapolis Symphony keeps a summer place back east, will it be a cottage on Lake Sunapee? If the chair of the mathematics department at Texas A & M drives five mornings into the sun from College Station for the month of August, does he aim for Penacook? In August Vermont drones with the sound of string quartets while motorcycle gangs converge on Laconia. (The rest of the year in New Hampshire it's the same noise, now performed by chainsaws and snowmachines.) Music festivals in Green Mountain towns, common as church suppers in New Hampshire, attract professors from the University of America wearing checked shirts out of the L. L. Bean catalogue. Saturday mornings, while a native takes his trash to the dump, the collegial hayseed ties his Volvo to the old hitching post and swaps stories with the salty character who runs the general store this summer, who last year managed Kuala Lumpur for IBM.

In the 1995 census it was discovered that seventeen indigenous Vermonters remained in the state; twelve spent their winters in Florida with their running-to-the-dump money. The rest had migrated to New Hampshire, from Malltown to Milltown.

Meantime, in the world at large, a conspiracy denies New Hampshire's existence and implies that Vermont borders Maine. Vermont has become the generic name for any place north of Boston, unless it's got lobsters. At poetry readings I find myself invariably introduced as resident of an old family farm in Vermont. Five hundred people have written me letters, correctly addressed, in which they asked me how the weather was up there in Vermont. Twelve visitors have written us notes, after a week or a weekend, saying how much they enjoyed visiting us in Vermont.

IN VERMONT deer are required to have shots. In Vermont people keep flocks of spayed sheep to decorate their lawns. In Vermont when inchling trout are released into streams, a state law requires that they be preboned and stuffed with wild rice delicately flavored with garlic and thyme. Vermont has decorator barns; Calvin Klein will sign your woodshed for $250,000. In Vermont you can buy boots precaked with odorless manure. Taylor Rental outside Burlington hires Yankees out for parties, each guaranteed to know three hundred amusing rural anecdotes, all of them ending "You can't get there from here." They chew nylon straw, they repeat "ayuh" over and over again, and they cackle hideously until you pay them off. In 1998 TransUniversal Corporation acquired Vermont, reorganized it as Yankeeworld, and moved it to Arizona on flatbed tractors.

In New Hampshire the state supper is beans and franks, and every recipe begins with salt pork, Campbell's cream of mushroom, and Miracle Whip. In New Hampshire breakfast and supper are both at five o'clock. In New Hampshire a brunch is something not to walk into when you are hunting coon. In New Hampshire convenience stores sell Fluff, Wonder Bread, Moxie, and shoes with blue canvas tops. In Vermont they have the forty-hour work week; in New Hampshire the forty-hour work weekend is standard. In New Hampshire people work a hundred hours a week cutting wood, setting up the yard sale, and misdirecting flatlanders; the rest of the time they make Vermont maple syrup and Vermont cheese.

Vermonters who commute from Brookline in BMWs call New Hampshire folk rednecks. (*Redneck*, n., commonly used by liberals and college graduates to describe people who can drive á nail.) Patten Corporation completed paving Vermont in 1947.

It is true that parts of New Hampshire have already defected to other states: Salem is a suburb of Boston; Nashua is Silicon Valley with frost heaves; Winnipesaukee has been Coney Island for as long as Coney Island; Waterville Valley is a component of Aspen. It is true that we used to have a governor who wanted to nuke Massachusetts. It is true that New Hampshire is known nationally only for its early primary and its Live Free or Die license plate. Once every four years a New Hampshire citizen has a fifty-fifty chance to be interviewed on national television, and we are the only state so far to fulfill Andy Warhol's prophecy about everybody being famous for fifteen minutes. Once every four years the *New York Times*, *Time*, *Newsweek*, and *USA Today* send reporters to the Ramada Inn in Concord to file stories about desolation, political rigidity, fecklessness, and stale hors d'oeuvres.

New Hampshire's license plate motto comes from a Revolutionary War hero, General John Stark, who may have been thinking more of Massachusetts than of George III. New Hampshire's obnoxious and independent bloody-mindedness derives from the seventeenth century, when the Bay Colony, sometimes abetted by London, tried to eat it alive. It derives also from the eighteenth, nineteenth, and twentieth centuries, as Massachusetts continues to cast cannibal glances north. Like the rural South, New Hampshire lives in a present that is the product of its history, and American history still lives in New Hampshire genes; mind you, we still vote for Frank Pierce.

Franklin Pierce, if you never noticed, was the fourteenth president of the United States, the only president from New Hampshire, and incidentally the only one not to be renominated by his own party after his term in office. If Rodney Dangerfield were authentic—and did not vacation in Las Vegas, Vermont—he would be Franklin Pierce. Vermont's only president, on the other hand, was Calvin Coolidge, elected to the highest office because, as governor of Massachusetts, he suppressed strikes.

In Vermont the state flower is the sushi bar, and the state bird is the electric hot tub. In New Hampshire the state lunch is a submarine sandwich with a tub of coleslaw. Both are manufactured in the great coleslaw factories of Secaucus, off the NJTP. Twenty-three years after his death, Robert Frost remains the poet laureate of Vermont; like the rest of Yankeeland decoration, this poet laureate no longer functions, but he sure is cute. In Vermont, in 1999, the license plate slogan was Eat Three Nutritious Meals a Day. In legislative committee this slogan edged out Experience Mozart.

Vermont plays double-A baseball in IBM's Burlington, as New Hampshire features the Nashua Pirates just off El Camino Real. But genuine New Hampshire folks play in the major leagues. Rich Gale won two games last year in Japan's World Series; he grew up in Littleton, with an effective summer season of thirty-eight days, counting Sundays. Still in the majors are Mike Flanagan, pitching for the Orioles, who like KC's Steve Balboni comes from Manchester; Joe Lefebvre of the Phillies, from Concord; and the great Carlton Fisk, most New Hampshire character of all, who grew up in the small Connecticut River town of Charlestown. It is rumored that one Vermonter clings to the roster of the California Angels.

Not far north of Carlton Fisk's Charlestown, west and across the river, is Woodstock, Vermont, which just now lacks a representative in the major leagues. Woodstock is why I hate Vermont—and what I fear for New Hampshire. This is the Woodstock that Rockefeller money embalmed in the shroud of a small New England town: instant "Ye" at every parking lot; cute boutiques elbowing each other down main street; a dear old country inn fabricated in 1969. Nostalgia without history is a decorative fraud, and condosaurus, having consumed Vermont, munches at New Hampshire's borders.

The Radio Red Sox, 1986

IN NORTHERN New England's September, as we drive past swamp-maples turning red, we keep our radios tuned to the calm urgencies of Ken Coleman broadcasting from Fenway Park. This year the month was splendid not only for leaves.

The Red Sox belong to New England, not to the city of Boston. Of course, the region is diverse: Nothing but the name unites Danbury, CT with Danbury, NH where I live. We hear that there are areas in tropical Connecticut—where leaves do not turn until Thanksgiving—in which Yankees fans hold out like Japanese soldiers in island caves. There are even followers of some National League club from New York. But in our northern boondocks, the Red Sox contribute to regional identity, and it is by radio mostly that we follow our team. Deep in the country you don't get cable; the Red Sox TV channel in Boston is UHF.

In the old days, tangible baseball belonged to the villages, and the married men played the single men on the Fourth of July; the major league game happened in newspapers and in imagination. Among other consequences, this abstraction meant that you weren't required to root for Boston. You weren't stuck by radio and television with an omnipresent media team; you could pick for cherishing any team you wanted. Most folks followed a club nearby, but my uncle Dick, as a boy in Tilton, New Hampshire, before radio, followed the Cincinnati Reds—an imprinting similar to a baby duck's upon its mother. The great Cuban pitcher Adolfo Luque ("the Pride of Havana") inspired him (twenty years in the majors, twenty-seven and eight in 1923), and although he still allows grudging admiration for Jim Rice and Roger Clemens, his heart still throbs for a stadium near the Ohio River that he has never visited.

My New Hampshire grandfather, less aberrational, loved the Boston Red Sox for decades before he saw Fenway Park. Born in 1875, he took the train one Saturday in the 1890s to attend a professional game in Boston, National League, and recited that game in precious detail while he loaded hay onto a hayrack fifty years later. I heard about Hugh Duffy. In the meantime, he had switched his affection to the American League Red Sox, and every day at noon cherished yesterday's game in the *Boston Post* that came by mail. My grandfather imagined his own Ted Williams with glorious specificity, based on recollections of batting and fielding when he played the game himself. In those years we seldom heard games on radio. They played baseball in the afternoon while we were haying; if rain kept us from haying, it kept them from playing; on Sundays listening to the radio broke the Sabbath.

One day late in the 1940s my Connecticut father, on vacation with his in-laws, drove my grandfather and me down to Boston for a Wednesday afternoon game. My grandfather was so excited that round red spots like a clown's makeup fixed themselves on his high cheekbones. He saw the famous left fielder, old number 9. He watched his shortstop, his first baseman, his tall left-handed pitcher—and he saw enormous Fenway Park with its vast throng of maybe ten thousand. The expedition was a success and in no way did it deepen my grandfather's affection for baseball and the Red Sox. Baseball was *there* always, an eternal game eternally stretched for the seventh inning, and when we paused for breath in the hayfield, my grandfather's clear storytelling voice would bring Smokey Joe Wood together with Johnny Pesky, Cy Young and Tris Speaker together with Mel Parnell, eternal teammates on the shadowy all-star team of a farmer's daydream. And this daydream was not merely private; it was social. Everybody talked baseball, even at town meeting in March. At the Grange or the post office in April, or on Old Home Day in August, my grandfather talked baseball with his old friends. Country people with horses and buggies did not see a great deal of one another, and when they met, the Red Sox formed a port of reentry for old conversations.

Things have not altogether changed. Now when we park the car and leave the motor running to pick up a cup of coffee at the Kearsarge Mini-Mart, old conversation continues in new mouths: "Did you hear that tenth inning last night?"

We get to Fenway more than once in forty years, but if we drive two to six hours to get there, it's hard to make the journey often. We rely on Ken Coleman and Joe Castiglione, the radio game with its background of noises, vendors and heckling, the rise and swoop of public hope and despair. Regular listeners learn to decode the announcer's pitch pattern, so that when bat-crack meets crowd-roar, Ken Coleman's first words, "Buckner hits a long . . . ," tell me *single, fly out,* or *possible home run* long before his words announce it.

Coleman is sixty-one and has broadcast thirty-one seasons of major league baseball with a soft attentiveness and the gentlest irony in the eastern United States. He's not given to false enthusiasm, artificial excitement, or gross charm. He's literate, friendly, and dependable; you trust the man, and that's how we want it. He brings the game in its folds and creases every day to millions of people driving pickups, milking cattle, and baiting traps, also to people drinking beer in barrooms, lazing on the beach, clipping coupons, and grooming polo ponies. Sixty-six New England stations carry the games, and everybody listens. The Red Sox with their beautiful archaic park are a radio team. Doubtless it is regional prejudice that makes the Mets, viewed from the north, seem as slick as network television.

Radio fans want to visit Fenway also; it's a validation. This year, we finally got there on September second and watched the Sox play Texas. Our seats were on the left-field foul line close to the wall. I could interfere with a ball without leaving my seat. O Fenway Park! (With some box seats in my uncle Dick's Cincinnati, you need binoculars to see home plate.) A few feet below us, we saw Gary Ward of Texas grab a single barehanded and snap it into second; we gazed as Jim Rice positioned himself to play a double off the wall like Bill Russell rebounding. We eavesdropped on the rage of their concentration. We watched their eyes.

We won. We came from behind and won it, eight to six. Al Nipper had some troubles, which allowed us a brief tour of the Boston bullpen, first Sammy Stewart and then Calvin Schiraldi, who relieved our anxieties with two strikeouts. But the high point of the evening was a walk. The Fenway crowd is knowledgeable, and the excitement—how do you explain this to a lover of football?—rose like a balloon as Wade Boggs, facing a left-hander who gave him trouble, fouled off strike after strike in the seventh inning until he worked a walk that set up Marty Barrett's two-run single. Fourteen pitches.

When the game was over, we drove back to New Hampshire, our headlights reflecting the fires of autumn as we hit the North Country. Sleepy the next day at the filling station, we heard a neighbor ask, "Did you hear Boggs get that walk?"

Living Room Politics, 1988

ON ROUTE 4 most houses raise an orange or a blue newspaper tube beside rural delivery's mailbox. These colors record party affiliation, like the royal blue in northern Greece after World War II; blue tubes take New Hampshire's ultra-right *Manchester Union Leader,* and orange tubes the liberal *Concord Monitor.* Now, in late summer of 1987, every newspaper, every day, mixes local news with national politics as candidates attend Rotary breakfasts, Old Home Day parades, and senior citizens' coffee hours. In photographs every day we watch Senator Bob Dole hoist an obligatory baby; we see Congressman Dick Gephardt smile as he shakes a hand.

Some years back, an ex-governor of Georgia started visiting New Hampshire three years or so before the primary he was aiming at. Now campaigning has become full-time, but it hots up in the summer before the critical February primary. By July of last year, 1988's candidates swarmed as thick as blackflies in May. Weekly papers, with columns by stringers resident in each hamlet, took notice, mixing the domestic with the national. In August Sam Bigelow, who writes about Andover for Franklin's *Journal-Transcript,* varied the usual item ("Welcome back to Don and Jackie Hazen, returning after a two-week trip down South") by announcing:

> The Merrimack County Republican Committee will hold its annual barbeque picnic next Saturday from 2:00 to 5:00 P.M. at the home of Paul and Sharon Nagy, Chase Hill Road . . . Special guests,

as of a couple weeks ago, included Congressman Jack Kemp, Dr. Pat Robertson, General Alexander Haig, and Neil Bush.

We could read the follow-up in the next Monday's *Concord Monitor:* General Haig and Congressman Kemp both disliked the White House peace plan for Nicaragua; Elizabeth Dole suggested that her husband is best qualified to become "the leader of the free world"; Kate Hislop, identified as "a little-known candidate," told us how we need to "cut the deficit, limit welfare, and deport illegal aliens"; Kemp answered questions about superconductors and the Persian Gulf; Haig punned, "Beware of Dole and Dole. It's only watered-down pineapple juice"; Pat Robertson, who canceled, sent two ex-Broncos (from Denver) to state his case; represented by his son, Vice President George Bush won the straw poll.

A week later the pretty town of Salisbury, on Route 4 a few miles south, celebrated its Old Home Day. This New Hampshire holiday, like everything else in New Hampshire, is a local option. Andover has none; Danbury and Wilmot hold theirs on sequent Sundays in August, each featuring Moulton's Band from Sanbornton ("continuous since 1889") in concert. In 1987 Salisbury's Old Home Day took place on Saturday, August 15, with a parade, picnic, and presentation of awards. Vice President Bush dropped by—the same day he dropped by Londonderry, Hopkinton, Webster, and New London—to award a clock to the eighty-year-old Citizen of the Year and to honor a young woman who won a national scholarship.

The Old Home Committee started planning the day's events last March without considering a vice-presidential visit. Three weeks before the event the selectmen heard indirectly that Bush would like to take part. One selectman later allowed, "At first we were not inclined." Another explained, "We didn't want it to be their party and not our day." They went along when they decided that a vice president would add honor to the honorees.

. . .

In primary season we are spoiled rotten. Don Marquis's phone keeps ringing; he handles social studies for Nashua secondary schools, and he hears himself saying, "No, Senator, no, I'm sorry. I told you, you can only speak to one assembly a year." We meet them all if we want to. The weekend after Salisbury's Old Home Day, Bruce Babbitt, the former governor of Arizona, spoke at Daniell Point in Franklin, confluence of the Merrimack and Pemigewasset rivers, and argued for a national sales tax to reduce the deficit. He met my uncle Dick Smart, registered Republican for fifty years, who had just switched parties and said how much he enjoyed the Democrats: He didn't have to wear a tie now; and in fifty years, he said, Republicans had never offered him wine.

The *Manchester Union* waited until December to choose Pete du Pont, the former governor of Delaware, from among the Republican candidates; until then, the *Union* seemed more interested in knocking the governor of Massachusetts, Michael Dukakis. Sixteen years ago the *Union* ran a successful campaign against another New England favorite son, Maine's Edmund Muskie. Now the front page thundered, "Dukakis has pulled off one of the fastest and most underhanded skimming operations on Massachusetts taxpayers in the history of political-money-grabbing." The issue was a pay raise.

Dukakis didn't seem to be around New Hampshire much last summer. Everybody else was. Congressman Dick Gephardt would be at Dennis and Margie Fenton's one night soon; there was a number to call or you could just drop by. The *Union*, one August morning, reminded us that Kemp would debate Gephardt at a college in Manchester the day after next. In the column headed "Campaign '88," we also read that a 1984 campaign coordinator for Walter Mondale had signed on with Senator Joseph Biden; Paul Laxalt of Nevada was meeting with advisers at Bretton Woods (two days later he withdrew, and a month later, Biden); the previous night Kemp attacked Dole again; Senator Al Gore was to meet with teachers in Concord for a twelve-thirty lunch on Thursday, visit Daniell Point in Franklin for coffee at four, and return to Concord sipping more coffee at six-thirty; and Senator Paul Simon would hit the Country Way nursing home in Keene that day, at six meet the Democrats of Peterborough, at seven-thirty more coffee in Goffstown.

In the common mercantile metaphor, politics in most of the country is wholesale; in New Hampshire it is retail. Wholesale is television advertising. Retail is continual coffee in living rooms. It's fortunate for the candidates that nobody in this state stays awake after nine P.M.

WHICH BRINGS UP, of course, the absurdity of this eccentric state's taking so much importance on itself. Roy Blount, Jr., tells about a Yankee who criticized the South for flying the Confederate flag. The Yankee bragged that the North didn't need a flag, and Blount answered that the North wasn't a *place*. New Hampshire is a place—as Milledgeville is and Birmingham isn't—and among other things it is the place of the first primary. Everybody has stories to tell. Merle Drown's father, known all over New Hampshire as the Cheese Man because he sold cheddar at all the fairs, managed to slip a hunk to JFK in 1960; the inevitable letter thanked him for "the welcome change from campaign fare." Merle and his wife Pat both teach high school; dark-horse candidates search out coffee hours with high school teachers. Four years ago (eight? twelve?) they talked with Fred and LaDonna Harris, with Annie and John Glenn. When Pat finished talking with Annie, two aides came up to her: "What did you talk about? What's your name?" Shortly thereafter Pat received a letter addressing the issues mentioned. We *all* get letters; first class mail outnumbers catalogues. Not since William Faulkner wrote me four letters with four different signatures, all postmarked New York while he lived in Virginia, have I received so many communications from important people.

Famous politicos cozy up to us, which infuriates flatlanders from New York and Massachusetts—which makes it worthwhile. Mike Barnicle, who apes Jimmy Breslin for the *Boston Globe*, can be counted on: "New Hampshire is to the country what Barry Manilow is to good music." On the other hand, the *New York Times* tries writing prose. A few years back, Francis X. Clines visited Danbury, on "the curving emptiness of Route 4." He interviewed five people and reported their cynicism about politics and politicians; two said they wouldn't even vote. Back on Forty-second Street, of course, everybody rushes to the polls.

Governor John Sununu of New Hampshire calls politics New Hampshire's second-favorite indoor sport. And one of our oldest. Dennis Fenton—at whose house Gephardt talked late last summer—is an Andover selectman, my second cousin, and a good Democrat. His political flavor goes back to our great-grandfather John Wells, the Copperhead who hated Lincoln although he fought for the North. Gephardt retailed politics in the Fenton living room because a Danbury blacksmith believed in states' rights one hundred and thirty years ago. When my grandfather and his siblings (Dennis's grandmother was Wesley Wells's sister Grace) grew up, Democratic politics crowded the table with quarrels at noontime dinner and at supper. As I hear stories about nineteenth-century New Hampshire, everything seems political.

Politics remains retail in New Hampshire because of our system of government and the history that established it. The state was founded on distrust of anybody you could not look in the eye. Settled by refugees from theocratic Massachusetts, New Hampshire has always struggled to keep its identity. The northwestern part, the upper Connecticut River Valley, was populated by emigrants from Connecticut and western Massachusetts who also resented control from afar—from central New Hampshire, for instance. Distrust of government, be it federal or state, decided the way we govern ourselves. Our enormous legislature started late in the eighteenth century, to keep the upper valley from forming another state. The New Hampshire House of Representatives marshals four hundred members to govern a state whose population edged over a million just a couple of years ago. Everybody knows his representative; my grandfather, a Democrat among Republicans, was elected representative seventy-five years ago. Jimmy Phelps, down in Danbury, was elected selectman when he was nineteen, and ran for representative when he was twenty-seven; the people who voted him in had gone to school with him. We talk every Friday when I pick up my mail.

Like everybody else in the United States, we distrust politicians; unlike everybody else, we find it hard to avoid becoming politicians. There are so many offices. My cousin Forrest, another great-grandson of John and Martha Wells, is selectman in Danbury; his mother Edna spent twenty-one years being elected trustee over graveyards in Danbury. Once a year we elect these officers, the same day we convene at the town meeting to tax ourselves. If we don't like the way our roads are plowed, we vote out the town road agent whom we voted in the previous March.

Sometimes we hear that Boston television, beamed into southern New Hampshire with its dense population of Massachusetts emigrants, is changing New Hampshire politics. But ask Walter Mondale. Four years ago he skipped coffee hours in favor of ads on television while Gary Hart answered questions in living rooms, with predictable results. For some candidates the living rooms are the hard part. It was in a Claremont living room that Senator Joseph Biden, irritated at a question from a high school teacher, boasted about his IQ and misrepresented his academic record. On the whole, I suspect that these face-to-face encounters are good for the candidates. In New Hampshire's primary season, candidates look in people's faces, not into cameras, when they answer questions; the little red light does not snap off until the question is answered.

I ARRIVED at the Fentons' house "to meet Dick Gephardt" just before seven-thirty. Cars were already dense; New Hampshire runs on its own time, the only place in the country where it is polite to be fifteen minutes early for dinner. The candidate was already there, wearing the uniform: blue suit and red tie. One hundred and twenty people ate cookies and drank coffee, standing around in the living room, dining room, kitchen, hallway, and garage. Congressman Gephardt shook hands: smiling, serious, presidential. Maybe *too* presidential? He has been criticized for looking like the president of the senior class. He spoke for ten or fifteen minutes and then answered questions. The first came from an old man who had just shelled out four thousand dollars for a corneal implant that took four hospital hours. Later questions concerned the arms race, Nicaragua, and the Persian Gulf war. Gephardt didn't evade the questions; it would have been hard to.

As I drove home late that night, at a quarter past nine, I thought about the privilege of the evening—to be repeated as other candidates would stand in other Andover houses, one of them doubtless our next president, addressing issues such as disarmament, import policy, the Gulf, and military adventurism. I like this privilege and I consider it useful. Newspapers set agendas, television photographs everything, but in New Hampshire we get to watch the candidates' eyes as they answer our questions; the rest of the country watches us watching.

Rusticus

OLD NEW HAMPSHIRE Highway Number 4, incorporated by an act of the New Hampshire legislature in the autumn of 1800, wound out of Portsmouth, a seaport that once rivaled Boston, drove west through Concord, north past Penacook, through Boscawen, Salisbury, and Andover on its way to Lebanon and the Connecticut River. These town names string history like beads. The Penacook tribe assembled each year on the banks of the Merrimack at the site of the present town. I grew up thinking Boscawen an unusual Indian name; it is Cornish, the surname of an admiral victorious over the French in the eighteenth century. In Andover, land was granted to veterans of the Louisburg Expedition against the French, but the first house did not go up until 1761, a year after the English conquest of Canada put an end to Indian raids. We need no reminding, now, that Lebanon is an Old Testament name.

Not that these New Hampshire towns lack a history of violence. At Penacook is the island in the Merrimack River where Hannah Dustin killed ten Indians in 1697. Forty years old, she was kidnapped from the village of Haverhill, in the Massachusetts Bay Colony, where she had given birth a week earlier. Her husband with their seven older children was working in the fields, Dustin nursing her infant under the care of a neighbor named Mary Jeff, when Abenakis attacked, burned her house, and brained her baby against a tree. The Indians took the two women into the forest, where they divided their prisoners into small groups, Dustin and Jeff companioned with a boy captured at Worcester. As the three captives began their journey north toward Canada, their guards were two braves, three women, and seven Abenaki children. While the Abenakis slept on the Merrimack island the three Bay Colonists stole their tomahawks and murdered all but one woman and one boy who escaped. The three ex-prisoners prudently hacked up the corpses of their captors, and when they returned to Haverhill received a bounty of fifty pounds for each scalp.

Cotton Mather tells the story, which he heard from Dustin herself, who survived into her eightieth year. We meet her again in Francis Parkman, who spells the name Dustan, but I first heard the adventure from my grandmother, told with some difference in detail as a family story about a heroic ancestor. Around the time my grandmother died, in 1975, the Liquor Commission of the state of New Hampshire contrived a Hannah Dustin commemorative bottle filled with bourbon: You twist her head off (as the Abenakis should have done) and pour yourself Kentucky's whiskey.

New Hampshire's state economy, without sales tax or income tax, is based on wickedness and ill health. The first state lottery was New Hampshire's in 1963; flatlanders buy truckloads of cheap cigarettes; a state monopoly keeps liquor cheap. Huge stores beside the interstates sell cases to visitors from Massachusetts, while highway signs primly warn about the dangers of drinking and driving. Novelty items, like the effigy of the female Indian killer, help New Hampshire's citizens avoid taxes. I begin my generalizations about the culture or ethos of northern New England by relating these two pieces of New Hampshire lore, with nothing in common except a woman's name and fiscal prudence. Perhaps if we add the woman of 1697 to her figurine of 1975 and divide by two, the product is present New Hampshire.

My grandmother was born in this house in 1878, thirteen years after her father moved here. The white farmhouse sits on a busy two-lane country highway, although the original Cape was presumably set back from the Grafton Turnpike (incorporated in 1804, not finished until 1811), which headed north after Highway Number 4 turned toward the sunset at West Andover. The saltbox went up in 1803, I assume on a wagon track where men led oxen. It would not go so far back as Hannah Dustin, for reasons that her adventure makes clear. Most settlement this far inland took place after the Revolution. Troops mustered out and migrated north from Massachusetts—doubtless including descendants of the Haverhill Dustins—or west and north from the New Hampshire seacoast, for independence and a piece of land. This house stands between Danbury and Andover in the town of Wilmot, incorporated in 1817 out of scraps and patches, including Kearsarge Gore. It remains quiet despite the traffic; we see only one other house from our house. We love our country solitude, interrupted by church, shopping, and occasional callers who stop by the dooryard; we love Mount Kearsarge, noble to the south of us; Eagle Pond, placid to the west; Ragged Mountain rising east behind our woodshed . . . But we love best the culture we live in, despite its bourbon figurines.

WHEN I WAS asked to write about New England mind or spirit, at first I thought, Fine. That's what I always write about. A reservation followed quickly: What do I know about the mind of Greenwich, Connecticut? or Fall River, Massachusetts? or Nashua, New Hampshire, for that matter? How can I generalize about New England if I cannot even generalize about New Hampshire? The novelist George Higgins, who used to review magazines in the *Globe* on Saturdays, once quoted the architecture critic Ada Louise Huxtable on New England: "It's a very Calvinistic life," she said. "It has beautiful symmetry and restrictions, and great intellectual elegance." Higgins was puzzled: Perhaps Huxtable had overlooked Brockton and Lawrence? When Huxtable continued by saying, "But you could say it's a little constipated," Higgins's puzzlement disappeared. "It's Cambridge," he deduced with relief.

Surely he was correct. The New Hampshire in which I live is as alien to Cambridge as it is to Brockton, and it is about *this* province that I allow myself to speak. If what I observe in Wilmot, Danbury, and Andover applies elsewhere, it will apply mostly to other parts of northern New England—not to Nashua nor to the low-tax Boston suburb called Salem, New Hampshire—and spreading west from Vermont into the poorer rural regions of northern New York and Pennsylvania, into the country towns of eastern Ohio, settled with New Englanders about the time these New Hampshire towns were settled, with handsome village squares and Federal buildings.

Not to mention the rural South.

During the year, I take brief trips away from this house as I read my poems at colleges. Every year I go to the West Coast once or twice; I visit Texas once a year, not only Austin and Dallas but Lubbock and Waco; I visit the exotic landscapes of Idaho, Colorado, Montana, Oklahoma, and Utah; I return continually to the various institutions of Ohio—and nowhere in the United States am I reminded so much of rural New Hampshire as when I read my poems at small colleges in Georgia, Alabama, and South Carolina. In a circle surrounding Atlanta—which could almost be Toledo—small colleges inhabit middle-sized Georgia towns: Columbus, Augusta. When I stay at the Carrollton Holiday Inn, I might as well sleep in Rhode Island or Montana. But when I walk or drive outside Rome, Georgia, or when I sit on the verandah in Cross Hill, South Carolina, although the architecture differs, although the accent is incorrect, I feel homely emanations rising from the red dirt. Resemblance begins with the sculpture, alive in the center of southern towns as it lives in Wilmot Flat, of the Civil War soldier and the soldier of the War Between the States—slim fellow eternally bronze, standing alert with musket and identical standard handsome features, with the minor discrepancy of uniform, of victory and defeat.

He stands more often in the South than he does in New Hampshire. He poses in Wilmot Flat, not in Andover or Danbury. Rich Andover raised a war monument only in 1923, five years after what the granite slab calls THE WORLD WAR, but the list of one hundred and forty-three Civil War soldiers takes pride of place on the monument's front. Poor Danbury—which my great-grandfather left for the New Hampshire Volunteers, Company F, 15th Regiment—fixes a small bronze plaque on the Town Hall. Among the fifty-one names, from Samuel S. Adams to Addison L. Woodman, I recognize families that survive in Danbury one hundred and twenty years later: Braley, Brown, Butler, Danforth, Farnham, Ford, Minard, Morrill, Morrison, Sanborn. I recognize the name of a cousin killed by cannonball at Vicksburg. My ancestor John Wells brought back to the cousin's family the contents of his pockets, and one object has come down to this house. I have already mentioned his ring of bone.

Only in small towns of the rural South and in northern towns of New England does this war survive: blockade, starvation, burning, attrition, sepsis, amputation, and charges into cannon fire. If you search the suburbs from Connecticut through New York and New Jersey, past Pennsylvania, skirting Gettysburg into Ohio, Michigan, and Indiana, if you search through the plains states to the West Coast from Orange County to Bellevue, Washington, you will not find this war. In the present United States, this war recedes into olden times, like Homer, the Roaring Twenties, the Crusades, Gilgamesh, and Will Rogers. It is preserved like a bottled fetus in the library and in the notebooks of genealogical eccentrics. But outside Atlanta and Birmingham, and north of Boston, the blue and the gray still march, bugle call and amputated limb, in the fierce cannonade of old memory. The past continues into the present because the plaque's family names remain on the land. Only in the rural South and rural New England do you find Americans who live where their great-grandfathers lived, or who know the maiden names of their great-grandmothers.

RURAL New Hampshire separates itself not only from Cambridge and Brockton. Let me call rural people a separate class, Class Rusticus. In order to talk of its uniqueness, I must speculate about the cultures against which it distinguishes itself. When we talk about

American classes by making revision of European class structures, I suspect we miss the point. Americans divide themselves not so much into economic classes as into ethnic, regional, and cultural groups, except that most of us belong to a single class within which there is considerable economic hierarchy. Massclass is singular because it shares goals and values, and because it does not care where it lives except in connection with these desires. (The names of desired objects alter according to the hierarchy, and your mobile home is my year in France.) When I assert Massclass, I do not deny that poverty and suffering assault its unluckier members. Depression or recession, unemployment, bankruptcy and foreclosure, failure and social welfare, are cyclical components of our economy. I speak of the commonness not of success and prosperity but of standards of success and prosperity. Neither do I deny the existence of a separate underclass, perpetually burdened by poverty, rendered almost unemployable by habitual loss, generation after generation nurtured and enfeebled by welfare. (I only deny, by definition, that these sufferers may be called working class.) At the other extreme, maybe there are a few families, with money around for several generations, who make an American upper class. Maybe. I remain skeptical of an inherited upper class in the United States, skeptical that its narcissism is secure. These people hold to superiority over rich Massclass managers only by the skin of their capped teeth, the way the lower middle class in older Europe paddled furiously to distinguish itself from workers. Black is a class, most of the time, a culture and a set of values distinct from Massclass from which some blacks emigrate into Massclass. I suppose that Hispanic is another. Emigrant is a one-generation class, culturally divided according to place of origin, the second and third generation joining Massclass America.

This digression means to claim: Rusticus is another class or culture; I live among this class as a Massclass emigrant. My mother and my grandmother were born in this house but my mother moved to Hamden, Connecticut—a suburb of New Haven—when she married, and I grew up among blocks of similar houses, a neighborhood where everyone shared four convictions: 1. I will do better than my father and mother. 2. My children will do better than I do. 3. "Better" includes education, and education exists to provide the things of this world. 4. The things of this world are good.

Within my Connecticut town the neighborhoods were distinct, and they were distinct according to hierarchies of money—the market value of houses, their size and proximity to each other, the number of stalls in their garages. In Hamden we lived on the western side of Whitney Avenue in a prosperous section called Spring Glen, a little more prosperous than Whitneyville, richer than Centerville and State Street. Because we were on the western side of Whitney, my father always said we lived on the "two-bit side"; east of Whitney was the "fifty-cent side." If I enjoy myself in ironies about Massclass, it is not with the notion that I thereby detach myself. I am a card-carrying member, Amexco, and one does not alter the habits and values of a lifetime by changing one's place of residence. I retain the markings: distaste for physical labor, fear and loathing of false teeth, desire for my children's education and comfort. Because my parentage was mixed, because I spent my childhood summers in this house, I kept at least a vision of something different.

THE CLASS OR CULTURE of Rusticus is alien to Massclass. Let us start with a stereotype of New Hampshire's citizenry as cherished by citizens of Boston: Rusticus women are fat; Rusticus men wear crew cuts; there isn't a full set of God-given teeth from Vermont's border on Lake Champlain eastward to Maine's Atlantic coast. Mr. and Mrs. R. inhabit a thirty-year-old trailer without calling it a mobile home, surrounded by two junked Buicks and a pickup that's all froze up next to the old freezer past the washing machine; they're somewhere between thirty-two years old and fifty-seven, but it's hard to tell; each weighs two hundred and twelve pounds, but he spreads his weight over his whole five foot eight and a half inches while she tends to be more concentrated at five foot one; the working truck wears a gun rack and an NRA bumper sticker; there's a sign for night crawlers and another for a yard sale; when the mill's going they gum Twinkies and TV dinners, but when they're laid off they settle for squirrel meat and potato chips; they have never applied for food stamps because they don't know they are poor and because people on welfare are liars and cheats. They vote Republican.

When Massclass visitors honor Rusticus with the epithet "redneck," they acknowledge an analogy to the rural South, and acknowledge as well the antipathy that one class or culture feels for another. "Redneck" is racist slang, like "hillbilly"; it demonstrates urban and suburban superiority while it conceals fear of the alien. But of course Massachusetts liberals, when they speak of the rednecks of New Hampshire, do not believe that they demonstrate fear of overweight people without teeth. They feel that they denounce right-wing politics, narrow and bigoted opinions associated with Alabama sheriffs named Virgil who shoot SNCC workers. These flatlanders may assemble some evidence to support their bigoted generalizations. There *was* a New Hampshire governor who praised the living conditions of Soweto; there *is* a newspaper that is not only the worst moment of journalism in the United States but the most grossly conservative. But things are never so simple as our righteousness makes them out to be. Even to characterize New Hampshire's politics as right wing is unhistorical, as if we called Hannah Dustin a racist for her position on the question of Native American rights.

Reading early American history, one becomes aware that the Revolution started not with the shot heard round the world but with the seventeenth-century landings at Virginia and Plymouth. It started with the extraordinary, habitual independence of these colonies from their sovereign across the sea. Our ancestors were ungovernable from abroad; they were also largely ungovernable at home. Within each colony, every unit separated itself as much as possible from every other unit—town from state, village from town, family or neighbor-group from village, and legislature from governor. On occasion we had to cooperate: to fence the common, to build a jail. *Some* law was necessary, but in spirit most colonists, Puritan or not, remained grossly antinomian. We were, after all, self-selected separators, alike only in that we all decided to leave the past behind and start over.

New Hampshire's history for three hundred years—I need to say it again—has been dominated by the necessity to separate itself from its rich neighbor. If New Hampshire had not made itself a porcupine, Massachusetts would have swallowed it alive. The generally separatist tendencies of Americans were exacerbated for New Hampshire by the power of Boston. When colonies became states, when the Union needed preserving, still Franklin Pierce's Democrats voted in the House against using federal funds for construction of highways and canals in states and territories. Ideas of states' rights, and states' consequent responsibilities, pertained not only to slavery and the South.

Although my great-grandfather was a Copperhead—like the New England fellow who named his son Robert Lee Frost after moving west to California along with others who bet on the wrong side—John Wells fought for the Union out of local feeling. He never spoke of the war, hated Lincoln all his life, and bequeathed to his posterity genetic adherence to the Democratic Party, which leaves my family, out of loyalty and DNA, eccentric in New Hampshire. When the Democrats nominated Al Smith, John Wells's offspring decided that the pope would not take over the West Wing; Roosevelt's New Deal seemed only sensible to the clan descending from John Wells.

Not so for my neighbors in general, skeptical not only of national government but of bigwigs in the state capital and, if truth be known, of the selectmen they themselves elect on town meeting day. If this politics is right wing, what do we call the National Association of Manufacturers, General Motors, ABC Television, conglomerates and cartels, *U.S. News,* or Ronald Reagan? Of course New Hampshire Republicans are conservative in their anticollectivism, but Reagan Republicans are collectivists of capitalism, and agribusiness is corporate collective farming, and U.S. Steel is stockholder nationalization.

In New Hampshire the ideal remains to work for yourself. Units of one are preferred: one-family mill, one-family farm, one-woman peddler, and one-man logger. Veteran hippies move in, turning Libertarian in a climate that is almost anarchic. All political labels falsify when they try to name particular cases. In the conservatism of Rusticus there is considerably more Thomas Jefferson than Alexander Hamilton, yet New Hampshire's voters pile up majorities for Reagan's banks, deficits, and big business. Political labels deny manyness and complexity. If Lincoln's Republicans were radical on slave territory, they were conservative to maintain the Union; if the secessionists were conservative of slavery, they were radical to secede. Radical and traditional. Magnolias, honor, Tara, and pure women erected a political lie of nobility to cover evil, the usual lie that helps us to think well of ourselves, to call ourselves good when we are vicious. Nineteenth-century chattel slavery—slavery in 1860—was morally as defensible as the Final Solution. The courage of evil is an imperial commonplace.

In the ethics of Rusticus, the noble lie that masks evil is Proud Independence. We cannot compare this vice to slavery, pogroms, or napalmed villages, but it is worth acknowledging that our freedom from taxation imposes suffering on the poor, on the insane, and on the otherwise handicapped; that New Hampshire, refusing to fund Medicaid, ruins families with ill children; that laissez faire with its abhorrence of zoning allows corporations to own dumps that murder ponds and probably people; that Proud Independence is an illusion of the many that serves the greedy few.

Not that notions of independence are without cultural benefit. For one thing, the culture of Rusticus encourages eccentricity, and eccentricity valued promotes the acceptance of diversity. Three quarters of the stories I hear—"Did you hear about the time old Meacham made skunk stew?"—celebrate divergent behavior; a few famous eccentrics, dead fifty years, get talked about every day in Danbury. Social results of this enthusiasm are varied and useful. In the countryside, and never in the suburb, old and young live next to each other, rich and poor, foolish and shrewd, educated and semiliterate. As in the country the sexes have traditionally separated their workloads less, as there has been less hierarchy among trades and occupations, so sparseness of population mixes neighbors at random, and the trailer or the shack squats two hundred yards down the road from the extended, huge late-eighteenth-century farmhouse spruced up with fresh paint on clapboard and shutters. At church and store, garage and rummage sale, the neighbors in their variety talk with each other. In the neighborhoods of Massclass, suburban ghettos quilt-patterned with hierarchy, old and young are as separated as rich and poor. Alienation breeds fear that wears the costume of contempt.

The social ethic of this varied Rusticus culture is niggardly in public and charitable in private; generosity is permitted as long as it appears voluntary, whimsical, responsive, and unplanned. Ideas of work live at the center of this ethic, and the finest Rusticus compliment is "She's not afraid of a day's work," pronounced *wuk.* Variety of competence is as valuable as diligence. Half of Rusticus men can build a house from cellar to shingles. Such versatility is historical. In the old days everybody was a farmer, including preacher and lawyer and doctor, and every farmer could turn a lathe or operate a forge. Further back, the farmer made shoes winter evenings while his wife made clothing. She began with the sheep's wool or flax fibers; she dried or carded, she spun, wove, cut, and sewed; she ended with dress, with trousers, with workshirt. Grandfather and grandmother Rusticus were part-time everything—wagon maker, candle maker—and their descendants remain jacks- and jills-of-all-trades, unlike the specialist citizens of suburbs and cities.

On the old general farm—eight Holsteins, fifty sheep, two hundred chickens, five pigs; ice cut from the pond in winter to cool the milk of summer; cordwood cropped for heat and cooking, for canning and sugaring and probably for sale; vegetables raised for the summer table and for canning; fieldcorn grown for the cattle's ensilage—man and woman worked equally hard. The women who worked just as hard as the men neither voted nor as a rule owned property. Nonetheless, it is not merely ironic to speak of egalitarianism in the workload of the sexes, because work makes pride, and equality of labor confers value. Of all the aggressions on the female inflicted by male industrial culture, surely the most destructive was enforced decorative leisure, useless ornamentation, despairing conspicuous inutility. In the growth of capitalism, the sexes in the middle and upper classes specialized: Men worked as women demonstrated by their leisure men's prosperity. This arrangement drifted down from aristocrats—where the man was equally burdened with uselessness—to the urban middle class in the late eighteenth century and became epidemic in the nineteenth century, along with female neurasthenia. Middle-class women were not allowed to do anything useful, and if their males died or failed or went crazy or alcoholic, there was no system of support—proving again the importance of males. As late as the 1930s, when my mother left the farm and accommodated herself to the Massclass life of Connecticut, wives did not take jobs. She had been a teacher, and only virgins taught school. Although my father's weekly wage was small, maybe thirty-five dollars, it was the Depression: As part of her acclimatization, my mother hired a girl, five dollars a week, to clean house, cook, and serve dessert for bridge on Wednesdays in a black dress with a tiny white apron over it.

Her mother, at the same age, made soap. Every night the whole family gathered in a circle around a high table with an oil lamp on it, as the women sewed socks, basted hems, knitted mittens, crocheted, and tatted. While the mother ruled her house-empire of power, the father remained all day outside in his domain of barns and sheds. Think of my mother growing up in this world and after the brief transition of college moving to Connecticut where the maid picked up the teacups after bridge on Wednesday afternoons. It is true that she ironed seven white shirts a week for her husband and seven more for her son. It is also true that on the New Hampshire farm, her mother sometimes hired help. When crews worked at harvest, my grandmother hired a woman who lived nearby to make pies all morning for ten cents an hour. Because this helper valued her self-esteem, she would go home in the early afternoon, eighty cents richer, change into fancy clothes, and return as a neighbor for whom my grandmother would construct a cup of tea.

This story reminds me of an anecdote Henry James tells. When he wrote *The American Scene,* returning from decades of English life to his brother William's summer place in Chocorua, he wrote lyrically of landscape—and with amused horror of New Hampshire's egalitarianism. New Hampshire lacked "the satire and the parson." Henry missed measure and order; he lamented "the so complete abolition of *forms.*" He appears shocked, for our entertainment, as he tells about a rustic, to whom he ascribes cynicism, "who makes it a condition of *any* intercourse that he be received at the front door." This rustic asks the summer person who opens the door, "Are you the woman of the house?" in order to deliver a message from someone he calls the "washerlady."

This is a story about manners, and therefore about *form,* like my grandmother's pie maker who turns up at teatime. In James's anecdote, the characteristic teasing humor of Rusticus is accomplished by careful misuse of language. (New Hampshire humor is always verbal: One common form derives from literalness: "Why is Dean pulling that big chain?" "Ever see anybody trying to *push* one?" Another is self-mockery of proverbial cautiousness: "Say, is Cal Morey your brother-in-law?" "Well, he was this morning.") When I lived in Ann Arbor, I suffered from the manners of ironic deference. People deferred to me because I wrote books, an activity with prestige in the academy, where worth is measured by column inches of bibliography; they fell into irony because they could not abide their own deference. Living on Route 4, I suffer from no such burden. It seems not to occur to anyone that I might think myself better than they are because I write books. Why should it be better to write books than to build houses or grow blueberries? Better is not an issue. I am doing what I want to do and what I can do; so are other people, if they are sensible and fortunate.

Not that Class Rusticus is without its own systems of superiority. If it were not known that I worked hard, I would feel disapproval. The general ethic praises work, and hard-working pillars of the community find laziness contemptible. Naturally there are lazy people about, working now and then in harvest or cutting summer brush on a ski slope or shoveling snow in February—feckless, agreeable, sitting around in the summer twilight with a six-pack. I mean to distinguish the self-appointed bum from the unlucky, from the insulted and injured, from the congenitally unemployable *poor.* Of course it is commonplace for Rusticus as Republican to deny the distinction.

Women of the rural culture remain indistinguishable as workers from the men. Bum-women lie about with their six-packs; pillar-women work fourteen hours, and now, like their men, labor at factory jobs before they come home to continue working. The forty-hour week is unknown; Rusticus works either eighty hours a week or none. If I brag to a neighbor that I have just frozen sixty pints of tomatoes, I hear a counterboast that puts me in my place: four hundred and eighty pints, of everything. A forty-hour week may pay the mortgage or the taxes; then we are free to improvise, to do what we want to do, to raise pigs and cut cordwood, fish through the ice, sharpen saws, tear down a barn, hunt deer, build a house. In the nineteenth century, farm boys took jobs at the hame shop in Andover because they had to work only twelve hours a day, six to six, only six days a week, and they paid you real money for it; it was a week on Hampton Beach compared to the farm. When the boss turned soft, around the turn of the century, and closed the shop at noon on Saturday, old-timers were contemptuous: "That's not a week's wuk!"

Once this ethic of work was common in the United States, when most people lived outside cities. Even Hamden was a town of farmers providing milk and produce for the port of New Haven. In the eighteenth century, Eli Whitney used water power (at the outlet of today's Lake Whitney, alongside Whitney Avenue) for his gun factory. When he built houses for his workers, Whitney's Village became Whitneyville, the section of Hamden where my father grew up. My great-grandfather Charlie Hall labored building the New Haven Reservoir in 1861, off Armory Street in Hamden near the old Whitney factory, and at noon he walked off his job and trudged three miles into New Haven, where he enlisted to fight for the Union. When he died during another war, in 1916, his Hamden had altered from a small town into a suburb of New Haven. It took another forty years and another war to complete its transformation. Hamden High School shot up in a farmer's field half a mile from our house in about 1940. After 1945 and victory came the Hamden Plaza farther down Dixwell, then the Hamden Mart, acres of shiny stores surrounding macadam parking lots that blacked over old farmland. In the 1960s and 1970s condominiums arose behind the stores, high on the hills overhead; traffic lights blossomed everywhere, bustle and confusion and change. By 1990 the shopping malls had turned dingy. Our history becomes thirty seconds of film collage, not slow like Eisenstein or a Marx Brothers movie, but accelerated like *Laugh In:* accelerated decay, decline, defeat. In Whitneyville where I watched the huge (as I thought) brick Brock-Hall building rise when I was in kindergarten, wreckers and bulldozers have leveled it and another condominium rises. Next door where I attended the opening of the Whitney Theater before the war, dozers wait to knock down the theater and the little row of shops beside it on Whitney Avenue in Whitneyville to make way for more condos. After condosaurus has ruled its moment, some disaster will wipe it out. Another creature will walk in its place while its cinder-block bones sink on top of Eli Whitney's gun workers' cottages and the bones of shaggy dairy horses.

Henry James in *The American Scene* spoke of New York as a "vision of waste" because of the destruction of good houses, "marked for removal, for extinction, in their prime." New York was vanguard and template. John Jay Chapman (1862–1933) was a New Yorker who admired the exuberance of his town but who had been modified by Massachusetts after a tour at Harvard. "New York is not a civilization," he wrote, "it is a railway station ... The present in New York is so powerful that the past is lost. There is no past. Not a bookshelf, nor a cornice, nor a sign, nor a face, nor a type of mind endures for a generation, and a New York boy who goes away to boarding school returns to a new world at each vacation." On the other hand, "In Massachusetts you may still stop the first man you meet in the street and find in his first remark the influence of Wyclif ... It is one-sided, sad, and inexpressive in many ways. But it has coherence."

If we consult George Higgins about "the influence of Wyclif," he may question our experience of Brockton. Nor would one find much coherence, now, even on Beacon Hill. New York is model for city and suburb from sea to shining sea. When Thomas Hardy wrote a preface to *Far from the Madding Crowd*, twenty-seven years after its first publication, he wailed a familiar complaint of alteration and loss. After lamenting the disappearance of rural customs, he went on:

> The change at the root of this has been the recent supplanting of the class of stationary cottagers, who carried on the local traditions and humours, by a population of more or less migratory labourers, which had led to a break of continuity in local history, more fatal than any other thing to the preservation of legend, folk-lore, close inter-social relations, and eccentric individualities. *For these the indispensable conditions of existence are attachment to the soil of one particular spot by generation after generation.*

My italics. The unhistorical may smile at the date of 1895; the present's creature thinks that, because people complained a hundred years ago as they complain today, the complaint must be constant and not the matter complained of. But a hundred years is a wink of historical time. Hardy's complaint was valid in 1895 and it is valid now.

What surprises me, I suppose, is the holding out, for despite Hardy's pessimism, and my own when I was young, there is resistance to the murder of the past. Rusticus is a series of eccentric individualities, complete with legends and folklore, and this culture persists.

Italian hill towns, settled by Greek colonists long before Christ, spoke ancient Greek halfway through the twentieth century. In New Hampshire we still speak Greek. Over the decades of Hamden's destruction, the look of the land around Eagle Pond has altered but not greatly. When I alighted at the West Andover depot in 1939, my grandfather drove Riley and the buggy past a series of dying one-man farms. The farms and the men and the horses and the depot are dead, and stonewalls that once marked pastures for a few cattle now keep pine trees from wandering into Route 4. But the houses mostly endure. In the culture of Rusticus, tearing things down is as wicked as fecklessness. Nothing separates Massclass from Rusticus more than rural dedication to preservation and continuity. When the University of Michigan, inheriting a beautiful Federal house on State Street in Ann Arbor, sold it so that it was torn down for a fast-food franchise—I did not make this up!—there was only a resigned shaking of heads.

Returning here, I told myself that I returned to house, hill, and pond, the nonhuman environment, and that, after all, my work was such that I could do it anywhere. Of course, I discovered or rediscovered that the people were dearer than the hills. (I had not suspected so, I think because I had made a decision in my twenties not to live here. In the spirit of Aesop's fox, I disparaged the New Hampshire present.) When I came back in 1975, to live where I wished to live, I found myself among other people who live where they do because they wish to and for no other reason. Ann Arbor (Berkeley, Madison, Hamden, Atlanta, and Shaker Heights) is largely composed of people who live where they live because that's where the job is. They will leave when a better job comes along elsewhere, the migrating laborers of prosperous Massclass. There's a commonplace, repeated at parties in Ann Arbor, that is standard on every campus of the University of America:

"One third of the people in this room were not in town last year; one third will not be here next year." The words go unspoken in Danbury.

Rusticus lives where he does because he wants to. Anybody with a skill and an appetite for work can make more money elsewhere. People who build houses can get twice as much an hour if they emigrate two hours south. Many leave to follow the money; then they return, shaking their heads, surprised that they will put up with less income for the sake of place, determined to do just that: not martyrs, just un-Americans of happy voluntary low income. People who remain here are self-selected partisans of place. Many were born here, after parents, great-grandparents, and great-great-grandparents. Many moved here because they liked the look and feel of it. Some came here because of a job and then refused to be transferred elsewhere. They are un-American because they prefer land, place, family, friends, and culture to the possibilities of money and advancement. Doubtless many Americans prefer something or other over money, but most of us feel guilty when we do anything except for money; we think that a man is not manly or decisive if he admits a motive outside money. But no one remains in rural New Hampshire for the money. Everybody living here hangs out a sign: *I don't care so much for money as I'm supposed to.* Therefore Massclass, in the shape of summer people, laughs at the native, and the native, secure in a secret superiority, laughs back. This is the cynicism of Henry James's rustic.

Indifference to money is not proof of virtue; ax murderers are notoriously indifferent to the wages of their profession. It depends on what you love instead of money, or on the mix of motives. Many people remain here not only out of love but out of dependence or perhaps inertia. Maybe it is happy to be place-bound or family-bound, but it limits one's chances to become a ballet dancer or an astronaut. In my family that has stayed here forever, I hear this limitation in many stories. Aunt X started normal school over to Plymouth, an hour away, but took sick and came home and never did go back: homesick. Uncle Z, with a job in a sawmill, worked only part-time because the mill was doing poorly; his weekly wage was minuscule. He found a job four hours west in Vermont, doing the same work at twice the money. Soon he was back at the old New Hampshire job, making do and looking for odd jobs to buy shoes for his children. He missed his brothers and his old mother.

Still, the love of place shows itself noble and honorable in a hundred ways. We returned to an 1803 house, including an unrevised 1803 chimney, which had gone with insufficient maintenance during my grandmother's eighties and nineties. I have mentioned that as we shingled, painted, replaced a chimney, and repaired, people constantly thanked us: "*Good* to see the old place coming back." It was extraordinary, this public delight in our restoration. Strangers parked their cars, as we worked in the garden, to praise us for keeping the old house alive.

The land (not the scenery) is dearer than I credited. Once at our church, our summer minister—pushing eighty, he lives in the farmhouse he was born in—asked us to come next week prepared to speak about something in the creation that we liked to look at. The next Sunday he could hardly get his sermon in, as his normally taciturn parishioners gabbled their passions: the Jack Wells Brook where it dropped over the little rapids; the noble stretch of double stonewall by Frazier's place; the patch of wild daylilies at the base of New Canada Road; the way Kearsarge changes color in dawn light month by month all year, green and blue and white and lavender; the gaunt and bony ruin of an old mill foundation.

The main link that joins us together, and separates country people from Massclass, that ties rural North to rural South, is connection to the past. We love the house, not just for its lines or its endurance, but because of people who were born and died here; we love the mountain, not only because it's beautiful, but because we know that the dead gazed at it every day of their lives and left behind testimony of their love. House and mountain connect us to the past. These connections may be strongest for true Rusticus, but these feelings do not require blood ties; blood ties only facilitate them. These connections are also strong for emigrants from Massclass who join themselves to the rural culture because they cherish its connectedness. They prevail not only among the inhabitants of white farmhouses but among shack people who approach the flatlander's stereotype. Not all shack people, of course; not all green-shutter people either . . . but connections in this culture *prevail.*

In the last decade or two, all the little towns have started historical societies (I belong to the Danbury, Wilmot, Andover, and Northfield historical societies), which meet sometimes for invited speakers with special knowledge—railroads, Shakers, watermills—more often with a neighbor who brings photographs to show and stories to tell. Historical societies sponsor museums: In the Wilmot Town Hall, in the Flat, we keep a room with old photographs, Civil War memorabilia, old farm tools, clothing, flags, and typed-up reminiscences; in Andover the elegant Potter Place depot, a glory of Victorian gingerbread, was donated to the Andover Historical Society as a museum. The depot itself is exhibit number one.

Historical societies may be fads, like the gentrification of old quarters in cities, but really they may represent deep mind-habits: They are storytelling turned into institutions. The section of Andover called Potter Place took its name from Richard Potter, celebrated magician and ventriloquist of the early nineteenth century, who spent his show-business fortune to build a mansion in Andover, which burned when my mother was a girl. He died before the railroad came, but when the new railroad built a depot near his house, the depot was named Potter Place. More than a hundred years after his death my grandfather told me trickster stories about Richard Potter as a "fellow used to live around here," who avenged himself on an enemy farmer by hiding in the bushes and casting his voice so that the brute heard a baby crying from his load of hay, emptied his hayrack, loaded it again, heard the baby cry again . . . My grandfather neglected to mention one piece of information about Richard Potter: either he did not know or it seemed unimportant that he was black.

In most of the United States you do not hear stories about a "fellow used to live around here" one hundred and fifty years ago. In most of the United States, you know that the lawn you water was desert or apple orchard or strawberry field until 1957—and that is all you know. We Americans dislike the past. Or we simply adore it and lump it all together as a glossy product of generalized nostalgia, *olden times*, a decorative and disconnected alternative to the present. The ornamental past enforces the dominance of the temporary.

W. H. Auden remarked that the mediocre European is possessed by the past and the mediocre American by the present. One must admit that many of the cleverest and most inventive Americans—Benjamin Franklin, Thomas Jefferson—were possessed by the present. Ralph Waldo Emerson, with centuries of accumulated knowledge and culture enlightening and burdening him, spent a lifetime celebrating our independence of history, authority, religion, and order; his intelligence served American disconnections. But if many bright Americans are possessed by the present, all dumb Americans are. An unexamined assumption of Massclass is that such possession is a duty, and the result is the torn-down Federal house.

In northern New England, in Wendell Berry's Kentucky, and in other rural places, the culture suggests and supports connection to a continuous past that lives in the air, in relics, and in the stories that old people tell. Everywhere are antiquarians, but without the linkage of stonewall and Civil War soldier in bronze, and without the same soldier in story, library antiquarianism is documentary and disconnected. It is better than nothing, because it gives evidence of our famine, of our need for the nutrition of historical connection against the thin, bare, accelerated moment. Perhaps the recovery of old quarters in Chicago, Washington, and Boston is not merely faddish but testimony of true hunger.

Americans can almost be defined as people who lack history, who emigrated here to escape a nightmare from which they could not awake. Current protests about the unhistoricism of the American young repeat and multiply complaints that started before the Revolution, complaints that the successful and blessed Revolution only accelerated. But a narrower present turns into a worse nightmare, and as always we divorce for the same reasons that marry us. In *The American Scene,* still in New Hampshire, Henry James spoke of the land "not bearing the burden of too much history." But he continued:

> The history was there in its degree, and one came upon it, on sunny afternoons, in the form of the classic abandoned farm of the rude forefather who had lost patience with his fate. These scenes of old, hard New England effort, defeated by the soil and the climate and reclaimed by nature and time—the crumbled, the lonely chimney-stack, the overgrown threshold, the dried-up well, the cart-track vague and lost—these seem the only notes to interfere.

The word is "defeated." This country north of Boston ended up more defeated (after Reconstruction) than the defeated South. Southern cotton mills started the decline and fall of the northern mills, and the opened western country took New Hampshire's farms away. Defeat may be melancholy but it creates historians; it provokes connections, while victors (New York, Minneapolis, Los Angeles—and Atlanta) remain trapped in shallow and prosperous modernity.

Neither the New Hampshire dirt nor the dirt of South Carolina extends deep into past time. We dig to find no Roman roads, only artifacts of the nomads who first trudged into this wilderness and hunted bear on these hills or trapped raccoon by these ponds a few thousand years before the Europeans arrived. When we dig in the soil of England, we dig into Stonehenge and Othona, yet England is young compared with the soil of Italy, Greece, Egypt . . . and China! While shaggy Homers improvised hero stories in analphabetic Greece, the Chinese assembled their first dictionary.

How much history does the soul require? Hardy's "indispensable conditions" are "attachment to the soil of our particular spot by generation after generation." How many generations is that? Three is too few; four or five may be sufficient. Let me proclaim Hall's law: When fifty percent of the local population remain aware of the maiden names of their great-grandmothers, or can visit the graves of ancestors born a century and a half ago, or can tell stories handed down from a hundred years back, the spirit's necessity for connection may be satisfied.

My family's version of Hannah Dustin differs so much from Cotton Mather's that it may derive from another seventeenth- or eighteenth-century ancestor, switched in the telling to the famous name. Of course the truth of it, unascertainable, never matters; the felt connection matters. Another story I remember concerns a male ancestor who fought the French and Indians. Retreating with an outnumbered patrol, my storied forefather volunteered to go back alone through the woods to the abandoned camp in order to retrieve the cooking pot that they had inadvertently left behind. He found it, but on his solitary return he heard the sounds of a war party in the woods. He hid in the hollow trunk of a fallen tree, and moccasined feet pattered over his shelter; he waited, he emerged, he returned safely home. Was the log big enough to hide the pot in? Did he set it upside down on the ground, hoping it might pass for a stump? No one could tell me. When I walk in the woods I look for a rusted pot.

Inhabitants of Danbury, New Hampshire, lack the hunger that citizens of Hamden, Connecticut, feel, and live in an air of connections—with stories of Indian fighters, of famous hermits on Ragged Mountain, of how people built the road through the bog, of how two hundred oxen pulled the mast-tree all the way to Portsmouth, of how the boys marched off to fight Johnny Reb. Connections to the past imply a future. Without past there is no future. If the present's partisan charges that Rusticus "lives in the past"—a sin against America—I claim that only our connection with the past validates the present; the exclusive present is a psychic desert. We Americans pay homage in the church of work to the religion of money and the present, but in our private houses we are despairing atheists. Epidemic despair derives from the violated need for connections. This denial started when we left Devonshire and Calabria, the Norwegian farm and the shtetl in Galicia. We left for good reason. Some connections braid ropes that tie us down; hierarchical structures prevent motion, invention, or discovery, in the name of the fixed relation of part to part, like the planets and the sun that circled the earth. Therefore we sailed two months in an eggshell across the tall Atlantic into a wilderness sparsely populated by a people that, Francis Parkman tells us, regarded us as a source of protein.

But the same forces that shot us loose released the acceleration of energy, which by Henry Adams's law (1904) doubles every ten years. Adams looked back on a life that began with the railroad, doubled into the dynamo's coal energy, and quadrupled toward petroleum with the motorcar and the airplane. Eighty years after the expression of his law, acceleration continues its regular progression. Now the human system—*that lived in one town for five hundred years—generations of stonemasons living on the same cobbled lane to build the cathedral, quiet centuries without technological change—interrupted for slaughter, for Crusade and conquest and Inquisition—has arrived at a panic-present of continual speed, Paris for lunch and New York for dinner, divorce tomorrow in Santo Domingo, and the human system requires pills, dope, alcohol, violence, possibly not greater in quantity, for the quantity has been constant, but violence wonderfully greater in quality; as Henry Adams put it in 1904,*

"Bombs educate vigorously"—falters, starves, and dies in the desert of volatility. Against acceleration, Rusticus and its emigrants raise entropy's flag with this strange device, not Excelsior but Lentior: SLOW DOWN.

E. M. Forster's "Only connect" implies a lateral or geographical connection. This good advice works best when the lateral crossing is bisected by a vertical that connects us to the dead, to the old persistent earth of graves and foundations, upward into connection implicit with the divine and the unborn, contracted with the earlier born, earlier flourished, earlier dead. In America outside the historian's library and the antiquarian's museum, the lived past thrives where people live among the dead, separated from the brutality of change, the filmic witness of buildings rising and falling in Hamden, the universe new every thirty seconds.

We are Lentior's vanguard, stewards of human connection. History records no straight lines. As the nuclear plants shut down, let the word go out: *The world of tomorrow is delayed until further notice.* While present-livers expend themselves in acceleration, speed canceling their bodies, let us spend quick lifetimes telling old stories while we stand on dirt thick with the dead.

I ♥ My Dish

Last summer we added the latest touch to our old house—to *remain* classic you need to keep up—by installing a twelve-foot satellite dish out back where the saphouse used to be. It's beautiful; we call it our David Smith, although I'm not positive that the sculptor ever worked in black mesh. When I'm eating dinner with my hosts in Idaho, out on a poetry reading, I hand snapshots of my dish around the table; when I come home after my journey I hug it.

Some people think it's strange that I love my dish so much; some people find me inconsistent to love both rural New England and an electronic gadget connected to outer space. Our veterinarian made a rhyme about L. L. Bean flannel watching the Playboy Channel. They ask me how my grandfather would have liked it. Well, I tell them, he would have loved two innings of his Red Sox between supper and shutting up the hens. By 1988, satellite dishes had become the real thing of the countryside—unlike picket fences—as common to backwoods New England as stonewalls, yard sales, green shutters, and junkers. If you drive past a handsome clapboard house with a white wellhouse, a painted barn, and no television aerial, you know that its owners drive up from Boston on weekends in a BMW. On the other hand, over on Route 104 toward Bristol, there's a trailer with *two* dishes in front. After long speculation, I have decided that *she* likes hockey and *he* likes basketball. Ma and pa dishes (double-dip two-scoop) are cheaper than divorces, if *he* goops at a twenty-four-hour Nevada shopping channel and *she* freaks on silent horror movies. In this house I like baseball, I like basketball, I like hockey, and in descending order tennis, soccer, Ping-Pong, volleyball, badminton, lacrosse, boxing, wrestling, arena football, football, roller derby, and golf. The ladder's rungs never give up, and neither does my dish.

At any given moment, this machine can seize something like three hundred alternatives out of thin air: news and news feeds, televangelists, fifty shopping services all flogging the same pink zircon, sitcom reruns, exercise shows, movies—and sports. The movie list in my *Satellite TV Week* runs to five hundred every seven days, but many never get listed. Most interstellar abundance never gets listed, but you develop a feel for what's lurking out there, among spacenuts, spacebolts, and flying saucers—*everything!*

We get French broadcasts from Canada: baseball and hockey, of course, but also European highbrow stuff. We get tons of Spanish. We've discovered a few programs in Italian, one of them various enough to include quiz shows and opera. Once I found a basketball game, small white guys without talent, with announcers speaking an unknown tongue. There's always news in English, not only CNN but the BBC three times a day and network news fed upstairs at three or four different times for the different zones. If you are driven to watch *The NewsHour with Jim Lehrer* at six, seven, eight, and nine, you can do it.

Mostly I watch live sports. On a Saturday in May I am embarrassed by riches and keep swiveling the dish. There's the NBA on CBS, at one and at three-thirty, on three satellites and four transponders. Because CBS is showing both Denver/Dallas (to most of the country) and Detroit/Chicago (for home folks), I can satellite from one to the other. In the autumn, on a Sunday afternoon, I can find every professional football game as it happens. Summer Saturdays I get NBC's baseball game of the week *and* its backup. Today I pick up the NBA from Telstar 302 because that's near Satcom 4, which is where I catch the Red Sox. I switch around at halftime, between innings, or during time-outs. From one to six I career from Chicago/Detroit to Boston/

Seattle to Denver/Dallas. From six to seven-thirty I read a book, because I must conserve sports attention for the Stanley Cup playoffs, Boston Bruins and New Jersey Devils at seven-thirty. Later, if I can stay up so late, the New York Knights take on the Chicago Bruisers at ten-thirty in arena football.

Mind you, this difficult schedule ("When the going gets tough, the tough get going") occupies me mostly on weekends. Weekdays, unless you care for taped 1978 lacrosse playoffs on ESPN, you often wait until seven-thirty to watch baseball (every night, April to October) or basketball (hundreds of college games, ninety percent of the NBA). But when the Chicago Cubs play at home on weekdays, you can sometimes take in a Cubs game at two-fifteen and a Braves game at five-thirty before the Red Sox at seven-thirty. When my teams play on the West Coast, I can watch an eastern game at seven-thirty or eight before traveling to California for a first pitch or tip-off at ten-thirty. On occasion, I hate to admit, I need to sleep; like everybody else in New Hampshire, I get up at five, and if I've been staring at Anaheim Stadium or the Forum until one in the morning, I feel a little logy by eight A.M. Sometimes during West Coast trips I go to bed at eight o'clock, like everybody else in New Hampshire, and set the alarm for ten-thirty.

If I don't get in these daily hours of sport, my work suffers. When the device was installed old friends worried for me: "They'll say, 'Whatever became of Hall?'" But within a month—about the time of my birthday, when my daughter gave me a T-shirt reading, "I ♥ My Dish"—I had altered my habits. Now I can claim that because of my dish I work twice as much as I did before.

It's a trick, doing a sixteen-hour day, seven days a week, without becoming a workaholic. In order to accomplish this feat, we must placate the It. The It, if you've forgotten, is an internal overseer that the wild psychoanalyst Georg Groddeck described and named, a creature that monitors everything we do. It is powerful, but fortunately It is very, very gullible. To work the hundred-hour week, we must deceive the It, because It needs to think that It's relaxing half the time. When we are young, It thinks that getting drunk is fun, and finds nothing so relaxing as a good vomit; late in life, It may find pleasure in watching *Jeopardy!*, or It may read Barbara Cartland or Robert Ludlum. One thing for sure: It demands Its way, and if you don't let It out for a walk, It will burn holes in your stomach. Because I station my It in front of the Boston Celtics (a.k.a. Red Sox, Bruins, Buffalo Chickenwings, Waco Whatevers) eight hours a day, It considers Itself pampered. With Its limited acuity, It does not recognize that between pitches I read magazines, manuscripts by strangers, unsolicited books, today's mail, newspapers, the *Letters of Henry Adams*, my outgoing mail, and page proof; nor does It notice that I floss my teeth, make late revisions in prose, and dictate tomorrow's letters. I used to work from five in the morning until six at night; now I keep going until eleven P.M. Paradise is thinking I'm not working while I work like crazy.

Meantime, I make progress toward the final project, which is to cut out sleep entirely, or at least to restrict it to fifty naps a day, each ninety seconds long and during commercials.

Not that you need to avoid commercials. Often you watch the feed from the arena or stadium to the TV station (known as the backhaul) and catch the game before commercials are added. A year ago I watched no Celtics games, because the away games were on Boston's Channel 56 (which doesn't reach this far) and home games were on cable (which doesn't market itself to a thin population; I get many signals for cable, from all over the country, often by paying a modest annual fee). Now, with my beloved dish, I watch *all* Celtics games; I receive not Channel 56 but the feed to 56 from Phoenix or Cleveland. Among other pleasures, I hear the announcers talk during commercial breaks. Mostly they yell at Louis in the truck or mock a cameraman for attention to cheerleaders, but occasionally I hear athletes described with especial candor.

For backhauls you need to push buttons and feel around in the sky. If you know from the paper that any game is happening anywhere, chances are you can find it, and while you are searching may find the high school basketball finals from Indiana or spring-practice intersquad football from the University of Nebraska. Sometimes it's difficult to know what it is you've found—as the "Bisons," let us say, put it to the "Bulldogs"—but often the ads, if you're getting ads, help you to decipher the signal's provenance. These days, I learn about used-car prices in Denver.

WITH RELUCTANCE I will admit that there may be a dark side to dish obsession. It might indicate, for instance, dependence on television, which is of course incorrect. It might indicate imbalance, which could lead to immoderate behavior, even to acts of violence. Law-abiding members of the National Dish Owners Association ("Fight Drugs: Buy a Satellite Dish") were shocked last year to read of the fanatic in Connecticut who chopped down his neighbor's oak tree because it blocked his reception. Folks like this ("When Dishes Are Outlawed, Only Outlaws Will Have Dishes") make it hard for the rest of us. Newspapers always refer to this fellow as "a self-described television addict," and quote him as saying, "Now I can get the Disney Channel." This vile collapse of morals and judgment ("Satellite Dishes Don't Watch the Disney Channel; People Watch the Disney Channel") may not be blamed on a mere wire-mesh contraption. Now, if that oak tree had been blocking ESPN . . .

THE DISH sponsors many visionary projects besides the abolition of sleep; I prowl thin air looking for geographical extension. Someday will we stumble on a live hurling match from Ireland, or the Moscow Dynamo, or Thai badminton semifinals? I guess not, given the technical differences among video systems; but of course technical problems never tamper with the powers of fantasy. I keep thinking of wandering not only in space but in time.

As it is, we spend the summer in reprises of winter's basketball, and on a cold dark day of December we find summer's game on half a dozen cable systems. I daydream of going further back, of finding a transponder that carries the young Babe Ruth pitching at Fenway, or maybe John McGraw's Giants wearing black uniforms, or Civil War troops negotiating rules for the developing game. Another possible avenue, open to daydream but cruel to hope, is the channel that gives different results, that shows the game as it ought to have been. On this transponder Calvin Schiraldi strikes out the Mets side in the ninth inning of the sixth game of the 1986 World Series. Or if he doesn't, Bill Buckner fields that grounder neatly and efficiently, the Sox pull it out, and in northern New England we go to sleep happy while New York writhes sleepless in defeat.

But the real question that haunts me: On which satellite, on which transponder, may we discover the future? If only we punch the right combination of numbers and letters, I keep thinking, the dish will grind itself into a new position, blurt some new science-fiction noises, and suddenly we will be watching the seventh game of *next* October's World Series.

The Rooster and the Silo

ON ROUTE 4 near us there's a cluster of old houses where West Andover used to be—five or six, this side of the track—and a great gap where the Viking Inn (Daniel Webster drank there) burned down not long ago. Nearby an abandoned schoolhouse falls in; there's a spruce trailer; there's an ugly ranch; there's a house that used to be a gas station; there's a gas station that used to be a house. Uphill off the highway there's an old Cape in trouble: The roof sags, six junkers sprawl about it, and a sign says FRESH EGG'S. Here and there a great old white farmhouse looks south or west, noble and cared for. There's a hollow of homemade houses, mostly small and oddly shaped, different from one another, improvised according to need and available material. *Architectural Digest* has not run a spread on them. Each speaks its own accent.

In the hamlet of Potter Place, besides the gingerbread depot that survives as the Andover Historical Society's museum, there's an old store that functions as a post office, open four hours a day, and there's the Potter Place Inn, which a year ago looked teetery. Because we don't often swoop down the old road, we watched its revival in quick cuts, like a television ad where they build a house in thirty seconds. The structure that seemed ready to topple, shabby on its last legs, squares clean rectangles and returns to health. Every old building shows diversity over its decades or centuries, and the direction is not always toward entropy. When we moved to this house in 1975 we repaired a swaybacked woodshed; we replaced rotten sills and clapboards. Bit by bit we brought the old place around, and the neighborhood thanked us. People sent postcards; people came up to us after church.

Not that opinions are uniform in this rural culture, even on the subject of preservation. There are always some, seeing a decrepit house, who want to "let the little red rooster run through it." This rooster burned down "Sabine," Uncle Luther's cottage. It would have been expensive to fix, but the man who torched it felt ashamed when he told me. I hold with William Butler Yeats, who wrote in *Purgatory*, ". . . to kill a house / . . . I here declare a capital offense." Killing is what we hate, not altering. We added a new room to this house ourselves—and ruined a roofline. In some protected towns they wouldn't let it happen. Some of us want zoning, want limits to growth—but we probably don't want the Code Man, villain of Carolyn Chute's *Letourneau's Used Auto Parts*. The Code Man has the social function of enforcing uniformity. When suburbanites move to the country they try to outlaw visible poverty. But if all houses in the countryside show green shutters, eighteenth-century lines, and white clapboard, it is no longer the country. It is Woodstock, Vermont.

Mind you, there's worse than Woodstock.

Twelve miles west of us in New London, diversity drowns under a tide of uniformity, as vast homogeneous condos parody the buildings indigenous to the old culture. Residences of a development named Hilltop Place mimic wooden farmhouses with barns attached, painted gray to look paintless but remain tidy. The paintless look refers to poverty, as if poverty were decorative. Many clusters of units include a weird round wooden tower, which, we suddenly realize, makes an allusion to silos. Do Hilltop's inhabitants, retirees from New York and Connecticut, know what silos are for? Marie Antoinette liked to play at milkmaid, but could she muck out a tie-up? Another mass condo, on the New London golf course, called The Seasons, flies uselessness like the flag of its raison d'être. On each side of the entry road the developers have erected stretches of white wooden fence, curved lateral lines against green grass, as pretty as a picture. But each fence begins and ends unattached, joining nothing, a chalk line without use or function. Even if it were attached, the fence is designed so that it could keep nothing in and nothing out. It is a fenceless fence, a motif, a meandering scalloped icon of decorative vulgar conspicuous waste that mocks the fences and walls men constructed to keep animals out of corn.

Diversity persists, under assault. Bless our trailers, our junkers, and our rotten but redeemable old houses. The real red rooster of this countryside is the designer silo.

Centuries of Cousins

LAST SUMMER I found myself at the historical society of a handsome village in central New Hampshire, near a lake popular with summer people for more than a century. Here were men with white hair and whiter trousers, wearing blue blazers with gold buttons, their faces tanned from tennis, never golf, their grandchildren shiny and polite. Drinking lemonade with an attractive, expensive family, I heard a Boston voice say, "Yes, you see everyone in New Hampshire, but do you notice how you never meet anyone who was born here?"

We have all heard these sentiments spoken of Florida, Arizona, California, Hawaii, and Colorado—islands of drift, holiday, retirement, and suntan; theme parks of the suburban American dream. I was shocked to hear these words spoken about my New Hampshire. But there are many states of New Hampshire, and now I was visiting the resort-state, an important component of New Hampshire's economy (fiscal and cultural) even before the railroads. When America prospered after the War of 1812, the White Mountains became America's Alps, obligatory for the affluent traveler. In the fifteen years before the Civil War, the new railroad invented summer people, vastly increasing the viewers and trippers. The lakes, the favored country towns, and the mountains multiplied their populations tenfold in July and August. A New Hampshire of dry summer breezes has prospered for a century and a half.

But the state I call my own is a twelve-month place, including mud and mosquitoes. My New Hampshire is the *Boston Post* cane for each town's oldest inhabitant; it is Old Home Day and the cellarholes that called forth Old Home Day; it is Prize Speaking Day and dressing up as Santa Claus for the elementary school's Christmas program. It is a rural culture derived from postrevolutionary eighteenth-century America.

This society started its decline a hundred and fifty years ago, but in the 1930s its habits still dominated our towns. As it survives now, we still find it in the South Danbury Church Fair. Women work all week cooking casseroles and bread, then toil in the sun on a Saturday afternoon to feed the multitude that line up at four-forty-five. Some who work at the fair grew up in Connecticut or Arkansas, Michigan or New Jersey, but found their way, one by one, to this place that they love. Others—among the men who set up tables and run the auction, among the women who cook—attended Sunday school inside the dark church fifty and seventy years ago.

In contemporary America this continuity is almost unthinkable—even if it is a continuity of diminishment. Danbury's population decreased beginning in the 1830s. The hill farms emptied out and citizens struck by poverty moved south to the mills of New Hampshire and Massachusetts, or west to the open spaces of New York State, Ohio, Iowa . . . Just now, as our year-round population increases, we begin to equal the numbers of a century and a half ago.

And I fear for the culture's survival. When summer multiplied us by ten for only a two-month season, our society survived and the summer economy helped it; after Labor Day we went back to being ourselves. Daily life alters when condos crowd with bathers and leafers and skiers and when retirees park Lincolns by the P.O. all year long. Under the assault, the church-supper universe fades. It does not extinguish like a blown candle but diminishes its relative strength, as water soaks salt out of beef. This culture survived the train, the radio, the automobile, and television, but it cannot survive yearlong outnumbering. Our new influx doesn't join the old; its numerousness overwhelms the old and installs in its place the dominant American suburban culture.

For one example only of what passes and what takes its place: Two miles south of us the Potter Place Inn used to be our most popular local restaurant. Everything was family style, too much food well cooked and well served in abundant serving dishes in a barnish room not noted for interior decorating, and the relationship among customers, hosts, and servers was familiar, you might say. The old owners retired and the place has seen its ups and downs. Just recently new people took it over and spruced it up; it looks good now, and the other night we tried it out. The prices have become New Canaan, and so has everything else. The hostess confided that our waitress tonight would be Karen, and Karen asked us if we cared to purchase a beverage.

By definition we Americans are a transient and changeable people; when our company transfers us every four years we cannot grow long roots. Therefore we and our neighbors, looking for something in common, find duplicate bridge instead of harvest festival. Maybe it's trivial to complain when a local institution becomes standard issue. It happens everywhere, even by Eagle Pond, and it's the lack of local variation that we complain of. We settle for Porsches and sailboats because we lack centuries of cousins; improvising a social standard, we make a coast-to-coast etiquette of *Have a nice day*; we purchase beverages instead of buying drinks; because we are changeable, we become interchangeable.

Country Matters

COUNTRY is the working farm or the farm no longer worked, empty barn presiding over hayfield returning to forest.

COUNTRY is village or small town set among hills or meadows, on the plain or in the desert.

COUNTRY is landscape uncluttered with people.

COUNTRY is an ethic, or an idea, that distinguishes itself from city and suburb.

On the other hand, there is Commercial Country Cute, a parasite that feeds on our genuine collective nostalgia for land, solitude, and rural culture. CCC is a product to be sold and a device for selling other products. To watch television advertising, you would think that America remains a rural nation. Mr. Bartles and Mr. Jaymes (as it were) flog sugarjuice by acting the part of hayseeds. Most egregiously we observe CCC in the marketing of real estate. When the old farmer sells his hayfield under the blue mountain, where he and his forefathers mowed and scythed all summer, the developer bulldozes stonewalls and sheds, builds roads, gouges a decorative pond, and erects brown-shingled odd-angled rows of medieval townhouses, called condominiums these days, with access to golf, tennis, and sailboating. Then the developer advertises his units, with layouts in the *Boston Globe* and the *New York Times*, as "Farm Cottage Village Estates" or "Daffodil Meadow Vue Mansions." When the developer names his roads, cut through topsoil constructed out of a century of Holstein manure, the poetics of commerce outdoes itself: "Brown Trout Creek Road," "Blueberry Muffin Lane."

Many consumers who buy these condos, for recreation or retirement, believe or wish to believe that they have entered the world of COUNTRY, when they have purchased only a daydream exploited for greed's sake. Unwittingly they leave Greenwich or Toledo for a place that their own presence, in overwhelming numbers, alters into New Greenwich and New Toledo. For COUNTRY is not merely place or space; it is a culture based on a sparse population and an ethic of liberty. Because our population is small, we can vote to tax ourselves when we attend town meeting. There's no town meeting when your town counts five thousand taxpayers—much less a million. This culture also derives from the natural world, making character subject to the round of seasons and weather. No roof covers the mall of COUNTRY life, making one even climate twelve months a year; we realize human stature under blizzards and beneath mountains.

Condos kill COUNTRY not on purpose but by multiplying citizens past the possibility of intimate citizenship. Where we had villages with outlying farms, we substitute developments with outlying malls—artificial towns with artificial marketplaces. Greed uses nostalgia, fabricating a connection between consumption and COUNTRY. When the new mall rises in Concord, New Hampshire, one motif will be Shaker architecture—ironic homage from the society of commerce to those celibate craftspeople who did not even practice private ownership.

Greed has been with us forever, under the name of avarice, one of the seven deadly sins; it is less often acknowledged that nostalgia has lived with us as long as avarice has. Nostalgia is no sin, but it can be dimwitted, especially when it considers itself a recent phenomenon: *Ah,* moons nostalgia, *back then we were an innocent people, pure, simple, and rural.* Just *when* were we innocent? In 1770 it was 1720; in 1910 it was 1860; in 1990 it was 1940. For the sixty-year-old of any generation, it was always fifty years ago.

But when it is not dimwitted, nostalgia can be as serious as it is perpetual. City and countryside have been with us always—and city has always regretted loss of COUNTRY. Nostalgia appears in the Sumerian epic *Gilgamesh,* a thousand years before Homer. Later, the city-states of Greece depended on outlying farms, and Greek literature regretted separations. Rome at its height squeezed a million and a half people into narrow streets of apartment buildings. The great Latin writers departed Rome for country estates, from which they wrote letters back to the city enumerating country pleasures. Horace's odes celebrated withdrawal to his Sabine farm, by which he separated himself from the bustle and vice of Rome.

The tradition of valuing the rural life over the life of city or court is as ancient as human history. COUNTRY is an ethical idea: a place of solitude, meditation, withdrawal, and honest feeling, as opposed to the courtly life of power or the market life of greed. The journey west for Gabriel Conroy in James Joyce's "The Dead," or the journey *North of Boston* for Robert Frost, stands for mental travel to origins and to the genuine—to places of retreat and of vantage from which we make disinterested judgment. In the city—the notion is—under the spur of competition our desires confront crowds of counterdesires, and we do not behave correctly; we lose ourselves to passions of self-aggrandisement: power, wealth, political importance, influence. In the clear COUNTRY light, on the other hand, we see without distortion and testify to what we see—unless, I suppose, CCC installs us, in some future generation, on The Farm at Eagle Pond Estates.

My New England

THE COUNTRYSIDE outside my New Hampshire house is the New England we know from postcards and calendars: covered bridges under the blue hills, trees fiery in early October, weathered barns in snow, March's sap buckets hanging from spigots driven into sugarmaples, low long farmhouses white with green shutters beside spring's golden daffodils, the green tent of the summer oak. This New England is only a portion of New England, but it is true enough, and so is the poverty that accompanies it, the shacks and the trailers. My New England is the old-fashioned part, north of Boston, and it is this New England that I will mostly write about. Though the suburban culture of General America takes over in the plupart of the six states, New England's past remains frail but alive in the spare countryside.

Summon the mind's map and begin a quick regional survey at the extreme corner of Maine's high Atlantic shores; this land is rough, cold, magnificent, relentless, and underpopulated. The long coast is rocks and lobsters, huge tides, fishing boats, and clapboard houses that age quickly under wind and weather. Inland, the little towns remain crabbed, comfortable without affluence, rough and raw. Enormous forests, crossing westward into New Hampshire and on to Vermont, are the home of loggers and of paper mills that shed their effluents as the wind blows and the waters run. But if we move south in Maine rather than west, driving down the coast following Route 1 and its tributaries to the coastal villages, we come to the summer place, which has occupied coastal and northern New England for a century and a half. The L. L. Bean complex at Freeport, open twenty-four hours a day, is the Vatican City of a mail-order industry that has long since outgrown its homemade signature. The lower coast of Maine is a scar tissue of Holiday Inns, lobster palaces, cottages, and great houses. Only the rich, in protected enclaves, keep the calendar look. "When private wealth takes itself to rural New Enlgand, to spend itself on summer comforts, it preserves allusions to the past. Our most New England–looking towns survive by infusions of pious wealth from New York and New Jersey, not to mention Iowa and Texas, not to mention Nebraska and Michigan.

Down the coast New Hampshire's brief, dense shore includes Portsmouth, where blocks of old houses, if you shut your eyes to electric wiring, retain vistas of the eighteenth century; it resembles a coastal town in the southwest of England, with clapboard instead of brick or stone. Boston's North Shore encloses the Boston rich. The islands of Martha's Vineyard and Nantucket, like Cape Cod itself, provide daily bulletins from the war between preservation and profit. The coast of Rhode Island, most urban of states, still harbors the cottages and yachts of Newport rich. On Connecticut's shore, Long Island Sound makes the best saltwater swimming of summer, warm and protected, with aeries of wealth and overcrowded public beaches.

Inland in southern New England the factory ruled during the industrial age, spawning great neighborhoods of workers, sponsoring influxes of immigrants to work the machines and eventually to populate the spreading suburbs. Old truck farms five miles outside the cities—New Haven with its guns and Waterbury with its brass; Worcester, Lawrence, Lowell, and Providence with their cotton and woolen mills—turned in the 1950s and 1960s into malls surrounded by ranch houses and, later, by condominiums flattening under the perennial gardens of television antennas. The dominant urban activity altered from manufacturing to shopping.

North of the mall belt, the population has typically varied from season to season. Cape Cod, the islands, and southern Maine and

New Hampshire were first to become summer places. Vermont took longer, and as late as the 1950s was less spoiled and ripe for spoiling. Even before the railroad, summer people came to Newport, Martha's Vineyard, and the North Shore, even as far as the White Mountains. Thoreau canoed and hiked; Emerson rode the stagecoach. Romantic sensibilities thrilled to the Byronic swoop of Mount Washington before America's truer alps, westward, opened with the railroad later in the century. In the meantime, trains from Boston took summer people straight to the mountains.

Rural towns engorged for July and August. For a century and a half, the year-round native, farmer or descendant of farmers, has profited from the birds of summer; hill people have mowed grass for flatlanders, cleaned their houses, sold them gas, and cheered when they left. Some native sons and daughters, who gardened and curried and baby-sat and washed Pierce-Arrows, developed a taste for the money they observed; they worked their way through UNH, took a job on Boston's State Street—and turned into summer people themselves.

Survival on North Country hill farms was hard work. For one hundred and fifty years, our population steadily dwindled. Exodus began in the early nineteenth century. In 1855 Herman Melville wrote about the "singular abandonment" of the "mountain townships." This diminishment accelerated later, and early in the twentieth century Henry James wrote about farms abandoned in New Hampshire. Even today, as you climb New Hampshire's wooded hills and mountains, you must watch to keep from falling into cellarholes deep in the forest. On the old farm sites, lilacs and roses bloom unseen, once planted and tended by farm wives; everywhere in dense woods you find stonewalls that testify to lost pasture, land once cleared by the muscles of farmers. Along disused trails you stumble upon abandoned graveyards.

In 1899 Governor Frank Rollins of New Hampshire decreed Old Home Week, a summer holiday of reunion, when the lost children returned to hills and cousins. Villages put on plays, dances, and church services; they mourned their dead, drank cider, spooned, listened to band concerts, and reminisced. When I first attended these ceremonies in the 1930s, at a Methodist campground in Wilmot—huge pines over tiny cottages and a band shell—nostalgia's energy endured: a longing for home and childhood, a passion of temporary return or reconciliation. The hurricane of 1938 uprooted pines, which crushed cottages. We still celebrate Old Home Day, but no longer do old natives drive here from Ohio or Delaware. The generations that departed died out, and their descendants lack connection. Now the people who return are often summer children who grew up to love the place of rest and exploration. Many new residents of the rural towns are summer people or children of summer people, attracted to northern New England as to another life, an alternative to Brookline or Stamford. They return—at retirement or earlier, by hook or by crook—to field, forest, and stonewalls, to ponds and to worn mountains.

They return also to a culture that differs from the society of city and suburb. I emphasize again: Universal to the northern rural parts is the value placed on eccentricity. Every village remembers heroes of strangeness, men and women talked about for decades after their deaths. My cousin Freeman Morrison, dead thirty-five years, is the daily subject of anecdote in my town: how he brought up a heifer virtually to speak; how he moved great rocks with a tripod contraption on the least excuse; how he preferred to work at night and shingled roofs by lantern. This passion for eccentricity provides amusement, which still expresses itself largely in talk, laconic wit ("Have you lived here your whole life?" "Not yet"), and narrative. Most anecdotes are told as true, and New England speech serves purposes of preservation. This cultural convention passes on the tales of the tribe, as our griots tell stories and the rest of us listen to remember.

These stories inculcate the culture's ideas of itself—like the story of the ox-cart man, which my cousin Paul Fenton told me. This house could have been the ox-cart man's house, and it has altered with the train and the motorcar. Our rootcellar beams, crudely squared off, still carry bark; when we put in new chimneys in 1976, we piled old bricks, one with the date of 1803. When my great-grandfather expanded the house in 1865, he also built a cowbarn slightly up the hill, away from the house, for safety in case of fire. The house sat on a narrow dirt road. Because the railroad had paralleled the road in 1848, iron power by 1865 had displaced the turnpike's matched teams of horses. Before I was born in 1928, the turnpike (turned into Route 4) had been paved for automobiles. As a boy I watched the last thrust of railroad authority as huge freight trains hauled World War II's steel to Canadian ports. Now, as one hundred and fifty years ago, there is no railroad here—at least there are no trains. The rails that gleamed like sterling in 1943 now rust and flake; bushes and pines push up through dirty crushed stone between pitted ties.

New England, never a single thing, has risen and fallen and changed and remained the same for three hundred and seventy years. No one could have built on the site of our house until after the English, aided by Colonial troops, defeated the French and removed from the Indians their source of muskets and powder. Not far south of us, Salisbury was a prosperous, fortified community by midcentury, but a farmer on its outskirts was liable to be scalped. New England's economy was coastal, as the great sailing ships tracked across the waters to the mother country, to France, to Holland, and to all Europe. There was, of course, the trade in slaves, molasses, and rum. It was not, thank goodness, our only trade. New England's several ports thrived, boiling with the goods of all nations, sailors on leave, and merchants trafficking. Most manufactured goods came from England; we shipped to Europe pig iron, dried fish, tobacco, and white pine, two hundred feet tall, for the masts of the Royal Navy. To the West Indies we carried poultry, beef, and lamb—alive in the absence of refrigeration.

Even today, the culture of the North Country derives from people who moved inland from coastal cities to wilderness late in the eighteenth century. The veterans and families who headed for the lonely north selected themselves to work harder than their brothers and sisters, with less comfort, in return for independence. Six Keniston brothers fought in the Revolution, one of them my great-grandfather Ben's grandfather. They grew up outside Boston and after the war scattered north along with thousands of their fellow veterans to the woodlands of New Hampshire and Maine and what would become Vermont.

Paul Fenton's ox-cart man brought the dream of liberty north after the Revolution. This independence was not so much the abstraction of the Declaration—lofty, glorious, and Frenchified—as it was a dream whereby the single unit of a family could exist in benign anarchy without regulation or cooperation. The liberty boys wanted each man his own nation, little city-states in the hills, small valleys dividing narrow units separated from each other by granite.

Separateness from others was not a price to pay but a reward to win. Settlers built rudimentary houses while they cleared ancient trees and moved rocks, making stonewalls. Because each family settlement required about forty acres for survival, they could not be crowded. They would never acquire money or save it, but they would contrive their own comfort. The natural world provided wood for warmth and ice for chilling; add a great garden, with a rootcellar for storing apples, potatoes, squash, cabbage, carrots, turnips; add one cow; add deer and turkey shot in the wild, sheep for shearing, maybe flax grown to make linen, bees and sugarbush for sweetness. In this society, men worked in woods and fields while women labored inside at ten thousand tasks. Notions of self-sufficiency became a brief reality—which still creates New England character, in the endurance of its superannuated dream.

The settlers brought values with them north from the coastal cities. They brought the Bible, most of them, and always the *New England Primer*, for education was linked to religion as Protestants required themselves to read scripture. Or, in the absence of religion, education turned almost holy. Out of seventeenth- and eighteenth-century preoccupations came the education industry that remains at New England's center: colleges, not to mention academies. (Rural New England's three major industries are yard sales, skiing, and prep schools.) After the first years of isolation, the settlers cooperated to build schools and churches. Young women, when they stopped studying, taught school until they married; if a New England schoolmarm didn't marry a neighbor, she trekked west. Outside school, education continued in winter parlors as fathers read aloud while mothers sewed in the evening. This society without many books remained ferociously verbal, with recitation its primary form of entertainment. In small New Hampshire towns, children still compete in Prize Speaking Day at elementary schools. In the diffuse centers of rural communities, in villages without even a store, we find a tiny library open six hours a week.

Although government was minimal, it was intense and local. From Massachusetts the settlers brought the town meeting; today we still go over, line by line, all items of the yearly budget. Government by everybody is next best to government by nobody. In sparse areas, everyone takes a turn doing things publicly required. Of course the value placed on local rule produced many Copperheads. If my great-grandfather detested slavery, he claimed that he had no business telling the South how to behave. I have told how this Copperhead fought in the Civil War out of local loyalty, and brought up his children to be Democrats. Thus my cousins are ferocious Democrats swimming against the conservative tide.

The Republican current flows from an eighteenth-century source. Though its headwaters are libertarian—anti-bigness, in government or in commerce—this conservatism votes for big-business Republicans. The individual ethic, in an age of corporations, works toward its own destruction because of its reluctance to restrict the use of land: "If it's your land, you damned well ought to be able to do what you want with it"—even when "you" is a corporation. Increasingly, the brown-shingled, sawtoothed medieval-village-townhouse condos come between the rural New Englander and the mountain he grew up gazing at. The covered bridge is stuffed and mounted; the mountain stream is posted, burdened with ownership; ski slopes sheer where sheep grazed; parking lots blacken the meadow for buses that carry tourists of the red leaf.

. . .

In the nineteenth century, subsistence farming was already a hard life. On the thin land it was difficult to be provident by saving against the lean years. Many children of Yankee farmers left off working the dour land. Mountain villages were abandoned, not for better farmland to the west but for southern mills, a regular wage, and a work week shortened to seventy-two hours. The United States had turned to manufacturing when the politics of war erected embargoes, when privateers and the British Navy shut off international trade. Cities that had been ports now became centers of casting, forging, leatherworking, weaving, and assembling. New Hampshire and Massachusetts made shoes and cloth—cotton, wool, and linen—while the South supplied raw materials, and New England became the South's England.

Technology also altered the New England farm. Farm machinery beyond the scythe and the pitchfork did not function well on hayfields studded with boulders at a thirty-degree angle. Our ancestors left the hill farms for the valleys, where they could use horse-drawn machinery, and for a while the valley farms prospered. With some flatland for haying, we could milk not one Holstein but six or eight and send our milk by railroad to the city, where mills employed milk drinkers who lacked a mooly cow in the backyard. Many of New England's small, diverse farms survived into the twentieth century, powered by pairs of oxen, by matched teams of workhorses, and by a sprightly mare to pull a buggy. If a farm prospered, the farmer acquired more land.

Along with land, education remained a value. Ben Keneston's daughter, my grandmother Kate, took the train five days a week to Franklin High School—six years of Latin and four of Greek. When Kate married Wesley Wells, he moved in and farmed with his father-in-law. Their three daughters—my mother Lucy the eldest—also took the train to Franklin High, and then the train to faraway Bates College in Lewiston, Maine, where the girls met the rest of New England. My father, who went to Bates from a suburb of New Haven, took Lucy to Connecticut, and thus I grew up in another New England, four miles from Yale University. New Haven, over two centuries, had translated itself from a port to a manufacturing town. By the late 1920s, when I was born, Hamden resembled the suburbs of Providence, Boston, and Portland. The house I grew up in was solidly made in a neighborhood of similar houses with six rooms, a small yard, and a garage. If the houses were alike, so were the children, the fathers and mothers, the dogs and cats. But in 1936, when we moved in, Spring Glen in Hamden still felt raw; farms remained visible underneath the tidy city blocks.

Or underneath my Connecticut grandfather, who appeared to be a businessman. My father's father, Henry Hall, was born and grew up only blocks away from our house, born in a time when there were no blocks but only the acres of Farmer Webb. Henry's father, Charlie, another Civil War veteran, worked as Webb's farmhand, among other tasks delivering milk to Webb's neighbors. Late in his life Charlie quarreled with the boss, quit the job, bought milk from another farmer, and continued delivery, his son Henry working with him, adding customers. When Charlie died, Henry expanded the dairy and joined up with the Brock family; together they built the great brick factory of the Brock-Hall Dairy in 1935. The business grossed millions of dollars in the early 1950s, but a decade later it had wasted away to nothing—its bigness the usual victim of a greater bigness, not to mention the automobile and the use of milk as a supermarket loss leader. My grandfather died at ninety-one, a widower supported by the utilities he had bought when the going was good, living bewildered in a suburban house on land where, as a boy, he had picked strawberries, ten cents an hour, for Farmer Webb.

When in the 1930s and 1940s I traveled from Hamden to New Hampshire, New Hampshire's farms were not agribusiness. When we went north in the Studebaker, we passed industrial poverty on the journey to rural poverty. In Massachusetts and Rhode Island, as in Connecticut, hard times were closed mills with men idle on street corners. In New Hampshire the farming depression had preceded the general debacle by a decade, starting just after the Great War. For a century the valley farmer had pursued his chores with the aid of hired hands; now he struggled alone. He could work on the road to pay his taxes, and because he had not borrowed money, he avoided foreclosure. But he was poor, and the valley farms came to resemble the subsistence hill farms of the century before: They produced food and warmth but no cash.

A few farms specialized in one crop—apples, strawberries—and thrived or at least survived. Mostly the aging farmers let their places go, and the white houses turned gray. Where matched teams and oxen thrived three decades earlier, one bony old horse pulled buggy, mowing machine, rake, and hayrack. Lacking help from men or oxen, the farmer gave up his poorer fields to bush and pine. More cleared land returned to forest every year, and the landscape moved backward from the nineteenth century to the eighteenth. Population continued to drain away, only reversing itself in recent decades. In the land boom of the seventies and eighties, even Melville's "mountain townships," emptied in the 1850s, started to fill up again. Some towns have regained their peak population of the 1830s but with a difference: Then, isolated families farmed subsistence acreage; now, retirement condos and vacation lodges crowd the lake.

I remember the field I first hayed, the summer of 1939. My grandfather was cutting a patch of stout hay a mile north of us on Route 4, widow hay from a field with no man left to farm it, and he had cut it and let it dry for two rainless days. Because this was the big day, we made it a ceremony. My grandmother packed a picnic lunch. My aunt Caroline was visiting with her car, and at noontime we joined my grandfather in the fields, spreading a cloth over the grass under an apple tree at the edge of the hayfield, eating sandwiches and hard-boiled eggs and custard pie washed down with milk and coffee.

When we had eaten and tidied up, the two women drove home with the debris. My grandfather lay on the grass under the apple tree and closed his eyes for a minute. Then he commenced raking with the horse-drawn rake, and when the piles were completed, he pitched hay onto the rack and I cleaned up the site, using the bullrake. This instrument was four feet across with tines ten inches deep and a long, bent handle; you walked pulling the bullrake behind you. Later I would take instruction in pitching-on and in loading the hay on the rack and treading it down, but now he did the heavy work while I learned not to catch the bullrake in a woodchuck hole and break a tine. We made hay as farmers had done for a hundred years. On the slow ride home he told stories. At the house my grandmother pumped fresh well water, frosting the sides of a pitcher. The cloth of this anecdote unravels swiftly: When I drive past the hayfield now, it has grown up to stout trees, not only fir and birch but hardwood.

The countryside outside my New Hampshire house remains beautiful: Mount Kearsarge in its glory changing with the seasons, pasture with intact stonewalls growing magnificently into forest, and population still sparse, independent, and eccentric. But if we imagine the future of my old hayfield-turned-woodlot—and if population continues to increase, if we avoid plague and war—maybe we see neither woods nor fields but blocks of houses crowded together, like my Connecticut grandfather's suburbs risen over the strawberry fields—and the countryside of New England gone, gone, gone, preserved only in paintings or photographs and in old books.

Fifty People Talking

RENA GUPTIL: Didn't use to be many come by that road. Drummers, sometimes, and Mrs. B. she kept two rooms over the front where they could sleep if they'd a mind to. Long about after the war, times nobody moved in and just about everybody moved out, 's when she closed up. That and the rheumatism. Now I don't know where they come from, cars all over the road day and night, seems.

SAMUEL WEARE: Oh, when he was a boy he was different all right, but not so much different as he turned out later. His grandfather let him raise that ox and he named him Perfect. He wanted to take Perfect to school with him, they was that close.

MORRIS GIANNELLI: I felt bad about it ever since. Now Eben he was some uncle to you? I felt bad about it ever since. He was dead before we got here, we never knew him, we never had no use for the house, just the land come with it that we used for the campgrounds, so we rented Eben's place out. Always troubles with the tenants. Finally these Campeaus, no-goods, they took off middle of January owing rent for two months, not telling nobody. It was cold, thirty, thirty-five below, and by the time I knew they was gone pipes was busted and then it thawed and then everything got soaked. Oh, it was a mess, you never saw . . . I got disgusted I guess, and I felt bad about it ever since, but I did it, then. We didn't have no insurance on it. I let the little red rooster run through it.

BETSY LAFLAMME: May took to herself after Roy died. They was mostly to themselves *before* he died, I suppose, but after the funeral—she went to the funeral, they wasn't many that did—she stopped coming to town for groceries. We figured Carl brought her a bunch when he stopped by. The last five years she never picked up her mail. Of course she never paid the town no matter how they dunned her. When Sherman was selectman he tried . . . but she wouldn't come to the door. At town meeting they wouldn't let Sherman put her house up.

MARCUS MAJOR: When I saw Wes down to the store I probably grinned. I used to jaw with him when I sold him cordwood. "Hell," said Wes, "I saw something about you in the paper." I said, "Well, you're likely to run into me any old place. I'm all over the place." "Yep," said Wes, "just like horseshit."

JIMMY BUCYK: Did I tell you about when Wash had his teeth out? They was bothering him some, mostly in the spring, and one day he says, "Jimmy, can you drive me to Doc Smith's?" When we got there I parked right in front, not like today, across from Holmes and Nelson's, Western Auto's there now, and he told me wait. Wasn't gone more than fifteen minutes. Doc Smith proposed to give him the needle but Wash said don't take the time. He came out of there with some cotton wadded up to his mouth but by the time we was home there wasn't no more bleeding and Wash was gabbing away like always.

SHARON SHERMAN: We never had anybody murdered before. I know Billy Chasen blames himself, letting old Pod keep the station open late. Pod liked it late at night, you know, nobody ever bothered him and he kept the radio going. Radio was still going when Chasen found him at five the next morning, lights on, cashbox open. They took the pennies, Chasen said, they took the pennies even . . . Chasen says he knows who done it but they can't do nothing.

BRUCE HUMBLE: When they opened him up they was cancer all through him. Of course they let the air in, so it grew real fast. That cancer took him real quick.

ANSON STEWART: Lincoln Bascomb wasn't much for doing chores.

When his stove went cold he chopped more birch—birch burns green, you know that?—and took off just enough logs to fill the firebox. He'd be out there with his saw before it was light on a cold morning. Sometimes he brought his hay in with snow on it. He planted corn in July so he never did take it in. Every few years, to pay his taxes, he'd sell off some more of his daddy's land.

LESTER FORD: Tuesdays when I made the run from Berlin I stopped to see old Chester. He smoked a pipe then and didn't that trailer fill up with blue smoke! Every week he remembered a new story. My, he could tell stories, even when he couldn't hardly move, his leg was so bad. When I got up to leave, he always said the same thing: "Told you a lot of lies."

MARTHA BLISS: It was hard to keep track but it was something like this: Old Herbert was married to Lois, I suppose twenty years ago, but she already had Yvonne, brought her with her, I suppose, and sometimes her boyfriend Hector stayed with them, at least folks said so, I suppose, and when Yvonne started to swell up, I suppose Lois said it was Herbert but Yvonne said it wasn't and that's when she married Lonnie but he hadn't been around town long enough.

MARK BROWN: I heard Lila telephone Bertha even though their houses wasn't fifty feet apart. "Bertha," she said, "go look at the sunset," she said. "It's pretty as a picture postcard!" Lila saw beautiful things every place she looked. I told her she rose her eyes up so high she couldn't tell she was stepping in shit. Hah-hah.

JOHNNY BUSO: At Blackwater Bill's, late August, after the first hard frost, old Lebow limped in to set at the counter two stools down from old Peter, took the coffee mug that Stacey handed him, and turned to Peter and asked him, "How did your garden fare?"

POLLY SHEPHERD: One thing about Lulu you could be sure of, she'd never tell you a thing straight out. If she was down to church playing the organ and you asked her wasn't it Sunday, she couldn't tell you just so. Why, I remember one day we was standing under the awning down to Henry's store, and the rain it was pouring down, and I asked her, "Lulu, do you think it looks like rain?" "Well," she said, "I guess maybe, might could be, maybe perhaps."

CHESTER LUDLOW: They was always rowdies here. If they didn't live in town they came to town to do their mischief. Halloween they piled gates and washing machines and motorcycles, even a snowmachine, right up in the square where their granddaddies used to stack outhouses.

LUCY BANKS: Papa died thirty years ago but I still say that's where I live, Papa's house. People don't stop by the dooryard the way they used to. Used to, it was the horse and buggy for some of them, Model T or Model A for most. Some are dead now I suppose. Most.

EDNA BEST: Everybody worried what Thelma'd do when Edward died. She couldn't drive and her daughter'd gone down to Rhode Island someplace, but then Thelma died first—we never could of believed it if we hadn't seen her there up to Melton's at the viewing, she just didn't seem like the kind to die—and Edward cooked for the fair, rolls and two casseroles and pineapple upside-down cake, the way Thelma'd done it.

LEROY WALLACE: He came from the city, I know that much, down Massachusetts way, a flatlander but not like the most of them I guess. Didn't want to have much to do with anybody, never went to town meeting much less church or the Grange. We obliged him.

J. G. MCNAIR: I knew both your great-grandfathers. How do you like that? John Wells he was the blacksmith talked funny, what do they call it, cleft palate. Other was old Ben Keneston used to drive his sheep twice a year, fall and spring, down the Bog Road. Something to see, those four hundred sheep.

HANNAH ROBEY: I used to sit on that porch with a man born 1856 and he told me about how the children, him and his sisters, told their father go hide because the drafting man was coming. Don't seem like I'm old enough to remember somebody remembering the Civil War. I guess I am. Old enough.

LUCILLE HUNTOON: That was when they still kept the pool hall, right down the street from the state liquor. Academy boys, they used to sneak into the pool hall, they wasn't supposed to, and pay somebody fifty cents go buy them a pint of William Penn. Lots got sent home. State of Maine Express came through here every night. Some teacher would put the boy on the train, telegraph his daddy he was coming home, want him or not.

BERTHA BUTTS: Hamilton was the market town back then. Friday nights they stayed open and Loren would drive us there, fifty cents both ways. Oh, it seemed like a big place then with the Newberry's and the Woolworth's both and the old A & P. You should have known it then.

RALPH GALLO: At town meeting our road agent talked about needing new equipment, talked for much as half an hour. He keeps the roads good. Bob our moderator, he called for a vote. "Everybody wanting to buy William his new front loader?"

GEORGE PARADISE: The Greek made that diner with blue-plate specials forty-five cents for meatloaf or chicken croquettes and mashed and two vegetables, bread and butter too. Never knew what happened to him. One day and he's gone, no more Greek.

EDDIE MCCARTHY: Met this fellow from York, Maine, and he says, "I seen you somewheres before," and I says, "I never seen you before in my whole life," and he says, "Did you ever catch a fish? A big haddock? Up in York, Maine?" And I swear, I couldn't believe it. I'd forgot, it's true, first time ever I went deep-sea fishing I caught that fifteen-pound haddock, they took my picture and he seen it. Way up in York, Maine.

FORREST MACK: When they started digging for the landfill I said to Sherm, "Ain't that where we used to went skating?" "Still do," said Sherm. "You ever seen them dig a landfill except where there's groundwater?" Sure enough by July the Jack Wells Brook looked like swill. Sure enough by August there wasn't a minnow left in Eagle Pond. Where was the state water folks when the brains was handed out? Sherm says they was out behind the Grange getting paid off.

LUCY BATES: We moseyed over to her house about four o'clock, she's got that new trailer over on Treatment Plant Road, so's we'd be there time for kickoff. Turned out, nobody watched the game anyway. Super Bowl or not. Turned out, nobody there'd seen a game all fall. She had a dish, the picture was real good, but we just talked. John Johnson he stood right in front of the set, couldn't see anything if you'd of wanted to.

REX MUMFORD: There was two places in Hamilton you could get a drink, right next door to each other. When my aunt Maybelle—she's the one had a car, schoolteacher, only car in the family—took me downtown with her, she lifted her nose when we drove past either one. They was called Eagle Tavern and Freddie's Bar and Grill, both gone now, but Maybelle was afraid, you see, she'd see her own brother come falling out.

MARGERY TIBBETS: On the common, there in the village—that stone, that's the soldier boys went off to all the wars. Some names you wouldn't believe, yard-sale names, was up to Canada back before we was a country, up fighting the Frenchmen. Lots in the Civil War, your great-grandfather too. Not so many in 1917. There wasn't so many around by 1917.

JEFF GETZ: Forty years that old place stood there with nobody in it. They kept shingles on it but they wouldn't sell it because they fought over who got the property after old Prescott died. It's on a back road, gravel, so I didn't go there in the winter but I liked driving past it when the weather was dry. Good old stonewalls over that way, never tumble, and Gambler's place is real pretty, and there's a pretty field. Well, every spring I was half scared to go there, for fear the roof'd fallen in after a snowstorm. Then Miss Borders she bought it, my goodness, and bit by bit she brought the old place back. I bet it didn't look any better a hundred years ago.

AUDREY HOOP: Johnny was always a good boy but not too smart I suppose. When he got himself married it seemed like something just switched on: "Time to get married!" He married Hildy because she's the first girl he saw after the notion switched on. Lots of us knew what she'd been up to but Johnny didn't. Then he got drafted and went to Vietnam and when he got home he found out what Hildy'd been up to—he couldn't miss it, no matter what; what she'd been up to was one month old—so he signed up for another tour and that's when it happened.

HAMP LEBOW: You knows that house down by Buffalo's old camp? Where they used to be the pink mailbox? Don't go near there if you can help it. When I sell lightbulbs for the Lions, I knock at every place but I don't knock there. Fellow there's so mean he shoots cats.

STELLA BUDGE: I taught forty years in that school, one room, anywheres from eleven to twenty-seven scholars at a time, and Percy was the smartest I taught in all those years. When he was six years old I said to Mr. Hubbard, "You see that little blond one? You remember: He'll be selectman!"

MARTHA MUSGROVE: When Emily died it was as if the blood dried up in everything—in school where she worked with the kids that had troubles, in church where she went every Sunday for sixty years, even in her family, that began to pull apart then. Everybody wondered for years what flowed them together because they was Republicans and Democrats, cops and crooks together.

MARTHA BATES: He was always filling in those ads they print inside paper matches: *Complete High School. Earn $20,000 in Spare Time. Get Big Money Working for Airlines. Drive a Tractor Trailer. Read Palms.* I brought him the mail when they was too much snow and he couldn't cross the meadow to the P.O. I bet I brought him one thousand Informative Treatises.

LUCY POPOVICH: Mrs. Roberts, she knows where the wild strawberries are. Before that, she's picked asparagus from the side of the road. Later the blackberries and blueberries. She knows a mushroom from a toadstool. You see her, May to September, walking beside the road with her neck crooked over from the rheumatism and a basket over her arm. She knows where everything grows. Where everything *is,* that grows.

DANNY DUMAINE: Lloyd and Andrew been running their gas station fifty years. Andrew can't promise anything. "Going to do that oil change this morning, Andrew?" "I suppose, might do, if we get lucky, if nothing happens." But Lloyd now, he's different. He has his sayings. When you're about to drive off, Lloyd'll say, "Drive like hell, you'll get there."

BILLY LITTLE: Nothing went right for Belle. She stayed with her old father because nobody else would and all he done was crab at her all day and all night for twelve years until he died. Then she took up with that fellow from Manchester—*said* he was from Manchester—but then one day he was *gone.* They said he had a wife come and get him.

BETSY WELLS: When I was a little girl I sat on the porch with Elzira my grandmother's sister. She taught a one-room school down by the old campgrounds for forty years. Elzira, she never got married. They said she was too particular. Mostly she stayed down to her cottage, but she liked to walk up to my grandmother's house for gossip. She knew everything and she never missed church. "Why did God make hornets?" I asked her. She said in the olden days people used hornets for rheumatism. She said I should be a lawyer when I grew up.

JOHN JOHNSON: He never had any money. If he had any money he bought land with it. Land-poor, he was. In 1916 he put up five hundred gallons of syrup. You know how much sap that takes? Forty to one, most years. Sold them for a dollar a gallon and bought two hundred and twenty acres. Huldah still sewed underwear out of flour sacks. Mind you, if they'd *had* some money, Huldah would've thought it was a shame to waste good flour sacks.

BETTY GOULD: Parker grew up here, sure, right where he lives now on Parker Mountain Road, where they don't have a mountain, but he never was one to mix much, back then, when he was a boy. So he went to college someplace and then I guess down to New York City and thirty years later he comes back to stay, right back to the old place stayed closed up after his daddy died. Of course when he comes back he's got this fellow George with him. People say things but I don't see as they make any bother.

LUCY LITTLE: Bob Smith kept that store for twenty years. Go there at six in the morning or six at night, Bob stood there smiling at you in his short sleeves. He was like the mayor, if we had a mayor, and a good sight more agreeable than any selectman we ever had, I'll tell you. He liked it, running the store.

ANNIE PARSONS WHITFIELD: We met Tuesday afternoons, first and third Tuesdays, and we *did* sit in a circle and we *did* do quilting. Must have gone on sixty years or more, my grandmother went with her grandmother. When Martha Bliss moved in down to the old store, that was the end of it. She talked so mean. Nobody wanted to come anymore. What a shame.

HERBERT MCNEILLY: I worked on the roads five years when old Mansfield was road agent. Oh, my. Old Mansfield he took the town for plenty, I'll tell you, and the town voted him back in every March just the same. Old Mansfield drove the dumptruck and *always* had a six-pack riding shotgun I don't know. When he quit—yep, he *quit*—the town found they was something like ten thousand gallons of gas not accounted for. They was nothing to do about it.

SHERMAN BUZZLE: You want *zoning* you go to Russia, back to Russia.

LOREN WHITE: The old Rialto down to Hamilton, I remember when they built it, bad times and nothing much else got built then. That was when them CCCs camped up on the hill and built the park they call, what?, Whitmore State Park. It holds up. We used to get free dishes Monday nights and a double feature too. Seems like it cost fifty cents. Course that was ten-gallons-a-dollar times.

BUNCH HAVELOCK: Look at old man Gossage, you'd never think

he'd been anywhere but that trailer out by Wells Creek. The age he was, though, they'd all been somewhere. I guess! He don't talk much but once down to the firehouse, they had some beer, and he told how they flew sixteen, eighteen hours in those little old airplanes—B-24s? 25s? They wasn't 747s, I'll tell you. Well they took off from some little island or other, nothing but an airstrip and a beer hall, where the Marines got killed on those invasions, Tarawa and Iwo Jima, burning Japs out of their caves. Well, they flew eight, ten hours all across the Pacific and dropped bombs on them paper houses, Japan. Tokyo I guess. They could see the fires a hundred miles off, when they flew back, eight, ten hours back. Can you imagine that? Old Gossage the gunner.

JANE JOHNSON: Town meeting got a little rough that year. Andy Bascomb got into a fistfight with Sherman Buzzle and of course the moderator would of usually got the constable to throw them out but Andy was moderator and Sherm was constable.

BOB SMITH: People'd come in here, or I'd go pump gas, they wouldn't—they *couldn't*—take off without they told me some story. Didn't matter what, just so it was some story. Some, they'd tell half a dozen. I didn't mind. I told them right back, to somebody else, keep them circulating like a dollar bill. Come bedtime was the only time the stories stopped. Good night.

MARTHA LUDLOW: I get so tired of politics! Chester don't talk about nothing else unless it's taxes, and what's the difference? I wish he'd got elected selectman that time, get it out of his system. Sherman Buzzle beat him. Seven votes. That was just before I had the appendix.

III
Daylilies

Daylilies on the Hill, 1975–1989

"Endurance is good," he said, "and best is the endurance
of magnitude." "Yes, yes," he answered, "of course:
centuries of cathedrals. On the other hand," he said,
"there is also the daylily."
                                        Bees wake in May, roused
by the cry of lilac; skunkweed raises green hands;
July's fieldmice skitter in cornrows; in August

blackberries darken themselves on Acorn Hill, as chilly
bees feel sleep arriving. At dawn in a warm drizzle,
June peas bush out beside lettuce leaves and asparagus,
old roses bud, and the goldfinch returns singing
as our dog Gus and I walk along Route 4 in first light,
no cars on the road. Fifteen hours later, we trudge again

through a cut hayfield, and twilight dew darkens my Nikes.
Fifty-five years ago I trimmed this field with a scythe,
pleasing my grandfather. To the west, foothills blacken
against a late sunset; overhead first stars. Branches
of dead elms fishbone up as empty in June as in January.
Two hundred years by the dirt turnpike, then by the blacktop,

they hoisted a magnanimous green. Now we set oak saplings
beside their stumps. Gus leaps at a moth, prances, and plumes

his gay tail high. Where we walk, the settlers' stonewalls
square out old pasture. When I pace in the family house,
the layered past shows forth in a hundred thousand things —
making house and land composite, alive and dead together.

In the back chamber, where we preserve broken beds and chairs,
tattery postcard albums, headless dolls, dolls' furniture,
wooden-runner'd sleds, butter churns, spinning wheels,
and clocks without faces, three highchairs stand in a row.
The newest is Sears's fancy pressed oak from nineteen eleven,
mail-ordered when Nan was born, where I took my turn

in nineteen twenty-nine; beside it the wicker highchair
where my mother and two years later her sister Caroline
gummed their toast; alongside, another highchair, smaller
and older still, that fitted my grandmother Kate, born
in the north bedroom in eighteen seventy-eight.

In February
seven-foot-deep snowfields will reflect a sky "as blue,"

my grandfather said, "as the seat of a Dutchman's pants."
When Gus leaps, running in snow, he will pause in the air
as if I dreamed him, and dry powder scatter in flurries
where he lands on the moondust snow.

When we first
moved in, we looped cable around the tilting saphouse,
tied it to an eight-cylinder four-wheel-drive GMC pickup

and pulled it asunder. Under a collapsed cornerpost
we found two flat white rocks and turned them over: BENJAMIN
KENESTON 1789–1863. I remembered also his stone upright
in the old graveyard, where his son, BENJAMIN CILLEY KENESTON
1826–1913, raised it—after this one cracked and he carted
the pieces home to set under four-by-fours for the new saphouse

rising on the hill with its fresh-sawed, yellow-fibered planks.
When the ice mountain receded thirty thousand years ago,
shedding gravel and boulders, leaving Eagle Pond behind
for the Penacook's trout, birds flew to the warming north
and shook seeds from their feathers to sprout in new dirt.
In the long drying, whippoorwills lay speckled eggs

and sang, and thrived on grubs and beetles for millennia,
but ten years of DDT concluded the whippoorwill race,
thinning shells until they fissured and embryos died.
Whippoorwills go out, go out—as if we watched house
lights go out, one by one, at night across the valley.
    Adding a new bathroom onto this old house, we sawed

through the irregular upright ash and cedar laths
of eighteen three. Light entered the dark mouse-precincts
long hammered shut, plastered and papered over almost
two centuries ago. We sawed through rough old boards
fastened by hand-forged nails over great sills of oak
hewn flat on two sides, and with their bark still clinging.

When we kindled a fire with wood two hundred years dry,
it blazed like kerosene.
                                        In June's nine o'clock twilight—
rosegold over foothills, like copper showing through tin
linings of pots worn thin by generations in the same kitchen—
June plays its tune of mitosis. New leaf cells split, double,
and double again; green goes more green; Gus's nose

twitches at new buds in this hazy undersea dark. He sniffs,
waving his tail in dog-rapture at a flowering bush's base,
at rhubarb's rags, at the twiggy, new-set apple trees.
    Driving for the *Globe* at five o'clock on a warm morning,
I discover the store opened up like a rind, burned
out, black, smoke still rising from beams and timbers

heaped among hulks of coolers and freezers. One back wall
totters upright: on a standing shelf exploded cans. Wine
bottle shards glint in an alley behind a black cash register.
Volunteer firemen, who have worked all night to protect
house and barn, drink coffee and eat doughnuts provided
by the Ladies' Auxiliary. A dozen young men chew and sip,

wearing boots and bright slickers—exhausted, cheerful.
Four kinds of baked beans, three casseroles of meatball stew,
salad, macaroni and cheese, Edna's red velvet cake, Ansel's
best rolls, Audrey's homemade ice cream: The church
fair copies itself every year, Julys turning into decades,
Repeating, growing smaller, like the barber's mirror'd wall.

When I wake early morning in summer, I want to live
a hundred thousand days: The body's joy rises with dead
elms rising, black empty scaffolding alongside hayfields
under blue hills. Three crows as fat as roosters peck
at a coon killed on macadam: Yellow beaks rip on Route 4
in New Hampshire.

On a rainy day, by the light of one bulb,

picking again through the back chamber, we find a narrow
cardboard box with faint old-fashioned handwriting on it:
Wool sheared from B. C. Kenestons sheep Carded
at Otterville Ready for Spinning April 1848.
Next morning is fair again, and the mountain clear,
while mist rises from spiky hayfields cut last week.

On the glorious Fourth of July in Andover, nineteen seventy-
six, we watched "Two Hundred Years of the Republic" parade: A girl
riding her shying horse; then the Bristol Shriners' band
wearing fezzes; then old cars, clowns, fire engines, one-wheelers,
oxen; then the floats of four churches, the Little League,
the 4-H Club, the Andover Volunteer Firemen, Future Farmers

of America, Boy Scouts, and the Rescue Squad—all fitted
to the theme "From Colony to Country." On the green, crafters
raised their stalls: fancywork, thrown pots, woodcuts, macramé.
After the baked bean and ham supper in the grade school
auditorium, we watched turtles race for the Lions; we threw
soggy baseballs at a target that, if we hit it, tumbled

a watery pailful on Sherman Buzzle, this glorious Fourth of July.
    Now I stand gazing while Gus searches out his tree
and lifts his leg abruptly against the ribbed bark of a stout
maple that *I* remember slim as a cornstalk fifty years ago.
I startle as overhead crows clamor *caw-caw-caw-caw-caw.*
    After Jane's daffodils go—before peonies and daylilies

rise red and yellow, before pink and white—overhead green
flaps broad flags from sugarbush, ash, birch, and oak
as it glories in the whole durable density of summer,
arrived in May, persistent through June rain, July heat,
August parch, and cool blue evenings of turning September,
departing into October's red.
                                        Stone grows; stone extrudes

each spring as snow recedes from the fields. Stone's gravel,
crushed by engines or glaciers, becomes small boulders.
Stone's boulder hunkers huge by the roadside where the young horse
Riley shied at a shape that bulked like a revenant mammoth.
    Moments carve medallions—weeks, days, and hours—images
that mount themselves in the mind's permanent collection:

With Riley the old horse, my grandfather and I cut widow hay
July and August unrainy hot mornings forever; afternoons
we rake it together and fetch it home: timothy, fescue,
clover. As Riley turns his head to watch, twitching
greenflies off his back, my grandfather Wesley pitches
forkfuls up, slow and steady. I build out stages of hay,

loading, between the rack's homemade split-pole rails.
Wesley works with the presence and practice of sixty years.
I watch him twist his fork in, balance, heave, balance,
and swing it over his head: so, so . . .

By the kitchen
window, under the canary, in many incarnations always
named Christopher, that preened in December singing yellow,

my grandmother Kate braided her long hair, looking south
toward dawn. She planned her day: Monday washing, Tuesday
ironing, Wednesday baking, Thursday cleaning . . . She made
soap twice a year; she darned socks, sewed buttons and seams,
crocheted and tatted after supper each night; she churned pale
butter once a week, put hens' and pullets' eggs down

in waterglass midsummer, and each morning under Christopher's
cage observed with gratitude: "Mountain's real pretty today."

Every day I carve these images of Wesley and Kate,
making reliefs or intaglios from summers more than fifty
years ago. This year as an old man I remember
the old people of this house. Last night I woke from sleep

seeing again the generous faces of Wesley and Kate.

The eagle my great-grandfather knew fished this pond night
and morning, single bird who kept house on Eagle's Nest.
Our forty acres of cold water gathered under borders
of birch, hemlock, and oak to breed pickerel, horned pout,
minnows, sunfish, trout, and perch.

Maybe I was eight or nine;

my grandfather hitched Riley to the buggy's shafts;
my grandmother took off her apron and pinned her hat.
Riley labored up New Canada Road to the Dobbins place
for the auction—a social rally, like Old Home Day
or the Fourth, or Uncle Luther's annual surprise birthday
party each August twenty-first. Freeman was there, his beard

wagging around his permanent smile as he talked without stopping.
My grandmother's old schoolmate Lucille turned up
to gossip with: Who's bedridden? Who's next to die?
I met my grandfather's old friend Merrill Huntoon,
blind, who pitched for Danbury while my grandfather
played second base. Peddlers' barrows at the crowd's

edge sold tonic, ice cream, Rawleigh's Salve, and Quaker Oil.
When the auctioneer banged his gavel we stopped talking.
Gradually I understood what was auctioned off. For the first
time I heard the dead lament their characteristic loss.
After Belle died, Victor couldn't keep the house alone,
and my grandfather gave him a bite of land for a shack.

Mr. Hall from Hill lifted up stuff for folks to bid on:
Ball jars by the dozen, a pram, apple peelers, old boots,
chairs, tables, quilts, feather pillows and mattresses,
boxes of pretty pictures (snipped-off Christmas cards,
pastels of babies cut from magazines, daguerreotypes
of matriarchs, bearded fathers and Civil War boys, dressed-

up daughters), a Shaker basket, hammers, saws, a level,
oil lamps, heavy wooden skis, diaries, pedal sewing machines
—whole lives of the dead going, gone, for a nickel or a dime.
On these summer nights, after Gus and I walk, I swivel
a satellite dish and materialize the Boston Red Sox
to get sleepy by, watching a few innings from Baltimore

or Fenway Park. A visitor from Boston pretends outrage:
"*What* would your grandfather think?" I imagine Wesley Wells,
after milking and locking up the hens, sitting to watch
Ted Williams or Nomar. He grins with pleasure, snorts
at failure, and, drowsy after five innings, goes to bed.
In eighteen sixty my great-great-grandfather complained:

"Now your modern inventions are just fine, like this railroad,
but . . . when I was a boy the twelve-horse teams carted
loads of ash for the hame shop, or grain for Johnson's mill.
You never saw such horses." Today I walk in a sandy trench;
small trees grow between ties over the yellowed stone
I remember new and white in wartime fifty years ago.

Hayfields shuddered with freight; sheep turned slow heads
at tremors of tonnage, war's iron rolling. When we heard
the four A.M. freight, we knew: one more hour on feathers.
    In September dawn, cold dew shines on hayfields. By noon
the still-tall sun brings back July: blue sky, a warm breeze
that wavers the pond's turning birches. I wait for the branch

that reddens first each year by Chester Ludlow's house:
then swampmaples carmine; then the whole clamor and glory.
    The fire that never went out went out in the range
where strongest coffee dripped winter and summer, where berries
boiled or cold-packed darkened blue Ball jars, where a reservoir
heated water for washing dishes, where home-rendered lard melted

to fry doughnuts, where the tough setting-hen boiled four hours
into fricassee, where the bread baked twelve loaves at once,
and mince pies and custard. While this fire went out, elsewhere
damp fire burned slowly in sills two hundred years old, and ants
carried oak away consonant by consonant. Now as the range
sits in all weathers behind the toolshed—beside mowing machine,

whittled ladder, bullrake, and pitchfork—its black castiron
burns itself down in the fire of rust that never goes out.
                                                            No cars
on Route 4 tonight, so Jane and I walk on the macadam. Gus pulls
as we keep to the white gutter line, visible in starlight
beside glacial New Hampshire sand. No sound as we turn back
except for the chill tinkling of dog license and rabies tag.

Ahead, the single porchlight projects its yellow oblong
over black grass, interrupted by trees. When Gus pauses
to sniff, his pale tail waves like ectoplasm under a sky
without moon or clouds, crazed by the ten million stars
I number by actual count this darkest autumn night.
  It must have been Ben Keneston who made this door

in eighteen sixty-five when he added a shed and a woodshed
to the old Cape he bought to move into with his family,
and hung it between shed and woodshed. He nailed five
vertical boards against two across. Shiny, ridged and scored,
never painted, the door shows scallops of wear on top
and bottom. To keep it shut against the open woodshed—

against Gypsies and Frenchmen—he chiseled an oblong latch,
two inches by five, out of rockmaple to swivel on a bolt
fastened to the jamb, with a thumb of wood nailed underneath
and a spike dangling from twine to fit a hole above it.
The same spike hangs from the seventeenth length of twine.
This hardened latch—dark brown, solid, with little bumps

and hollows like a turnip's—wood that turns pages in the book
of connections, wood touched ten thousand times by dozens
of hands—shines like Saint Peter's toe.
                                        Warm rain in the morning:
Gus stretches, yawns, mutters, and remembers to mark his maple.
As I drive to town for the paper, headlights on at five-thirty,
wipers swoop against cool drizzle, repeating themselves.

I pass the burnt store, half cleared away, the dank air
still thick with creosote.
                              We drive late on a night
of ripe sweetcorn in blithe air, tomatoes ripening. By Route 11
our headlights immobilize a family of five raccoons, pirates
of corn conspiring, bright eyes shining.

At Christian Endeavor
young Edna led us, her face passionate with goodness and humor,

as we sang Sunday night hymns early in the nineteen forties.
Because I loved trains, I raised my hand every week to sing
"Life Is Like a Mountain Railroad," and every week we sang
Edna's favorite, which Fred played again on a bright day
as we carried Edna from the South Danbury Christian Church,
where she spent the Sundays of seventy-two years, in a box

with bronze handles to the long car and the Danbury graveyard,
Ansel standing in silence—: "I come to the garden alone
while the dew is still on the roses."

Uncle Luther remembered
the Civil War. As he sat on the sunny porch, in the captain's
chair where his father lived out his last summer,
I asked him questions. *I* was nine, aware that Luther would die,

who remembered a countryside busy with young men and women.
He let me see how decades lapsed, the people packed up
and departed, fields grew, and the wooden houses tilted inward
to collapse into cellarholes. Stories continue as the earth
continues. And the best way to preserve topsoil, as the man said,
is to pave it over: Do I pave it over by writing it down?

Do I glass it in?

I sat by my grandfather's side at church;
he wore a brown suit from my father's closet as Luther preached
his sermon without notes. Above the pump organ my grandmother
Kate's black sequined hat tossed as she played "Rock of Ages,
cleft for me." When we stood for a hymn I saw her mouth
a great O. If I wriggled, my grandfather's Sunday
face looked down, and his right hand fumbled in his pocket
to fetch me a Canada Mint.

On March third last year, the sap moon
disappeared behind clouds, wind rose, the temperature dropped,
and in the morning four inches of fresh snow covered
the disgrace and ruin of the yard where Sherman's snowplow
tormented turf. Snow recovered its scabby layers on hayfields.

By noontime sun dazzled from new snow as the air warmed.
Therefore in the hills today, under old snow and new, maple trunks
three hundred years old start their yearly work. If tonight
freezes, tomorrow's sun will release sweetness into our buckets.
An elm by the road—taller than the house, four feet thick,
two hundred years old—leans ripping and creaking as the saw

tears it through. It poises, its topmost branches trembling
as it starts to sag, lowering slowly, sliding and tearing,
inch by inch, tilting, leaning, groaning, until the trunk
shreds its last fibers loose and streaks through shocked air
to strike the ground bouncing its great stiff length out—
and settles still.
In March, the melt fissures snowfields

that hover detached from hillsides beside ditches where water
runs day and night without pausing. Gray layers that remain
on hayfields must have fallen last year in December.
This ancient snow lay where it fell all winter, diminishing
in January's thaw or as the determining moon circled
toward this moment of melt. Now, underneath a damp vanishing

lid, woodchucks sleep without stirring toward spring.
Or maybe a restless one knocks on the underside of the snow.
This photograph—in the fold-down desk my grandmother earned
with coupons from Larkin's Soap, after she stopped making
her own soap—shows an old woman in a Mother Hubbard
beside a bearded man next to their middle-aged children

as shiny as boiled eggs, and in front a young mother who holds
a baby feathered in lace. The baby in the photograph
married, bore nine children, had twenty-five grandchildren,
buried two husbands, survived ten years alone, broke her hip,
and was buried in the graveyard under a granite marker
that carves her name and the dates of her life. Maybe . . .

I do not know her name.
Daylilies rise from the hill.
The structure persisted against assaults of poverty, hurricanes,
education, ignorance, money, Massachusetts, automobiles, war,
drought, secession, fire, flood, and the closing mills.
Now it sickens of outnumbering as the Nashua developer builds
seventy houses on Dobbins Hill.
Morning and night now, Gus and I

walk past blond elm stumps cut close to the ground, smoothed off
by a highway crew. Gus meditates ruin. Daylilies
collapse on the hill; asters return; maples redden again
as summer departs again. When we stroll the Pond Road
at nightfall, western sun stripes down through dust
raised by the yellow pickup passing five minutes ago:

vertical birches, hilly road, sunlight slant and descending.

IV
News from Eagle Pond

The Darkened Parlor

THE *Oxford English Dictionary* confirms—what we'd guess from *parliament* and *parler*—that parlors started as places for talking, rooms in monasteries where monks could speak to visitors. Soon aristocrats used the word for a private conversation place, separate from the public great hall. Not until the nineteenth century, it appears, did the word come to mean our parlor: "the 'best room' distinct from the ordinary living room." By 1880, *Scientific American* could boast that in the United States "almost every well-to-do mechanic has his parlor, or 'best room.'"

None of these sources mention one common use of parlors, at least in New England. In Robert Frost's "Home Burial," the grieving mother reproaches her husband's insensitivity by referring to "what was in the darkened parlor." Their dead boy's body lay there, and bodies lay in parlors for New England centuries as long as funerals took place in people's houses. When we changed our burying habits, we called the undertaker's establishment a funeral parlor.

My family never used parlors for much else. Sometimes we've used them for weddings, sometimes for sickness, sometimes for courting (a heatless parlor encouraged hugging), and sometimes for coffee when the minister came. The parlor at our place is a pretty room, but in my grandparents' day the furniture was uncomfortable—parlor furniture was by definition uncomfortable—acknowledging that the room was not for daily life. Now we keep a loveseat there—it turns into a bed for solitary visitors—and a recliner for a mother's arthritic back. Even though we fill it with comfort, even though it's our prettiest room, we seldom sit there.

It's the southwest corner of the original Cape, with windows that gather southern and western light. The western windows front on a busy road, which makes it noisy with pickups at dawn and dusk all year, and noisier all summer with the traffic of vacationers. We use it as a gallery for family pictures, grandparents and even great-grandparents, mostly photographs but one silhouette of a great-great-great, and one pastel of my grandmother looking beautiful and idealized at twenty. Around the wall there's the original wooden chair-rail, to keep us from denting plaster. Against the inside wall there's a fake fireplace, with a parallel fake in my study—the opposite room at the house's northwest corner. Our false fireplaces puzzle me. The house is old enough for real fireplaces but there's no structural evidence, down in the rootcellar, that we ever had them. The rootcellar is clearly as old as the house.

Why did we ever need a parlor, with the comfortable living room adjacent? All over New England, old houses carry this extra room, and no new house gets built with one. Sometimes in a made-over old house we find an unusual enormous living room—evidence that a modern owner, after the advent of central heat, conflated living room with parlor. It makes a room like the aristocrat's great hall, large enough for presidential candidates during quadrennial coffee hours.

My grandmother Kate put our parlor to practical use, for twenty years, when she ran a part-time business. Many farm wives, in families perpetually long on land and short on cash, raised money with a sideline. My grandmother made and sold hats, calling her work by a fancy name: In a photograph on one of my bookjackets there's a one-word legend over this house's front door: MILLINERY. Nobody can read it because the publisher printed the photograph backward.

Poking around in our back chamber, I once came across a thicket of iron pins that stuck upright ten inches from a round base, objects that bewildered me until I realized: These hat stands stood on tables

Kate erected in the parlor, fall and spring, when she opened her shop. Neighbor women pulled up their buggies and stopped inside to try the new fashions in hats. Sometimes Kate hitched up her own buggy and drove her millinery to remote farms in the hills. She not only sold new hats, store-bought and homemade, but refurbished old ones—a new veil, an artificial flower—for true Yankees who wouldn't buy something new when they could make over something old.

Twice a year Kate took the train to Boston, to look at the new fashions, to buy hats and hat material. When my mother was a little girl, sometimes she accompanied her mother to the city on these millinery expeditions. At ninety my mother Lucy still remembers an enormous Woolworth's with its long, long, long counter of penny toys; she could pick any one she wanted.

The Model T ended the parlor's commerce. People drove to Franklin (fourteen miles away, population five thousand) to shop for millinery, and everything in the universe, at its department store, Holmes and Nelson, where the change scooted from cashier to clerk by a tiny trolley that hurtled along wire tracks. This vast emporium, oddly enough, has shrunk into a Western Auto.

When my parents were married in the living room in 1927, their wedding presents sat on tables in the parlor. In some houses, people were married in the parlor—the same room they were buried out of—but ordinary life never inhabited parlors. When the family gathered in the ordinary evening, they gathered around a central table in the living room, warm in winter from the Glenwood, where a high bright oil lamp cast its light. Some read books, some did homework; sometimes one elocutionist read aloud while others sewed and listened. The girls practiced fancywork they learned from their aunt Nannie. My grandmother mostly darned, tatted, knitted, crocheted—and for twenty years made hats. Everybody kept *busy*, in the living room—and the parlor stayed empty, the door closed in winter, shades drawn in summer, useless . . .

Or nearly. When Aunt Nannie went crazy, she was crazy in the parlor. I remember the scary summer of 1938 when I was nine: senile dementia, screams and long disconnected monologues. She died in September, was buried the day before the hurricane, and her coffin set in the parlor. When my grandfather Wesley died fifteen years later, his coffin was the last to set there. My grandmother, who lived until 1975 and ninety-seven, was buried out of our church, two miles down the road, by the same undertaker—who was so pleased at how well he prepared my grandfather that he took Kodachrome slides of Wesley in his coffin.

My mother remembers that it was Aunt Nannie who stayed up all night with Nannie's father's body, my great-grandfather Ben Keneston, when he died in 1913. Somebody stayed up all night in the parlor with the corpse, my mother tells me; it was only one night, because they put bodies in the ground quickly those days, before the country culture embraced embalming. You stayed up all night, she adds, just in case . . . You don't want a cat wandering in there. I say: But I thought cats weren't allowed in the house back then; they patrolled the barn and the grainshed. Well, my mother said, maybe someone stayed up, just in case, you know, a rat . . .

Sometimes, late in the day, when the western sun sheds its canary light across the floor, Jane and I sit reading in the parlor, enjoying Kearsarge handsome through the south window. But mostly we let the parlor remain a people-free zone, a room set aside from ordinary life. Maybe it's good to preserve a best room—for rituals of courtship and marriage, for disease and dying—to remind ourselves how central they are, these matters on the periphery of our lives.

Graveyard People

WALKING OR DRIVING Route 4 in New Hampshire, we come upon little graveyards every few miles. When we leave the paved two-lane highway for the dirt roads that curve uphill taking us backcountry, sometimes we find minuscule stonewalled burial grounds that served one family. In the towns hereabouts, voters each year elect a citizen trustee of graveyards, seeing to it that available funds (small endowments or line items in the town budget) keep them properly trim and tidy.

In Andover there's an eighteenth-century acre where my oldest New Hampshire ancestors lie, and past it the large Proctor Cemetery to take care of the nineteenth and twentieth centuries. In one or the other lie my grandparents, some of my great-grandparents, back to some great-great-greats. Here Jane and I, a dozen years back, bought ourselves a place near a ravine, under great birches and white pines. Sometimes I walk the dog in Proctor—any excuse to haunt a graveyard—though never on a Sunday, not to mention on Memorial Day: Gus's devotional micturition could prove offensive.

Sometimes Jane and I walk on a dirt road past Andover center, off Route 11 on the way to Franklin. A couple of miles in, without a house around, we mosey in a small graveyard with or without the dog, reading inscriptions and imagining past lives. Jane discovered here the early-nineteenth-century grave of Samuel Smith, his stone standing among the stones of his three wives—all named Susan. This is a place of many Smiths, of Swett and Fifield, of Downes and Morrill, of Clay,

Clark, Sleeper, and Cilley. Many local citizens bear these names; many of these names flutter among the leaves of my family tree.

Down the road from our house, only half a mile, there's a little burying ground set on a slope; each marker digs five or six inches deeper into the ground on its northern end. Afternoon sun colors the granite tawny and points sharp shadows on the hill. (When I pass this graveyard, late afternoon in leaf season, someone has always parked to use a camera.) But why is this graveyard here, far from a church, with houses only every half mile? A Wilmot historian lets us guess, telling us that this area was East Wilmot once. We live in a small flap of Wilmot that tucks across Route 4 between Danbury and Andover. We were to be East Wilmot, making with Wilmot Flat, North Wilmot, and Wilmot Center a quadripartite township. It turns out that some citizens, after the Civil War and before the Spanish, planned a church here, and I suppose that this cemetery is a churchyard that never acquired its church. Here I find Brown, Currier, Sleeper again, Waldron, Tilton, Braley, Charles Scales 1842–1902 of the 18th N.H. Infantry, and Bussell as well as Buswell, which is the same as Buzzle—and Boswell, for that matter.

A mile farther north, just this side of our South Danbury Christian Church, my grandpaternal great-grandparents lie in the half-acre South Danbury churchyard. My grandfather's father John Wells lies here, 1841–1927, veteran of the Civil War, who flies a small frayed flag like so many of the New Hampshire dead: *Co. F., 15th Reg. N.H. Vols.* An iron rail surrounds this place protecting Currier, Sleeper, Cilley, and Morrill again, as well as other names I count among neighbors and cousins: Peaslee, Huntoon, Stevens, Pinard, Ford, Glidden—I visit Ella Glidden's grave, beautiful old woman I knew as a child at church, widow of a farmer who hanged himself in his barn—Langley, Eastman, and Perkins. For decades this graveyard hunkered under low hills dense with black-green hemlock, protected by arboreal darkness and comforted by the density of black-green embrace. A developer cut them down and the graveyard seems vulnerable now.

Graveyards are most taking when we least expect them. As we

drive up Kearsarge, toward the halfway spot where we can picnic or park to climb, I am startled every time to catch sight of a small densely shaded graveyard. It takes my breath away to park here and walk among the eighteenth- and nineteenth-century slabs of granite and slate. How could anyone have farmed up here, with the land so high and cold and scrappy? Farm they did, as the stonewalls tell us, and cellarholes when we walk in the woods. Old people still remember the one-room Kearsarge schoolhouse that stood on this road. How beautiful it must have been up here, and how isolated in winter, for the long generations of these bones.

For the most part, we no longer live close enough to graveyards. Doubtless this failing accounts for crime, drugs, racism, the S & L scandal, and Senator Helms. When we live by a graveyard, we enjoy quiet neighbors, yes, but neighbors eloquent to remind us of our present end. Sensible people agree: A day spent without the thought of death is a wasted day. The sight of a gravestone, weighty not only in its granite, allows us perspective on problems as pressing as burnt toast, taxes, and head colds.

Village people kept their churchyards nearby, like the dead field at Stoke Poges that Thomas Gray celebrated:

> Beneath those rugged elms, that yew-tree's shade,
> Where heaves the turf in many a mould'ring heap,
> Each in his narrow cell for ever laid,
> The rude Forefathers of the hamlet sleep.

The eighteenth century in England produced a whole school of graveyard poets, Gray the latest and best. In America the elegy—especially over the death of a child—became the most common poem of the nineteenth century. (When Lydia Sigourney collected a book of seventy such laments, Mark Twain claimed that she had added a new terror to death.) Reading the names and dates on the old stones, as we root around in boneyards, we note the omnipresence of death for our ancestors—so many dead children, so many wives dead and husbands remarried and new dead infants of new brides. Is it by a reaction, now, that we avoid any confrontation with death? Contemporary memorial institutions—like Forest Lawn—attest to avoidance only.

It's not only New Hampshire that makes splendid or touching graveyards. For a couple of years I lived in the English village of Thaxted, not Stoke Poges but prettier, where wild graves thrived in their tussocky beauty around the great fifteenth-century church. I wandered among them every day, passing the almshouses to get there.

In Rome my favorite place is the Protestant Cemetery. We went there first, like everybody, to see Keats's grave, beside Shelley's, near the first-century pyramid of Cestius, where Rome's stray cats congregate. On our first visit, after homage to the poets we discovered the densely populated main part of the cemetery, and I wandered among the dead I had read about in twenty years of leafing among late-nineteenth-century letters and biography—those great generations of Europeanized Americans and Romantic Englishmen, sculptors and forgotten novelists and painters, remembered by readers of Henry James's letters or Henry Adams's. These English and American artists, Roman dilettantes, ended residing in the damp, shady, crowded, cat-ridden, monumental alleys of the Protestant Cemetery. I walk among them as if I were reading leisurely Victorian letters or weekending at the villas and country houses of the fastidious dead.

But we care most for home granite. Especially I love that Andover half acre where my oldest ancestors remain. My great-grandfather, who resides in Proctor Cemetery, was Benjamin Cilley Keneston. His father was plain Benjamin, distinguished from his son by the giddy vacancy of Cilley, who lies in the tiny old graveyard as he otherwise inhabits our parlor, in the shape of a daguerreotype and a photograph.

The former shows him looking young, but he was born in 1789 and Daguerre didn't invent his process until 1839, so he wasn't young; his hair is as long as a hippie's around a meaty sensuous face, and his young-looking bride beside him grins with an expression like a leer.

The photograph shows the same man old: same vigorous hair but the eyes wild and cheekbones stark. His must have been a difficult life. I know that the handsome young woman in the earlier photograph died and Benjamin married her sister. I know that children died; this morning I walked again in the graveyard to see for myself. Yes, he buried two daughters, each dead at nineteen—Abigail, from his first wife Miriam, dead in 1836; Elvira, from his second wife Hannah, dead in 1842. Benjamin himself lasted until the middle of the Civil War, joining his daughters in 1863. Near him in the old graveyard is his father Jonathan, who fought in the Revolution, my great-great-great. Before Jonathan? Stone records dim out. My personal interest dims out also, since I cannot couple the dead with a house or a plot of land, or visit their graves.

But there's no need to know the dead personally, or to be descended from them, to enjoy their company in their last places. It's peaceful to loiter among representatives of the majority, in Roman cities or in English villages or down the road, acknowledging with serenity that we will join their ranks. In "Church Going," Philip Larkin, writing as an agnostic, spoke of churches and their surrounding yards as "places to grow wise in / If only that so many dead lie round."

Grandfathering

THE OLDER I get, the more clearly I recollect a morning when I was a child of eight or nine and attended an auction on the side of Ragged Mountain. Maybe "clearly" is the wrong word, because I know how memories can distort what really happened, in the service of later ideas and experiences. As I tell this story, I change names and alter circumstances a little. Do I alter other circumstances without knowing that I do? Probably. If I don't remember the auction clearly, I remember it with strong feeling—and with irony.

The Dobbins place had been sold, and old Victor Dobbins was clearing out his family's generations of accumulation. He couldn't take care of the big house anymore; I doubt he could pay town taxes. Like many cashless farmers, Victor used to work the roads to pay his taxes, but now he was too old to haul hardpan for New Canada Road. (I remember a large white mustache, yellowish over the mouth, a blue cloth cap, faded blue overalls, and a body that moved slowly, dragging the weight of its pain.) Because Victor had no place to go, when he sold the old farm my grandfather gave him a morsel of pasture land across New Canada, where the old man could raise a small camp with the help of our cousin Freeman, who could build anything if he had time enough. The land my grandfather gave Victor was only a third of an acre, shaped like a bite in a slice of bread, and he owned many acres of pasture and woodlot—but it touches me to remember that my grandfather gave the land away. *He* had no money but he thought nothing of giving away a houselot—of course the land had virtually no cash value then. By auction time, I suppose that Victor had moved a few chairs and tables and beds into his camp, skillets and forks and woodstoves and an icebox. Everything else was to go. The old place was crowded with *stuff*, like any house where five or six generations, following each other, have never thrown anything away. For the auction, the inside accumulation traveled outside, some things piled on tables, others leaning against weathered clapboard from which the paint had largely fallen away. Indoor possessions like quilts and chamber pots looked alien in the open air, as if they blinked and squinted in sunlight. At first the mere spectacle took my eyes, as the social occasion took my attention. Peddlers set barrows at the crowd's edge, one with yardgoods and another with cutlery. A tinker strung pots and pans on a rope stretched between an ash and a maple. Freeman had brought his pack, from which to sell Quaker Oil or Rawleigh's Salve if anybody required medical supplies.

People came from a distance. Neighbors and strangers prowled among the goods stacked by the house, fingering and raising to the light. I overheard conversations that exchanged information about kin and old schoolfriends. My grandfather and grandmother greeted old friends as they did on Old Home Day; I was introduced a hundred times as Lucy's boy and, yes, it don't seem possible . . . Bored, I wandered off to visit Riley, tied to a maple at the edge of a hayfield among other horses and buggies. Black Model A's, with an occasional blue Buick, occupied the Dobbins yard and the ditches of New Canada Road. I found no nine-year-olds to play with—just a few shy small children holding close to skirts and overalls. I wandered gazing at the furniture gathered in the daylight air: four mirrors, two beds, stiff upright dining room chairs, a kitchen table painted farmhouse green, wardrobes, dressers, chests, a Morris chair . . . I examined stacks of bedding, boxes of papers and photographs. Another corner of the yard was heaped with pitchforks and scythes, a bullrake with missing teeth, harness, axes, sapbuckets, saws, ice saws, milk pails, and milk cans. My grandfather had said something about maybe picking up a good scythe.

Dimly, I think I understood right away that I was watching the end of something old, the emptying out of something that had been full. As a child in New Hampshire I was witness to many conclusions, and eventually learned the history of this vanishing: Once, somebody had cleared this land—oak by oak, boulder by boulder; maybe the first Dobbins of New Canada Road was a soldier who mustered out of General Washington's Army and trudged north to cut his own land from the woods of a stony hill; or maybe the farm went back further, and Dobbins lugged his musket from this farm to join General Stark and fight Burgoyne at Bennington . . .

Once Ragged Mountain was dense with farms and farmers—the land clearer in 1790 than it was in 1935. The settlers were people with land and without cash who never considered that they lacked anything at all. If we refer to their enterprise as subsistence farming, the adjective reveals our grudgingness, not theirs. For them one notion shone as bright as the king's gold in his coat of arms: *The land was their own land.* Later the turnpike, the canal, industry along the rivers, and especially the railroad turned our economy (and our culture) toward cash. It was a long story, which took many years to conclude. After the middle of the nineteenth century, these hill farms began to extinguish—like the dying whippoorwill now, or like houselights that go out, one by one, across a night valley. Beyond the Dobbins place, the Trumps had abandoned their farm in 1917 and their place collapsed into its cellarhole before I was born. A mile up New Canada, Jim Blasington still worked his farm; two miles farther Freeman grew his own food and worked on the road for taxes. My grandfather sold milk, wool, eggs, timber—and got by.

That day at the Dobbins auction I watched the clearing out of yet another old place that had carried many generations on its stony back. Four years later the Blasington house burned down and Jim moved in with his brother Cedric. Five years later still, Freeman died, and in a decade his stout camp crumbled.

This Dobbins house would not fall down. Somebody from Cleveland had bought it for a summer place. For the next ten or twelve years, my grandfather and I would hay these fields each summer, keeping the acreage tidy for the Ohio people, helping to feed my grandfather's Holsteins so that he could sell blue milk to H. P. Hood & Sons in Boston.

Now the auctioneer held up farm implements for bidding on. My grandfather bought a scythe with a sound snath and an almost new blade for seventy-five cents. The buggy went—the animals must have gone earlier—and then the kitchen things: My grandmother bought two dozen Ball jars for a quarter. (A dollar was a lot to spend.) When bales of clothes began to go, I started to wake up. I had begun with a dim sense of conclusion; now I understood what was concluded. This waking is what I remember—my eight-year-old vision of time and devastation. There were top hats, women's hats with veils, out-of-style overcoats, housedresses, fancy aprons, skirts, gloves still in their Sears boxes, and handkerchiefs. There were albums of photographs and postcard albums; certificates of marriage, baptism, and death; temperance pledges; diaries; and box after box of letters. These boxes—waking, I understood—were stuffed with the lives of dead farmers and farm wives. These lives went for a nickel each, going going gone, as the auctioneer from Bristol dispersed the accumulation of six generations.

The auctioneer's voice chanted rhythms of loss on the summer air. When I went home I wept for the Dobbinses—and I wept for you and for me. Upstairs in our back chamber were broken chairs, chests full of dead people's clothing, captain's chairs, boxes containing pretty Christmas cards, snapshots of kittens and cousins, wads of old letters tied together with brittle twine.

THE PEOPLE from Cleveland who bought the place got their eggs from my grandmother: "nice folks," they were. When *they* died, as people tend to do, the new people added an enormous heated indoor swimming pool to the old Cape. The pool reached into the field where we hayed, and beyond it the same owners added two tennis courts paved with a green composite. No more haying there—and a little later, my grandfather took his own turn dying. What remained of the hayfield was mowed by one of the new people's handymen, sitting on a tractor that pulled six lawnmowers behind it. When Victor Dobbins died, the new people bought his camp to protect themselves. Because Freeman had shingled the roof, the shack stayed upright, though the windows broke and the inside filled with leaves. When the new people died, six hundred acres went on the market, all woodlot now, and recently a developer approached the town planning board for a permit to build seventy houses.

Permit not granted. Not yet.

Now in my sixties, and a grandfather myself, I walk with Gus up dirt New Canada Road past Victor's still-standing camp and past the old Dobbins place concealed under a complex of improvements. Not long ago a real estate agent telephoned to offer me the third of an acre my grandfather had given to Victor. He offered me the land as a courtesy, he said, because it nipped into my woodlot. I don't tell this story against real estate agents or anybody else; I tell it against the memory of an auction I attended fifty-odd years ago, against history and waking to loss. The agent suggested that twenty-five thousand dollars would be a fair price because the old shack would allow the purchaser to raise a building without a new permit; the new building would be grandfathered, he told me.

The Company of Cattle

A FEW YEARS AGO we mail-ordered a plywood Holstein. When she arrived and we unpacked her, we were delighted. This two-dimensional black-and-white creature was small, a lot smaller than a real cow, but from a distance she looked amazingly real. Her flat surface, artfully painted, provided an illusion of depth; she seemed about to stick her neck forward and bellow *moooooo* with concentrated bovine energy. We propped her up by the back of the barn, as if bossy walked into the field after milking to take refreshment from the green grass. She was our family cow, like the single mooly cow that early settlers kept for milk and butter.

From the road, her white bulk showed against the unpainted vertical boards of our barn. My cousin Dennis Fenton, driving down Route 4 from the north, told me later how he almost drove into the ditch when he looked up and saw our creature. Last winter, pleased with the success of the experiment, we expanded our herd. We sent away for a calf, or a "baby cow" as the advertiser listed her, lacking confidence that contemporary Americans know what a calf is. This summer our plywood mother and daughter stand by the old watering trough outside the tie-up where my grandfather spent his life milking eight real Holsteins—a great leather sisterhood of huge pink lips and long tongues, their tails swinging at flies, producers of copious milk and manure.

The tie-up and its barn go unused now, or used only by barnswallows and bats, and joined to the barn is the unused grainshed, over the carriage shed where a buggy rots. When I visit our plywood herd, I stick my head in the grainshed sniffing old smells, looking at the empty tubs that held grain, a corncrib, and an elegant wooden contraption for shelling beans. Maybe because rats spent a hundred years sneaking into this shed, dodging barncats, they still visit to nibble on soft wood and chew hunks out of rotten harness. This was the place I fed my chickens from, where my grandfather fetched oats for Riley and grain for the big milkers.

My cousin Dennis and his wife Marge were the last farmers in the family. With his milking machines, Dennis drained fifty-five head of registered Holsteins all by himself, twice a day—three-thirty to five o'clock, morning and afternoon. Dennis alone scooped up the manure and spread it on his hayfields; Dennis alone hayed his acres and stacked his bales. The only thing he bought ready made was ensilage. Then, as he entered his fifties, Dennis understood that he couldn't continue to do everything, and at payable wages he couldn't hire anyone to help him out. So Dennis and Marge sold their animals, fifty-five registered Holsteins going going gone, total divestment, not only the cattle but the milking machines and the great frosty gleaming tank that cooled the milk. At the rear of the auctioneer's tent, I watched two Japanese bid on some prize animals. A year or two later I visited the island of Hokkaido in Japan, where I was startled and gratified to find April snowdrifts, birch trees, and great dolorous Holsteins swishing their tails, some of them maybe exiled from the stony cousin-fields of New Hampshire.

Never have I wanted to farm as Dennis and Marge did—I milk Holstein images, not Holsteins—but I miss their cattle. I used to show off their farm, when I drove visitors to Eagle Pond from the bus depot in Concord. Now as I drive by the Fenton place I say nothing. Dennis's brother Paul has developed the acreage into house lots. There's a handsome stone gateway leading into the fields where cattle used to graze. Now I must seek out unfamiliar cattle to gaze at. One great dairy farm remains on Route 4, below the old Fenton place, where the valley widens at the north end of Boscawen. I gaze at the Holstein sorority there—huge female harlequins in their black-and-white costumes gathered sleepily together in slow abundance under the shade of a maple or amid lush green fields.

Does my cow-love appear excessive? I doubt that such love will afflict my grandchildren, not brought up in the company of cattle. I remember years back when Jane and I drove through the spring countryside with a friend raised in the suburbs of Detroit. The mild air carried some information: Farmers were spreading manure. Jane and I—she grew up across the road from a working farm—breathed deeply of the dark odor and spoke of it lyrically. Our friend laughed, telling us ruefully that the smell made him think of one thing only: the Detroit Zoo.

(I remember also the actor who played my grandfather in an autobiographical play of mine. When I showed Jim Greene how to mime milking, he told me what a city boy he was. Trying out for a television commercial, he had been asked to improvise conversation as a farmer with his wife. The actress, also trying out, improvised: "I'm afraid our old cow is sick." Jim answered, "Oh, he'll be all right." The actress whispered, "Cows are female." Jim was shocked: "*All* of them?")

Most of our visitors at this farm, which is no longer a farm, don't miss the animals because they never knew animals. It's commonplace to note—still, one must keep on noting it—that few of us associate the word "cow" (or even "steer") with the reddish substance we buy wrapped up in cellophane at the meat counter. Chicken is something we buy after Frank Perdue has cut it up: Only older sorts, and a minority of rural people, retain notions of the absurd feathered filthy squawking stupid ornamental magnificent citizens of the chickenyard, great fecund Rhode Island reds bopping eggs out one a day, a grand magnifico rooster strutting the henyard as lord of the harem. And there's no such thing as a calf—only a baby cow.

When Jane and I pass a herd of cattle, they look lazy and contented. Jane has expressed the wish to return, next time, in the form of a cow, which is understandable, yet I guess there's a downside if you should happen to return as a male of the species. One time Dennis telephoned us: If we wanted to see a calf born, we should drive over right now. Friends from Long Island were visiting, and we four cramped into the Saab and drove to the Fentons'. We watched in wonder and delight as the huge mother struggled to give birth while the rest of the herd—sisters and mothers and daughters and granddaughters and cousins—stood in a respectful fascinated circle watching it happen. Dennis helped by tying a rope around the emerging calf's front feet, pulling as the mother pushed, and the little bullcalf stood upright and made his first small tentative moo. The attendant sisterhood responded by dancing, making little leaps in the air, mooing raucously in celebration, cheering and rooting. They all wanted to help lick the calf clean, and Dennis had to discourage them.

Our friends have never eaten another ounce of beef. Or so they consider. I glimpsed the shadow of the cattle world when I spoke to Dennis a few minutes later. I was afraid that his little male was doomed to be stuffed with milk solids and injected with chemicals in the cramped pen of a veal factory. No, said Dennis; just then the cost of milk solids compared unfavorably to the price of veal. No, said Dennis, the butcher would pick up this boy tomorrow, and a day later, as Dennis understood it, the bullcalf would be cans of creamed chicken.

We have no problems with our plywood herd. We need not agonize about eating their flesh. As advertised, they are easy to take care of, no manure to scrape onto the pile underneath the tie-up, no grain or ensilage or hay to fetch and stuff under their steamy noses. They do not dry up, or squeeze out tottering small duplicates of themselves, or freshen and overwhelm us with the tonnage of their frothing milk. And at least they *look* like cows. As they stand on the hill beside the watering trough, they grant us the bounty of an illusion, our plywood herd standing in for the animals we grew up with, loved, served, and were served by.

The Thriftiest State

MY UNCLE DICK suggests that in New Hampshire we piececut our history lesson; we think our perfect union was founded not on *No taxation without representation* but on *No taxation.* It is good to live in New Hampshire if you are a road—roads are cared for—but it's no good being old or poor or a public school. We needn't dwell, however, on insufficient welfare; we needn't bring up no kindergarten or state aid to education. We are stingy on a soul-level far deeper than the tax-level. In fact, New Hampshire is foremost among fifty states in thrift, prudence, parsimoniousness, frugality, and saving. I could speak of stinginess to forestall criticism: I'm thrifty; you pinch pennies; he's a stingy, miserly son of a bitch.

It is a happy boast. When shoes wear out, we resole from the five-and-dime. Frayed shirt collars turn to a second life. Automobiles run on transplants and prostheses—that used transmission, this electrical tape—while we save good used bricks from old chimneys and repair clapboards using taped hammers from our great-grandfather's tool-boxes. Thrift ties us to our ancestors. Newspapers and cardboard boxes make insulation so that when we open the walls fifty years later, we find time capsules of the old world among mouse nests and tiny bones.

When I ask neighbors—at church and Blackwater Bill's and the mini-mart—if we deserve our reputation, everyone smiles with acknowledgment. "Just take a look upstairs," they tell me, or "Check out the shed." One after another, they say, "I was just going to throw it away"—an old pillow, stained, with half the feathers gone; the wheel of a dead wheelbarrow; a homemade ladder missing three rungs; a sweater made of mothholes; a calendar from 1937—"but then I thought, 'Well, you never can tell, it might come in handy.'" *Live Free or Die* shouldn't be the slogan on New Hampshire's license plates; we ought to drive our dented rusty cars wearing the motto *It Might Come in Handy.* The first time New Hampshire faced an energy crisis, we reduced our use of oil by forty percent—not because we bought new woodstoves but because we'd never thrown away the old ones. We scraped rust off the Glenwood that we'd tucked into a dry place under the barn, bought new stovepipe down to the store, and burned maple while Massachusetts shivered and went broke.

We keep junkers in our front yards not only for their beauty—as Vermont sculptors think, who live in SoHo ten months a year—but for function; who knows when the hood ornament of a 1957 Plymouth might come in handy? New Hampshire writers swear by the same notions of possible usefulness. We cock our ears at every yard sale or coffee hour, trying not to look as if we're listening, to hear Phyllis tell how her cousin buys two-ply toilet paper but uses only one ply at a time. We write it down; might come in handy. Dot Heath tells me, at church, how her husband Everett sometimes buys a sandwich, down to the store, that comes on a shiny white plastic plate. When he's finished, Everett sets the plate beside the sink for Dorothy to wash; later, Everett dries it. And everybody I talk to has heard of someone who hangs wet paper towels over the range to dry; "not if they're real dirty," somebody adds.

For several years, when I belonged to the Andover Lions Club, I sold lightbulbs door-to-door every October. Emily Peasly was almost ninety years old and took a long time answering my knock in the early twilight. Every year I explained about our three-ways, our packages of hundred-watters, and our mixed packages that held two sixties, two seventy-fives, and two hundreds. Every year she turned me down after asking, "Do you have a fifteen-watter?"

Examples start in our own backyard. When we tore down the saphouse my great-grandfather built, we found that he had propped one four-by-four on a flat piece of stone—which was his own father's broken headstone. Replacing the frost-cracked marker from the old Andover graveyard, he had taken the broken granite home and put it to use. Probably Freeman Morrison helped him with the saphouse, who died thirty-some years ago as the thriftiest man in the thriftiest county of the thriftiest state. Freeman never threw anything away. When he ate shredded wheat he saved the cardboard partitions because they fit into boot bottoms and he didn't need to buy a Cat's Paw at Newberry's. When Free shot his annual deer, he ate everything edible, used the hooves for weights on piles of picked-up newspapers, and tacked the skin over the boards of his shack to keep the wind out. When he wished to bathe himself, and the ice was out of Eagle Pond, he waded into the water fully clothed with a bar of soap—he made the soap—and washed his clothes and himself at the same time. Therefore, Free emitted a characteristic effluence; maybe it kept the blackflies off. And what did Free gain for all his frugality? Independence. He never worked for anybody's wages unless he wanted to. To live without money was his greatest freedom. New Hampshire's parsimony is a remnant—archaeological evidence—of the old cashless economy. Frugality once dictated the way we performed every chore. When I started haying fifty years ago, my task was thrift. I "raked after," using a great bullrake to sweep up strands of hay that the pitchfork left behind; then I carried the fringe in my rake to deposit its blond swoop, like bangs, on the forehead of the next haystack. When I mowed, I scythed corners the mowing machine couldn't reach.

Frugality endures, even among the young. My daughter Philippa adheres to the thrift culture, even though she lives in the city of Concord. She uses her supermarket checkout receipt for her next grocery list. She takes milk containers, beheads them, stuffs one inside the other, covers the result with contact paper—and makes light strong blocks for her daughters to play with. She spends Saturday mornings at yard sales—and her playroom looks like a daycare center. The yard sale has replaced the auction. At the old auctions we measured our thrift when the auctioneer held up boxes of fabric squares, liberated from worn clothing and ready for patchwork quilts; or remnants of wool for braiding into rugs; or broken furniture and barn equipment, potential for repair or salvage; or complete runs of farm magazines and weekly newspapers; or bottles with century-old labels on them. Now much of the same stuff—detritus from this region of keepers—migrates from yard sales, prices multiplied, to antiques shops.

Frugality is one of our major industries. (Ezra Pound once listed, as his chief source of income, "low overhead.") At the South Danbury Christian Church we hold a coffee hour every Sunday; cheese and crackers, cake, cookies, doughnuts. This hour lasts about twenty-five minutes, thrifty in itself, but it's our utensils I want to mention. We throw away paper cups because experience shows that they don't take soap too well. We have no such problem with disposable plastic spoons; we take them home, wash them, and use them again week after week, year after year. They come in handy.

Golden Codgers

When I spent summers on this farm as a child, I came to love old people generically—and by old people I suppose I included (like AARP) anybody fifty-five or over. William Butler Yeats in a poem speaks of "all the golden codgers," and all codgers were gold for me. Middle-aged neighbors were boring; they sat and listened, adding no stories. The codgers started with my grandparents Wesley and Kate Wells and moved on to uncles and aunts and cousins. Uncle Luther, who was Kate's older brother, was born in 1856 and old enough to remember the end of the Civil War. Aunt Lottie, my grandfather's sister, was famous as a girl for hefting hundred-pound sacks of grain. Freeman Morrison was our cousin who lived alone—moving rocks for fun, grafting an apple tree with six varieties of apple, in love with an ox—and who in company couldn't stop talking, spooling out the threads of everything that ever happened. The codgers were not only blood relatives. They could be our neighbors Charles and Sarah Whittemore, Charlie so sick, who used water from our well during a drought. They could be widows at church who told me Bible stories and shy tales of courtship when they were young. They could be old friends reunited with my grandparents at Old Home Day. I loved listening to my grandfather reminisce with a blind man about a baseball game played in Danbury in 1890; they joked and teased about a strike-out fifty years ago. When old people told stories, they constructed a miniature vanished world as small, clear, and immaculate as an architect's model city.

When I was a child, other children bored me; so did their parents. When I returned to New Hampshire thirty years later, I found the former middle-aged turned into wise tribal elders dispensing wit and lore. All that earlier time, they had memorized the tales of the tribe. Coming back, I listened to Paul Fenton tell stories. Paul was my grandfather's nephew, then in his seventies, who had high cheekbones like my grandfather and who (like my grandfather) signaled his recollection of a good story by a light that kindled his eyes. It was Paul who asked me whether I ever heard about the fellow used to live around here who filled his ox cart every fall with everything the family made or grew . . . Or I listened to Huldah Currier, named after the Old Testament prophetess, who was widow of John the RFD man. She told about the first day John tried to deliver both the Danbury and the South Danbury routes using a horse, as Fred Clark (Danbury's retiring RFD man) advised. He couldn't finish the route by horse—darkness fell—and had to switch to the untrustworthy automobile. Or I listened to Les Ford, who told about the fishrod factory down to Potter Place; I could see the foundation stones. Or I listened to Myrl Phelps, probably my age but a codger by choice, who told stories about Freeman and Wesley, or about Danbury's first local hydroelectric power plant, whose owner supplied electricity when he felt like it.

One day I came calling on Gifford Wiggin of Danbury—retired logging entrepreneur and road agent, semiretired land speculator. By the time I found Gifford, deep into his eighties, he liked to take the air sitting beside his house in the village on Route 104, just a hundred yards east of Route 4. I parked in his yard and watched him peer forward to recover my name from my face. As I walked toward him, his face wrinkled, crafty over his ragged white mustache: "I know who you are." Then he stepped inside to fetch another chair. It was early spring, unseasonably warm late in April. Nobody had told the blackflies, so we were able to sit outside, enjoying sun and fresh air in two aluminum chairs woven with pastel plastic strips that Gifford set in a warm corner where the kitchen joined the garage. Despite the warmth, Gifford wore a cap and a woolen plaid shirt over a blue sweater. When you're eighty-seven, you never quite warm up.

It was Gifford's grandfather—he answered my question—who first settled the family in Danbury, coming north from Concord about the time the railroad went through late in the 1840s. Gifford's father was born over to the Broughton place—used to be the Broughton place—a hundred and seventeen years ago. Speaking of his father made him think of a triumph. "I bought a hundred and fifty acres, which my father and my grandfather owned before me, bought it for eight hundred fifty dollars from John Currier." (That was Huldah's late husband, the RFD man; everyone dabbled in land.) Gifford's face, lengthened by vertical lines, broke sideways into a grin. "Just sold it for thirty-five thousand to a doctor." I admired Gifford's business shrewdness as much as he did—my admiration tempered by knowing that John Currier died thirty years ago.

"I won't have so much when the government gets through with it," Gifford added. Like most people in Danbury, Gifford grew up Republican, his Republicanism a Civil War legacy. After Watergate and the resignation of a president, Gifford found himself no longer able to support the Grand Old Party. "I got disgusted," he told me. "I used to be Republican, voted straight ticket. Now I guess I'm an . . . *independent.*" Gifford felt silly to be an independent. But he surely was—in his radical conservativism.

Gifford was not a churchgoer but he knew that I went to the South Danbury Christian Church, which his grandfather helped to found, chipping in a hundred dollars for a pew. Another who contributed—Gifford told me what I knew—was my own great-grandfather Ben Keneston. Gifford could remember all four of my New Hampshire great-grandparents, the only person alive who could. "That part of Ragged Mountain where the ski slope is, that was Keneston's, where Ben came from." Gifford remembered my great-grandfather driving his sheep over Ragged from pasture to pasture. "Quite a sight," Gifford said. "Ben used to feed them on hemlock, cut a mess of it." Then Gifford recollected my other New Hampshire great-grandfather, John Wells, the blacksmith who fought in the Civil War. Gifford recalled John Wells's political passion, a great debater despite his cleft palate—"tongue-tied," as Gifford put it—who handled the rebuttal as long as he debated among neighbors. When Danbury debated another town, John Wells had to sit and listen—frustrated to distraction—because the other town couldn't make out his speech.

We sat in the unexpected warmth, undisturbed except by an occasional trailer truck pulling from Bristol toward Danbury. Automobiles were still wonderful for Gifford, and they filled his talk as their noise filled the afternoon. He asked me about the import I parked in his yard, and found my ignorance frustrating; I didn't know anything except the mileage I got. Gifford remembered the first car he ever saw, only one cylinder but it did make a racket. He and his little brothers and sisters were playing outside when the driver clattered and chugged and smoked into the farmyard, lost, inquiring the way to the village, terrifying chickens. The children had no idea what it was. "We was all upstairs hell-bent!"

The first car to take up residence in Danbury was a Stanley Steamer, bought by Dr. Knapp—not young Dr. Knapp, who spent a year up to Hanover and then went to the First World War, but *old* Dr. Knapp, who also bought Danbury's second car, a two-cylinder Reo. Gifford remembered when Fred Clark, although he delivered the mail by reliable horsepower, bought himself a four-cylinder Maxwell. Remembering Huldah's story, I asked Gifford if Fred Clark ever tried to deliver the mail from his Maxwell. "He *tried* to," said Gifford, and laughed again. One form of transportation led to another, and Gifford reached back to tell me how trains used to take on water at South Danbury. Stagecoaches met the trains; Mr. Shepherd kept a coach with four horses that would take people clear to the campgrounds over to Wilmot, as much as eight miles away, for Methodist camp meeting or for Wilmot's Old Home Day every August.

We approached my own recollections, as I could remember eating homemade ice cream at the Wilmot campgrounds with my grandfather at Old Home Day, a memory that goes back at least as far as

August 1938, because in September of that year the hurricane blew white pines onto the little houses of the campgrounds. Gifford remembered from his youth a thousand people coming to Old Home Day. I remembered as many as two hundred; when we celebrate Old Home Sunday now, late August, we fill only a small church—as the great-grandchildren of the New Hampshire diaspora barbecue ribs in San Diego.

Forgetting the past, or shrugging ourselves away from it, is our American birthright. Everybody's family left home to come here. Restlessness is the birthright, or maybe the curse, that the talk of golden codgers militates against. Old people and their stories remind us that earlier times existed, a thousand or a million times connecting us to everything that came before us. Such connections imply a future to which our present delivers only a constantly shifting prologue. If we exist entirely within the buzzing clicking present tense of earphones and fax machines, who can believe in continuity with a future? In 1911, Gifford Wiggin recollected, Mr. Shepherd ordered a couple of Stanley Steamers built to haul people, replacing the stages, but people still called them stages. Words endure past the things they name. When I sat with Mrs. Fortune at the West Andover post office in 1944, waiting for the man with the green Ford pickup to drive from Springfield with the mail, we called it the stage we waited for.

After an hour of talk, Gifford interrupted himself to stand up. "Got to go upstairs and check on my wife." I knew she was bedridden. It took Gifford a long time to stand; motion was an assemblage of small pains. Ten minutes later he limped back, telling me that all was well; she was asleep. I figured that maybe Gifford himself needed some rest. I stood up to go, admiring this codger's spunk and humor. As I rose, of course, I stretched stiff limbs. I turned to go, but Gifford thought of one more thing to say: "You going to put this in a book?" I said oh, maybe, sometime. Gifford looked crafty again. "Don't believe everything you's told," Gifford said.

Not long after my visit, Gifford's wife died. Gifford kept on, without someone to take care of, clearly depressed. One day his sons borrowed Gifford's guns and hid them away. After a while, Gifford recovered enough to walk to the store each morning and sit for an hour on the windowseat—holding forth, teasing, joking, remembering. I saw him once a week. After he turned ninety I heard that he was in the hospital; then Gifford was dead. The Danbury store's windowseat is empty of Gifford's stories; but aging is never in short supply. With old age comes talk and stories. Although there are old storytellers everywhere, city and suburb, the rural culture admires eccentricity as it honors age—often the two go together, as age permits independence denied the young—and breeds a line of golden codgers. Because New Hampshire's small towns tell stories, its culture hangs on despite ski resorts and television. Whenever I find anyone older than I am, I gather what I can so I can tell it aloud or put it in a book. As my eldest granddaughters turn four, I start telling them what I know, to entertain them with stories of the old times that I remember well and of older old times I've heard about. Loving this country place, I want my grandchildren to catch this love as if it were permanent measles.

When I visit the store now I see Billy Morris, who is younger than I am but his beard comes white and he likes to remember things. At the post office I exchange a joke about old winters with Prosper Fifield. With Jimmy Phelps—son of Myrl, the storyteller—usually I talk longer, until each of us remembers chores to do. My cousin Audrey taught Jimmy when he was six, and among the decades of six-year-olds she remembers Jimmy as smartest of all. He was elected selectman when he was only nineteen, state representative when he was twenty-seven, and then deputy House leader. He has retired from the State House now, to concentrate on his construction work, but he remains Danbury's town moderator. One day as he tells me a story about a governor and a snake, I notice to my surprise that Jimmy is developing crow's feet. For one instant I recognize Jimmy as a golden codger—in his late eighties, fifty years from now—with ten thousand good stories and eyes that tell you when he remembers one.

Various New Englands

MOST OF MY LIFE I have lived in various New Englands. I grew up in suburban Connecticut, a suburb of New Haven called Hamden, an area called Spring Glen where six-room houses squared out the tidy blocks. The homes looked alike; fathers drove the same cars; boys walked to Spring Glen School wearing the corduroy knickers that their mothers had bought at Malley's and Shartenberg's. There were other centuries in the neighborhood, but we paid little attention to them. Just down the road was the New Haven reservoir that my great-grandfather Hall had worked to construct. A day laborer, one noon in 1861 he walked off his job into the city to enlist for a year in the Civil War. (After his twelve months, he returned and was drafted and hired a substitute.) Not far from the reservoir were the remains of Eli Whitney's factory where he attempted the mass production of firearms in 1798.

In the summer, taking the train, I left the middle-middle-class precinct of Spring Glen to visit this farm, where there were no cars or tractors or modern conveniences like money or electric iceboxes. For refrigeration my mother's father stored the summer's ice under sawdust beside the cowbarn, great transparent oblongs he had sawed from Eagle Pond in February. At the Boston & Maine depot, my grandfather waited with Riley, who pulled a buggy that bumped us a mile to the house. Weekday summer mornings Riley hauled the mowing machine, afternoons the rake and a hayrack, as my grandfather and I collaborated to gather hay for the winter cattle, sheep, and horse.

There were no blocks here—only old farmhouses needing paint, cellarholes where houses had fallen in, and shacks of the shack people. Of course I preferred the domain of want to schooltime's suburb. A disappearing land and culture became the garden of poetry.

My New England altered to Harvard, to Cambridge and Boston—urban and academic and fierce, dominated by wealth, class, and intelligence. After that I flitted about, as Americans are supposed to do: two years at Oxford, a year at Stanford, back to Harvard on a fellowship. Stanford was the farthest from New Hampshire; England was closer because of the daily presence of history layered in the earth, solid in architecture. When I taught in Michigan for a decade and a half, its environment felt as far from New England as California's. Michigan's past was Henry Ford and the battle of the overpass, only twenty years earlier. Ann Arbor was lively, gregarious, and agreeable. When I lived there I accepted its assumptions and did not look wistfully eastward. But the soil was thin: not enough corpses. When I returned, I lived fully in New England as if for the first time, and cherished the qualities and sensibilities that I had acquired without acknowledgment.

The difference in this sensibility is historical. In New England there are malls and franchise highways and tracts and office high-rises and Wal-Marts and cloverleaves and condos that could be lifted intact and translated to California or Texas or Indiana without seeming out of place. Yet within miles of these monuments of the moment we find an old barn still standing incongruous in the city, or a mummified granite Victorian edifice still in municipal use, or a patch of stonewall that embodies the energy, hope, and fatigue of eighteenth-century farmers clearing their land, avid for the liberty of the one-family farm. Or we find a country town complete with village green, white wooden church, and Civil War monument—a town that rich millowners and retired executives have populated and preserved. History is the New England earth. It is a layered history, not so many levels as Troy but present enough to keep us aware that we are not the first inhabitants here, that we come, we go, and others will follow us. An ox track becomes U.S. Route 4. Canals become straight and weedy streams interrupted by ruined locks. Railroad lines become paths for skiing or biking or hiking or snowmachines. Few remain railway lines. A track not far from my house runs one passenger train a day, each way, and you can travel north from D.C. to Pennsylvania Station to Hartford to Brattleboro to my depot in Claremont, or north from Claremont to White River Junction. Even some rituals persist. In country towns a few elementary schools still hold Prize Speaking Day, when pupils recite "Little Boy Blue" and the Gettysburg Address.

In my neighborhood there are families bearing names familiar from the lists of Revolutionary and Civil War dead. There are also names that recall the migrations—descendants of Canadian French who came to chop trees, Italians who labored in the quarries, Poles who worked in the mills. History is present in newcomers from Vietnam and Cambodia. I met my first Kurd last year in Boston.

It seems only half a life to live without connection to the past. When we visit England there are Roman roads and the ruins of villas and fortifications. Italy and Greece take us further and more grandly back; Mesopotamia, India, and China even further. New England is to the rest of the United States what Europe is to New England. For me, as I push toward eighty, there is comfort in these connections. Through literature and thought, through Egyptian pyramid and Greek Parthenon, we find links to our ancestors who imagined these monuments or—most of our predecessors—slaved to build them. Perhaps the most intimate connections are more domestic than monumental: the wooden bowl, the ornamental bead, the rusted apple peeler, the glass bracelet that a Roman infant wore. In New England the fragments of centuries stitch us together, not so many years as Italy's, not so few as Ann Arbor's. New England is: empty mills, new inventions, wooden scythes, a Mother Hubbard wrapped in paper and stored in a chest, a snowmachine, biotechnology, and contrails from Logan Airport streaking the blue air above the cellarhole of a farmer who came north after the Revolution to build his land.